THE IMPOSSIBLE PEACE

THE
IMPOSSIBLE PEACE

Britain, the Division of Germany
and the Origins of the Cold War

ANNE DEIGHTON

CLARENDON PRESS · OXFORD
1993

Oxford University Press, Walton Street, Oxford OX2 6DP
Oxford New York Toronto
Delhi Bombay Calcutta Madras Karachi
Kuala Lumpur Singapore Hong Kong Tokyo
Nairobi Dar es Salaam Cape Town
Melbourne Auckland Madrid
and associated companies in
Berlin Ibadan

Oxford is a trade mark of Oxford University Press

Published in the United States
by Oxford University Press Inc., New York

First published 1990
First issued in Clarendon Paperbacks 1993

British Library Cataloguing in Publication Data
Deighton, Anne
The impossible peace: Britain, the division of Germany and
the origins of the Cold War.
1. Great Britain. Foreign relations with Germany. Policies
of government, history 2. Germany. Foreign relations
with Great Britain. Policies of British government, history
I. Title
ISBN 0–19–827898–5

Library of Congress Cataloging in Publication Data
Deighton, Anne, 1949–
The impossible peace: Britain, the division of Germany and the
origins of the cold war/Anne Deighton.
1. Great Britain—Foreign relations—Germany. 2. Germany—
History—Allied occupation, 1945– 3. Germany—Foreign relations—
Great Britain. 4. Great Britain—Foreign relations—1945–.
5. World politics—1945–1955. 6. Cold War. I. Title.
DA47.2.D47 1990 327'.09'044—dc20 89–49374
ISBN 0–19–827898–5

Printed in Great Britain
on acid-free paper by
Biddles Ltd, Guildford and King's Lynn

For Megan and David

PREFACE

This book originated as a doctoral thesis written between 1983 and 1987 in the University of Reading, when I was a postgraduate student in the Department of Politics. The staff, now colleagues, of the Department of Politics at Reading have provided a very supportive atmosphere in which to work and teach; in particular Peter Campbell, Keith Sainsbury, Barry Jones, and Peter Jones have read and commented helpfully and positively on my work. My greatest thanks go to my doctoral supervisor, mentor, and friend Avi Shlaim, whose judicious blend of coaxing and badgering ensured that my thesis was completed in four years, and who contributed to proffer very positive encouragement from Oxford when I was revising the thesis for publication. Professor David Fieldhouse—who was a most rigorous tutor when I was an undergraduate—has continued to give me incisive yet always constructive advice, and I am very grateful for his interest in my work.

My thanks also go to Piers Dixon, who allowed me to spend many very profitable hours reading his father's invaluable papers and diaries as well as commenting in great detail on sections of the manuscript; and to Sir Alec Cairncross, who read sections of my work in an earlier form, and who put at my disposal his letters written from Berlin in 1945–6. I am particularly grateful for the conversations I have had with Sir Frank Roberts, Lord Franks, and Lord Gladwyn, and for the insights they gave me into the period. During the course of this research I have also met and benefited directly and indirectly from the ideas and kindness of many other people: Geoffrey Warner (who has given me much good advice, and whose treasured copy of *Foreign Relations* I borrowed for nearly a year), Christopher Hill, Lawrence Freedman, David Reynolds, Robin Edmonds, Joseph Foschepoth, Beatrice Heuser, and Anthony Gorst among others.

The Social Science Research Council (now the Economic and Social Research Council) generously funded me for three years of research. I remain indebted to the patience and skill of the Librarians and Archivists at the University of Reading; the Public Record Office; the Bodleian Library, Oxford; Churchill College,

Cambridge; and also to staff at the Reading University Computer Centre for their time and help. Copyright material from the Public Record Office appears by permission of HM Stationery Office.

Aelwen Goldstein, Elspeth Drew, Angela Lane, Margaret Kendrick, and especially my mother, Elizabeth Deighton, have all given me great friendship over the past five demanding years. Finally, I am enormously grateful to Graham who has welcomed and supported this enterprise in many ways, at a time when his own professional life was at such an exciting and absorbing stage. I am afraid that he got a lot more than he—or I—bargained for, when I embarked upon a Master's Degree as a part-time student seven years ago. Our children, Megan and David, have cheerfully accepted the distractions of research, and even learned to word-process with me. They are a continual source of delight, and it is to them that this book is lovingly dedicated.

CONTENTS

ABBREVIATIONS

ACC	Allied Control Council
APW	Armistice and Post-War Committee
CAB	Cabinet papers
CEEC	Committee for European Economic Co-operation
CFM	Council of Foreign Ministers
CCG	Control Commission, Germany
COGA	Control Office for Germany & Austria
COS	Chiefs of Staff
DBPO	*Documents on British Policy Overseas*
DMG	Deputy Military Governor
EAC	European Advisory Commission
ECE	Economic Commission for Europe
EIPS	Economic and Industrial Planning Staff
FO	Foreign Office
FRUS	*Foreign Relations of the United States*
LOI	Level of Industry
OMGUS	Office of the Military Governor of the United States
ORC	Overseas Reconstruction Committee
PHPS	Post-Hostilities Planning Staff
PLP	Parliamentary Labour Party
PRO	Public Record Office
SED	German Unity Party
T	Treasury papers
UNO	United Nations Organization
UNRRA	United Nations Relief and Rehabilitation Agency

Zonal division of Germany, 1945

INTRODUCTION

ON 8 May 1945 the Germans surrendered unconditionally to the Allies and the war in Europe was over. But by the end of 1947 the Allies were engaged in the elusive and intractable conflict that we know as the cold war, a conflict that has dominated contemporary international relations as well as the historiography of the postwar years.

Scholars have long argued over the origins and nature of the cold war. During the 1950s and the early 1960s Western opinion was dominated by the so-called traditionalist view of the cold war, expounded, in many cases, by those who had been active in government during these years. They have left us a prodigious outpouring of memoirs, diaries, and 'inside' accounts of the international politics of the 1940s and early 1950s. According to these traditionalist writers, the Soviet Union's desire to expand her power and influence outside her borders was checked only by the defensive, protective policy of the United States. The cold war was in essence an American response to a Soviet challenge that was posed within an acutely bipolar world setting.[1]

Then, during the Vietnam war and the crisis of American self-confidence that followed, scholars took a fresh look at the 1940s. A new school of thought emerged, a revisionist school, whose members were mostly left-wing or marxist in their orientation

---

[1] The writings of contemporary foreign policy-makers form the core of early writing on the cold war. See e.g.: Dean Acheson, *Present at the Creation: My Years in the State Department* (New York: Norton, 1969); Harry S. Truman, *Year of Decisions, 1945* (London: Hodder and Stoughton, 1955); Harry S. Truman, *Years of Trial and Hope, 1946–1953* (London: Hodder and Stoughton, 1956); George F. Kennan, *Memoirs* (London: Hutchinson, 1968); Walter Bedell Smith, *Moscow Mission, 1946–1949* (London: Heinemann, 1950); Charles Bohlen, *Witness to History, 1929–1969* (London: Weidenfeld & Nicolson, 1973); James F. Byrnes, *Speaking Frankly* (London: Heinemann, 1947); James F. Byrnes, *All in One Lifetime* (New York: Harper, 1958); Lucius D. Clay, *Decision in Germany* (London: Heinemann, 1950); *The Papers of Lucius D. Clay*, ed. Jean Edward Smith (Bloomington: Indiana University Press, 1974); Joseph M. Jones, *The Fifteen Weeks* (New York: Harcourt, 1955); Robert Murphy, *Diplomat Among Warriors* (London: Collins, 1964). Traditionalist works include: Herbert Feis, *From Trust to Terror* (New York: Norton, 1970); J. W. Spanier, *American Foreign Policy since the Second World War* (New York: Holt Rhinehart and Wilson, 1980); Arthur Schlesinger Jnr., 'The Origins of the Cold War', *Foreign Affairs*, 464 (Oct. 1967).

and, as such, highly critical of the role played by the United States in the postwar era. For the revisionists the United States was the real villain in the cold war. The Soviet Union, they argued, was weak, dispirited, and economically exhausted by the end of the war, and more interested in simply rebuilding its war-shattered economy than in extending its boundaries. The early cold-war years were depicted by them as the onward march of American capitalism, which sought atomic hegemony, power, influence, global and East European markets, and used the myth of Soviet expansionism to mask the true nature of its own foreign policy.[2]

With the opening of many state archives during the 1970s and also with the relaxing of international tensions, scholarship has thankfully become more detached and less focused on the polemics of Soviet–American rivalry. Much new material has become available, and so-called 'post-revisionist' scholars have begun to reassess the old assumptions and tired arguments of the cold-war debate.[3] They have asked new questions of the cold-war period,

[2] Major revisionist works include: Gar Alperovitz, *Atomic Diplomacy: Hiroshima and Potsdam* (New York: Vintage, 1967); Joyce and Gabriel Kolko, *The Limits of Power: The World and United States Foreign Policy, 1945–1954* (New York: Harper, 1972); Walter LaFeber, *America, Russia and the Cold War* (New York: Wiley, 1976); D. F. Fleming, *The Cold War and its Origins* (London: Allen and Unwin, 1961); Richard M. Freeland, *The Truman Doctrine and the Origins of McCarthyism* (New York: New York University Press, 1985).

[3] On 'Post-revisionism' see the comprehensive survey by John Lewis Gaddis, 'The Emerging Post-Revisionist Synthesis on the Origins of the Cold War', *Diplomatic History*, 713 (1983). Major post-revisionist works include: John Lewis Gaddis, *The United States and the Origins of the Cold War, 1941–1947* (New York: Columbia University Press, 1972); Daniel Yergin, *Shattered Peace: The Origins of the Cold War and the National Security State* (Boston: Houghton Mifflin, 1977). On Anglo-American relations see: Robert M. Hathaway, *Ambiguous Partnership: Britain and America, 1944–1947* (New York: University of Columbia Press, 1981); Terry H. Anderson, *The United States, Great Britain and the Cold War, 1944–1947* (Columbia: University of Missouri Press, 1981); Robin Edmonds, *Setting the Mould: The United States and Britain (1945–1950)* (Oxford: Clarendon Press, 1986). On Germany see in particular: D. C. Watt, *Britain Looks to Germany: A Study of British Opinion and Policy towards Germany since 1945* (London: Oswald Woolf, 1965); Philip Windsor, *German Reunification* (London: Elek Books, 1969); John H. Backer, *The Decision to Divide Germany: American Foreign Policy in Transition* (Durham: Duke University Press, 1978); John Gimbel, *The American Occupation of Germany: Politics and the Military, 1945–1949* (Stanford: Stanford University Press, 1968); Avi Shlaim, *The United States and the Berlin Blockade, 1948–1949: A Study in Crisis Decision Making* (Berkeley: University of California Press, 1983); Bruce Kuklick, *American Policy and the Division of Germany: The Clash with Russia over Reparations* (Ithaca: Cornell University Press, 1972); Hans A. Schmitt (ed.), *US Occupation in Europe after World War II* (Lawrence: Regents Press of Kansas, 1978); Robert A. Pollard, *Economic Security and the*

less influenced by the partisanship and polemics of earlier decades. In particular, the contribution of actors such as Britain and France, as well the Scandinavian countries and the Germans themselves, is being examined. Since the British archives for the 1940s and 1950s have been opened under the Thirty Year Rule, Britain's part in the making of the cold war can now also be examined with the help of official records. Her role had hitherto been largely ignored, partly because the economic and military pre-eminence of the superpowers and the bipolar nature of the developing cold war dwarfed Britain, despite her status as a world power with her Empire, her Dominions, and her wartime record. The first wave of studies on Britain after the records were made available were general, and often largely chronological in character. But there are now more studies which assess Britain's role in the postwar period, and there are now also some helpful reflective studies by those 'present at the creation'.[4]

Origins of the Cold War (New York: Columbia University Press, 1985); Gier Lundestad, *The American Non-Policy towards Eastern Europe 1943–1947* (Oslo: Universitetsforlaget, 1984); R. L. Messer, *The End of an Alliance: James E. Byrnes, Roosevelt, Truman and the Cold War* (Chapel Hill: North Carolina University Press, 1985).

[4] Earlier books on Britain in this period include: J. W. Wheeler-Bennett and A. J. Nicholls, *The Semblance of Peace: The Political Settlement after the Second World War* (New York: Norton, 1972). The pioneering book on Britain and the cold war published after the British archives for the period were opened was: Victor Rothwell, *Britain and the Cold War: 1941–1947* (London: Jonathan Cape, 1982). This was followed by Alan Bullock's indispensable third volume of his biography of Ernest Bevin, *Ernest Bevin: Foreign Secretary, 1945–1951* (London: Heinemann, 1983). See also Elisabeth Barker, *The British between the Superpowers, 1945–50* (London: Macmillan, 1983); Margaret Gowing, *Independence and Deterrence: Britain and Atomic Energy, 1945–1952* (2 vols., London: Macmillan, 1974); Kenneth Harris, *Attlee* (London: Weidenfeld & Nicolson, 1982); Ritchie Ovendale (ed.), *The Foreign Policy of the British Labour Governments: 1945–1951* (Leicester: Leicester University Press, 1984); Ritchie Ovendale, *The English-Speaking Alliance* (London: George Allen and Unwin, 1985); Alec Cairncross, *The Price of War: British Policy on German Reparations* (Oxford: Basil Blackwell, 1986). Eyewitness accounts and memoirs include: C. R. A. Attlee, *As it Happened* (London: Heinemann, 1954); Francis Williams, *Ernest Bevin: Portrait of a Great Englishman* (London: Hutchinson, 1952); Francis Williams, *A Prime Minister Remembers* (London: Heinemann, 1961); Duff Cooper, *Old Men Forget* (London: Rupert Hart-Davis, 1953); Hugh Dalton, *High Tide and After: Memoirs, 1945–1960* (London: Frederick Muller, 1962); Piers Dixon, *Double Diploma: The Life of Sir Pierson Dixon, Don and Diplomat* (London: Hutchinson, 1968); Lord Gladwyn, *Memoirs of Lord Gladwyn* (London: Weidenfeld & Nicolson, 1972); Nicholas Henderson, *The Birth of NATO* (London: Weidenfeld & Nicolson, 1982).

Between 1945 and 1947 the pattern of the cold war was not yet defined, the great postwar alliance systems were not yet fashioned, and inter-Allied planning was to be based upon hopes for effective co-operation through a world organization. The three great powers of the wartime alliance—the United States, Britain, and the Soviet Union—as well as France, all perceived themselves as world powers. Their interests and conflicts were economic, strategic, and ideological and spanned the globe. Economic leverage and military might in both conventional and nuclear forces did not yet dominate international relations, for this was a period when the arts of diplomacy and negotiation held sway, while the lessons of war were digested and the shape of the peace decided. The later perspective of a rigid bipolar antagonism is therefore unhistoric and inaccurate when applied to the early postwar years.

This book seeks to make a modest contribution to post-revisionist scholarship by examining Britain's part in the process that was to lead to the division of Germany after the war. A divided Germany still remains the most potent symbol of the cold war, of the ideological conflict between East and West, and of the new, global balance of power. The German problem was not the sole cause of the cold war, but was its principal battlefield, particularly during the 1940s. Germany's geostrategic position in part contributes to this. She lies at the heart of Europe, straddling east and west, and holding the key to the balance of power there. The Ruhr region was the economic powerhouse of Europe, and it soon became clear that economic recovery in Europe would be very difficult without the revival of the Ruhr. But in 1945 not only was Germany's economic future and political orientation unclear, but even the physical dimensions of the country were uncertain.

Worse, the experience of Germany's part in two world wars had left her rivals and enemies with deep scars. Europe had borne the brunt of German nationalism and military ascendancy. And the effect had been devastating. Neither France nor the Soviet Union could easily forget Germany's ability to penetrate their borders. Even after her crushing defeat, Germany was therefore to remain the object of great power diplomacy, and although the appalling effects of the reparations policy after the First World War were fully realized, there was little empathy towards a

German perspective in the rebuilding of the postwar European political system. Thus international tension between East and West was heightened by a mutual fear of a resurgence of German power.

This fear was intensified because the Allied powers had yet another stake in the future of Germany through their military occupation. The wartime agreements gave Britain and France and their more powerful partners, the United States and the Soviet Union, a joint responsibility in the organization and control of the occupation zones, and a political commitment to determining their future path of development. The agreement concluded at Potsdam in August 1945 was based on optimistic assumptions that the wartime alliance against Germany might be extended into peacetime. An Allied Control Council, staffed by American, Russian, British, and French officials, was to control Germany in preparation for the day when an adequate government for the country was eventually established.

However, in Britain such assumptions of four-power co-operation seemed increasingly unrealistic, even before the war ended. In official circles there were increasing doubts that Germany would continue to be the sole threat to the postwar order in Europe. The potential threat from the Soviet Union itself loomed even more ominously, because of her size, alien ideology, military might, and domination of Eastern Europe, despite her wartime alliance with the Western democracies. As the war progressed, the consequences of a Soviet advance westwards could not be ignored.

An expansionist Soviet Union, possibly controlling a communized Germany, would require a very different kind of peace settlement from that commonly envisaged during the early stages of the war. The wartime experience of the Soviet Union was such that it was clear she would never co-operate in any revival of a Germany she could not control, perceiving this—correctly—as a potential threat to her own security. Britain's traditional preoccupation had long been to preserve a balance of power on the European mainland, and it became increasingly clear that eventually this concern might lead her to build a coalition of states to contain the power of the Soviet Union. But to do this would mean the support of France and maybe, in the future, even of Germany. The wealthy Ruhr region was part of her zone of occupation and was a powerful, though expensive, card for Britain. It could be controlled to prevent its revival as part of a strong, nationalistic Germany or as part of a Russo-German combination. Its wealth might also be a potential source of strength for the West, should this ever be necessary.

But the Soviet Union was not simply a threat to the European balance of power. She was a world power with interests that stretched to Turkey, Iran and the east, to the Straits and the Mediterranean, and as such was a source of danger to the global balance of power. The experience of the war had also shown that Europe was too weak to act alone. American help would be essential in Europe and across the world if the Soviet Union were to be contained effectively. But, as John Lewis Gaddis, one of the finest post-revisionist scholars, has argued, in the early postwar period 'American omnipotence turned out to be an illusion because Washington policy-makers failed to devise strategies for applying their newly gained power effectively in practical diplomacy'.[5] To sustain American interest in Europe and to forge an anti-Soviet coalition became the fundamental objectives of British foreign policy, and one that policy-makers felt that, with her great-power status and tradition of diplomatic success, Britain would be able to fulfil.

But such a radical reappraisal of the Soviet wartime ally would clearly not be immediately acceptable to British public opinion and to the Americans themselves, and indeed was not easily arrived at in Whitehall itself. This new operational code for British policy was arrived at in a war-weary domestic environment that was increasingly dominated by fears of looming financial disaster.[6] The issue was also not a black and white one, but one that could only be clarified with the passage of time, as beliefs about Soviet intentions and behaviour were clarified and reinforced. Such an assessment would also need, eventually, to be 'sold' by the British, both at home and, indirectly, to the American Congress. So between 1945 and the end of 1947 Britain confronted the dilemma of this long-term Soviet threat with what can be described as a dual policy. The appearance of great power

[5] Gaddis, *United States and the Origins of the Cold War*, 356.
[6] Alexander George, 'The Operational Code: A Neglected Approach to the Study of Political Decision-Making', *International Studies Quarterly*, 12 (1969).

co-operation was publicly maintained, but the remorseless focus of British policy was directed to securing an effective Western alliance to contain Soviet might in Germany, in Europe, and throughout the world. As his American counterpart Dean Acheson later commented, Bevin's 'policy was to unite the western coalition against Soviet pressure, economic, political and military. He conceived of this as a common task at the heart of which lay Anglo-American and French solidarity'.[7]

The principal forum through which this policy developed was the Council of Foreign Ministers (CFM). The Council was established at the Allied Heads of State meeting held in Potsdam in July–August 1945, as the framework for preliminary foreign minister-level discussions on the peace treaties, including a peace treaty for Germany. Thus the British, the Americans, the Russians, and the French were publicly seeking to continue their wartime alliance in their forging of a global peace settlement, and complementing the contribution to world peace that the United Nations Organization would bring. British diplomacy at the Council, however, was to be paralleled by a determination not to lose control of the British zone or to allow Germany to slip into economic chaos and despair, which might incline the Germans to communism. Britain worked to isolate and contain the Soviet Union and to forge a combined policy over Germany with the Americans and, eventually, the French. By 1948 it was possible to declare this publicly. But in securing this new balance of power in Europe Britain herself was ultimately to have to accept a role as the United States' junior partner in Western Europe.

The chapters that follow trace the development of Britain's dual policy through the Council of Foreign Ministers that sat in London, Paris, New York, Moscow, and London again, until it was adjourned indefinitely in December 1947. Ironically, it was the preparation for these four-power meetings that provided the impetus for the formulation and clarification of the dual policy. The meetings became a source and platform not for four-power harmony but for an increasingly close Western understanding, stepping-stones to the cold-war confrontation that the Berlin Blockade first dramatically exemplified.

[7] Radio transcript, 25 Apr. 1957. BEVN II 9/13 (Churchill College, Cambridge).

This account sets out not to provide a general history of the Council of Foreign Ministers from the perspective of the four participating powers, but rather to outline British policy towards Germany as manifested in the Council in the years 1945 to 1947. American, French, and Soviet policies towards Germany will therefore deliberately be examined only in the context of their influence upon British perceptions and policy, for this is a study of just one actor in the cold-war drama—Britain. It is British perceptions, British priorities, British strategies, and British behaviour during the period of transition from hot to cold war in Europe that is the central concern of this book.

A study of the content of British foreign policy necessarily involves an examination of the way in which this policy was formulated and implemented, in particular the relationship between the permanent officials at the Foreign Office and their political master Ernest Bevin, a relationship that has attracted a certain amount of controversy. The force of Bevin's personality and drive, particularly at the Council meetings, was remarkable. But so was Foreign Office determination, backed by the Chiefs of Staff, both to sustain and to control the implementation of a policy to contain Soviet power. Officials maintained this thrust, despite Bevin's other preoccupations, vacillations, and illnesses, until secure in the support of the Labour Party and of public opinion, and, most important, of the Americans.

Thus between 1945 and the end of 1947 Britain was able to act almost for the last time as befitted her status as a great power. The overlapping uncertainties of Germany's future and of Soviet intentions required a redefinition of the European balance of power that was eventually to lead to a divided Germany. Four-power harmony and peace in the immediate postwar world were impossible targets: instead Britain was to lead the way to contain the genuinely feared threat of Soviet communism in Europe.

PART I
From London to Paris
September 1945–July 1946

1
LABOUR IN POWER

Expectations and Constraints: The Wartime Legacy

NO new Government inherits a clean slate, and in foreign policy-making few are bold enough to wipe it clean. For the Labour Government in 1945 both the domestic and external pressures for continuity were remarkable. Clement Attlee and Ernest Bevin, Prime Minister and Foreign Secretary respectively after 26 July 1945, were already in office, playing important roles in the wartime Coalition Government and involved in high-level discussions about the shape of the postwar world. They then took over the reins of power while the critical Heads of State meeting at Potsdam was still in progress. This critical turning-point between war and peace was no time to review British policy.

It was not initially expected that Bevin would become Foreign Secretary, and he himself had anticipated going to the Treasury. But he was preferred for the Foreign Office because, it seems, he was less openly anti-German, less left-wing, and more of a political heavyweight than his rival, Hugh Dalton. Attlee later remarked that he thought 'affairs were going to be pretty difficult and a heavy tank was what was going to be required rather than a sniper'. Bevin was also preferred by senior Foreign Office officials because Dalton had a reputation of being opinionated, as well as sympathetic to Soviet claims against the defeated Reich. Certainly, Foreign Office Permanent Under-Secretary, Sir Alexander Cadogan, felt that 'we may do better with Bevin than with any of the other Labourites'.[1]

Both in the Soviet Union and in the United States the election victory was viewed with some concern. The Labour Party's

---

[1] David Dilks (ed.), *The Diaries of Sir Alexander Cadogan* (London: Cassell, 1971), 776; Ben Pimlott, *Hugh Dalton* (London: Jonathan Cape, 1985), 411 f.; Dalton, *High Tide and After*, chap. 2; Michael Charlton, *The Price of Victory* (London: BBC, 1983), 47; Alan Bullock, *Life and Times of Ernest Bevin: Minister of Labour, 1940–1945*, ii (London: Heinemann, 1967), 39; Rothwell, *Britain and the Cold War*, 228 f.

triumph presented communists with the challenge of social democracy in action, a 'rival in the new life', as Attlee put it, and also raised doubts about the continuity of the wartime alliance. Indeed Vyacheslav Molotov, the Soviet Foreign Minister, told Bevin that 'Churchill and Eden used to be friends of the Soviet Union but you and Clement Attlee are old-fashioned imperialists'.[2] In the United States a general unease about the prospect of socialist reforms was at least tempered by the knowledge that the experience of the Coalition Government had well prepared the Labour leaders for office.[3] Ironically it would later prove easier for a socialist government to convince Americans of British suspicions of Soviet intentions in Europe.

During the war the Coalition Government had obviously publicly emphasized the importance of defeating Germany, and the BBC, the national press, and all ministers concentrated on the need for total victory over the Germans. National daily and weekly papers were broadly sympathetic to the wartime heroism of the Soviet Union and public feeling remained staunchly anti-German.[4]

Within the Labour Party itself the problem of the postwar German settlement revealed a wide divergence of opinion. The wartime debate centred on the question whether the whole German nation was responsible for nazism, a view which was encouraged by Lord Vansittart and Hugh Dalton and attracted substantial grass-roots support, but less left-wing and intellectual support; Aneurin Bevan and Labour Party chairman Harold Laski were two who represented a moderate line against the 'mania of anti-Germanism'.[5] The National Executive Committee of the Labour Party advocated reparations and controls on Germany,

[2] Dalton's diary for 5 Oct. 1945, quoted in Avi Shlaim, *Britain and the Origins of European Unity, 1940–1951* (Reading: Graduate School of Contemporary European Studies, 1978), 114. On Soviet reaction to the general election see Barker, *The British between the Superpowers*, 19; Williams, *A Prime Minister Remembers*, 71.

[3] David Williams, *Labour Britain and American Progressives* (Fabian publication, no. 53, 1947).

[4] Hugh Thomas, *Armed Truce: The Beginnings of the Cold War, 1945–46* (London: Hamish Hamilton, 1986), 216 f.; Watt, *Britain Looks to Germany*, 30 ff.; Barker, *The British between the Superpowers*, chap. 1: she calls this chapter 'When ignorance was bliss'.

[5] Michael R. Gordon, *Conflict and Consensus in Labour's Foreign Policy, 1914–65* (Stanford: Stanford University Press, 1969); Trevor Burridge, *British Labour and Hitler's War* (London: André Deutsch, 1976).

although the question of Germany's postwar borders was left open. The gap between the Labour Party and some of its ministers was to become even more striking over future policy towards the Soviet Union. Many in the Party hoped that Anglo-Soviet relations would be very good after the war. G. D. H. Cole thought that Soviet democracy was a legitimate form of democracy, and Laski, Stafford Cripps, and Dalton all argued that closer relations with the Soviet Union should be possible under a socialist government. The Labour Party election manifesto reminded voters that it was Tory fears before the war that had meant that Britain had missed the chance to establish a partnership with the Soviet Union and that the Labour Party would apply a socialist analysis to the world situation.[6]

Many in the Labour Party also hoped that a Labour government in power would break from the traditional continuity of British foreign policy, and Attlee himself had advocated this before the war. In the House of Commons debate of 20 August 1945 Michael Foot was to plead with the newly appointed Bevin that 'the Foreign Secretary . . . will not insist too eagerly upon continuity in our foreign policy, because a great part of the prestige of the Foreign Secretary in dealing with these matters arises from the great electoral victory in this country. Much more arises from that than from the legacy that was left him by his predecessor.'[7]

There grew a sizeable pressure group which was to attack Bevin's foreign policy, challenging him to pursue an independent foreign policy, away from entanglements with either the Soviet Union or the United States, but mediating and building a Third Force in Europe with other socialists. Naturally such views were widely debated within the Labour Party itself, although the influential Leonard Woolf, editor of *Political Quarterly*, was one of those who argued that the relation between socialism and questions of foreign policy was nearly always remote and obscure.[8]

---

[6] G. D. H. Cole, *An Intelligent Man's Guide to the Postwar World* (London: Gollancz, 1947); House of Commons, *Debates*, 16 Aug. 1945, vol. 413; *Let us Face the Future* (Labour Party Election Manifesto, 1945).

[7] House of Commons, *Debates*, 20 Aug. 1945, vol. 413.

[8] M. A. Fitzsimons, *The Foreign Policy of the British Labour Government 1945-1951* (Notre Dame, Ind.: University of Notre Dame Press, 1953), 24 f.; Leonard Woolf, *Foreign Policy, the Labour Party's Dilemma* (London: Fabian Research Publication, 1947), incl. foreword by Harold Laski.

This was a view with which Bevin concurred. His and Attlee's experience of war was very different from that of the bulk of their party members, growing as it did from the practical experience of policy formulation. As Minister of Labour and Deputy Prime Minister respectively, they had both been on the Armistice and Postwar Committee (APW), which was perhaps the most influential ministerial body of the Coalition Government, and had therefore had practical schooling in the analysis of postwar problems. Bevin took a keen and active interest in problems of foreign policy, making a regular and intensive study of the Foreign Office telegrams which came to him as a member of the War Cabinet. He told Molotov in October 1945 that he had been a party to the Tehran and Yalta conferences and had supported Churchill in all the decisions that had been taken.[9]

Unlike Attlee, who had a middle-class upbringing and whose conversion to socialism was an intellectual process fired by social work in East London, Bevin was born illegitimate, brought up in poverty, and worked his way up through the ranks of the trade union movement. He was not a man to be taken lightly or trifled with. He was egotistical, sensitive to criticism—especially from within his own party and from intellectuals—and often very touchy. His officials have subsequently been very enthusiastic about his vision and his strength of character, although their comments tend to cover the whole of his period of office rather than just the early years when he was still finding his way. He instinctively distrusted communists since his days of trade union politics, and the Soviet Union's heroic war effort did little to soften his deep dislike of both Soviet governmental methods and ideology. It seems Bevin also instinctively disliked Germans (and Jews and Catholics too). Gladwyn Jebb, who was one of his closest advisers, later revealed that Bevin 'had all kinds of awful prejudices', and of the Germans Bevin reputedly told Brian Robertson, the British Deputy Military Governor in the British zone, that 'I tries 'ard, Brian, but I 'ates them'.[10]

The lessons of the First World War and the interwar years were critical for Bevin's education. They appear to have led directly

[9] Williams, *Ernest Bevin*, 241; CP(45)202, 4 Oct. 1945, CAB 129/3; radio transcript, 23 Apr. 1957, BEVN II 9/13 (Churchill College, Cambridge).

[10] Bullock, *Ernest Bevin: Foreign Secretary*, chap. 3; Charlton, *Price of Victory*, 46.

to his exceptionally strong line during the war over the dismemberment of Germany, although there is no direct evidence that in 1944 he openly supported the Chiefs of Staff view that dismembering Germany would provide an insurance policy against Soviet aggression. Rather, he seems at this stage to have supported dismemberment primarily as a means of stamping out any revival of German aggression. His dislike of a central administration for postwar Germany continued right up to and beyond the Potsdam Conference. But the most important lesson he learnt from interwar history was the danger of appeasement and he publicly acknowledged that appeasing Hitler had brought Britain to war, for 'we all refused to face the facts and landed ourselves in it; because we were hoping against hope that this trouble would not arise. It did arise, and it is just as well to acknowledge it, and having acknowledged it, to do our damnedest to get out of it.'[11]

But Bevin was fully appraised of the arguments which raged in government circles during 1944, and he was not so naïve as to presume that the only threat of the postwar period would come from Germany. His first biographer notes that Bevin came to Potsdam 'fully aware of the tensions that existed, and with a shrewd assessment of the scope of Soviet ambitions, a much shrewder one indeed at this stage, than that of the Americans'.[12]

Even as he made his debut as Foreign Secretary at Potsdam, Bevin also asserted Britain's role as the major European actor and her strength as a great power. Britain was to take the lead as the major European actor with a display of determination and strength and was not to be 'barged about'. Indeed, the new American Secretary of State, James Byrnes, commenting on Bevin's performance at Potsdam, feared that 'his manner was so aggressive that both the President and I wondered how we would get along with this new Foreign Secretary'.[13] However, Pierson Dixon, his astute Principal Private Secretary, admired Bevin's 'wholly delightful assumption that, of the three, we were still the biggest', and Cadogan also was impressed by his strong personality.[14]

---

[11] Quoted in Fitzsimons, *Foreign Policy of the British Labour Government*, 24 n.
[12] Williams, *Ernest Bevin*, 241.
[13] Bullock, *Ernest Bevin: Foreign Secretary*, 25; Byrnes, *Speaking Frankly*, 79.
[14] Dixon, *Double Diploma*, 170; Charlton, *Price of Victory*, 46 ff.

Attlee and Bevin, but Bevin particularly, had staked out a
position on Labour's postwar foreign policy during the last months
of the war. Despite the hopes of many in the Labour Party, his
emphasis was on the continuity of policy with that of the Coalition
Government. 'I cannot help feeling', he told a Yorkshire regional
conference in April 1945, 'that on the questions of our defence,
our foreign policy and our relations with other countries, there
is an imperative necessity for the will of the nation as a whole
to be expressed. I feel that a complete knowledge of the facts is
essential to both the Party in office and the party in opposition.'[15]
The issues to which Bevin thought the Government had to address
itself were the economic reconstruction of the world and,
significantly, the prevention of the substitution of one form
of totalitarianism for another. This is what the Coalition
Government had aimed for, and the basis of the Labour
Government's policy should be in keeping with this. Indeed, as
his former colleague but political opponent Anthony Eden
elaborated, 'the greater the measure of agreement there is between
us at home, the greater will be the authority of my right Hon.
friend abroad'.[16] This perception of the fundamental difference
between foreign policy which he saw as above the rough and
tumble of party politics, and social domestic policy was to lie
at the heart of Bevin's conflicts with his own party.

Both Bevin and Eden also saw a bipartisan foreign policy as
a way of assuring Britain's world status. Always a 'majorities'
man, he did not see that disagreements either in the party, or even
in the House of Commons, could possibly enhance Britain's
position abroad. One of the most striking features of the transition
from Conservative to Labour Government in 1945 is the
continuity that was achieved, both in personnel and in ideas. The
influence of wartime thinking in Whitehall about the postwar
world thus bears closer examination, for it was to be Whitehall
officials who set the agenda for postwar British policy.

From 1943 onwards there were lively and protracted discussions
within the British Government about the postwar world, the place
of both Germany and Soviet Union in Europe, and in particular

[15] Quoted in Bullock, *Life and Times of Ernest Bevin*, ii, 349.
[16] House of Commons, *Debates*, 20 Aug. 1945, vol. 413.

about the role Britain would play. Attention focused specifically upon how to avoid a repetition of the débâcle that had followed World War One.[17] The weight of history lay heavily over these discussions as the Chiefs of Staff revived the notion of Britain's traditional interest in ensuring a favourable balance of power in Europe. The most famous exposition of this had been by Sir Eyre Crowe, who had minuted in 1907 that the 'check on the abuse of political preponderance [by neighbouring states] . . . has always consisted in the opposition of an equally formidable rival, or of a combination of several countries forming leagues of defence'.[18] In the same vein the Chiefs reminded officials and ministers that 'our policy in Europe in the past has been to maintain a balance of power with the object of ensuring that no Great Power should be capable of dominating the Continent'.[19] Appeasement had been a terrible mistake, an indication of moral cowardice, and in the postwar world any hint of weakness was to be avoided, wherever the threat to democracy and peace came from—and the Chiefs made it clear that the primary threat to future peace would be the Soviet Union.

However, where the line between appeasement and the recognition of other powers' justifiable interests lay was never made clear in discussions. Planners were instead determined not to repeat their failure to settle the German problem effectively after the First World War, not to allow the Americans to withdraw from Europe once again, and not to allow another breakdown in Anglo-French relations.

Within British government circles there had been several centres of discussion about the postwar world. Winston Churchill himself was of course deeply involved in talks about the shape the postwar

[17] For discussions of wartime debates in Government circles see Burridge, *British Labour and Hitler's War*; Keith Sainsbury, 'British Policy and German Unity at the end of the Second World War', *English Historical Review*, 94 (1979); Trevor Burridge, 'Great Britain and the Dismemberment of Germany at the end of the Second World War', *International History Review*, 3/4 (1981); John Baylis, 'British Wartime Thinking about a Post-war European Security Group', *Review of International Studies*, 914 (1983); Graham Ross, 'Foreign Office Attitudes to the Soviet Union, 1941–45', *Journal of Contemporary History*, 16/3 (1981); Anthony Gorst, 'British Military Planning for Postwar Defence, 1943–1945', in Anne Deighton (ed.), *Britain and the First Cold War* (London: Macmillan, 1990).
[18] Quoted in Fitzsimons, *Foreign Policy of the British Labour Government*, 4.
[19] PHP(44)27(0) Final, 9 Nov. 1944, CAB 81/45.

world would take and by 1945 was moving towards a vision of a postwar order that embraced an Atlantic relationship and a Danubian federation of south German states, based on a sharp appraisal of future Soviet threats to the European balance of power.[20] But Churchill and Eden were often in disagreement about postwar planning, for until the last months of the war the Foreign Office continued to emphasize the importance of containing German power. As long as the Soviet Union did not have cause to feel threatened by the Western Powers, in particular over Germany or Poland, there seemed no reason to doubt her willingness to co-operate. Moreover, nagging doubts about the direction and reliability of American policy when the war ended reinforced the need for Britain to work with her major European wartime ally against any revival of German power. The Foreign Office officially embraced Roosevelt's notion of a postwar world in which four great powers, the United States, Britain, the Soviet Union, and China, would operate collectively under the aegis of a new world organization.[21]

In April 1944 Churchill had created the APW out of the Armistice Terms and Civil Administration Committee with a brief to plan for the German and European postwar settlement. This Cabinet Committee met frequently and was very influential, not least because Churchill had deliberately kept under check the importance of the Foreign Office and the Cabinet.[22] The APW Committee was assiduously chaired by Attlee, and Bevin, who was also a member, took a continuous and active interest in its work.

But it was the Chiefs of Staff, and the Post Hostilities Planning Staff Committee (PHPS)—a joint Foreign Office/Chiefs of Staff Committee—who revealed by far the most outspoken views on the new balance of power in Europe that might emerge after the war. This Committee was chaired by Gladwyn Jebb until the Foreign Office abandoned its membership in November 1944. It produced papers as prescient as they were controversial and in its assessment of Britain's security needs after the war concluded

---

[20] Henry Butterfield Ryan, *The Vision of Anglo-America: The US–UK Alliance and the Emerging Cold War, 1943–1946* (Cambridge: Cambridge University Press, 1987), Part I.

[21] Gladwyn, *Memoirs*, chaps. 8–9. See also references in n. 17.

[22] Burridge, *British Labour and Hitler's War*, 169. In July 1945 the APW Committee was renamed the Overseas Reconstruction Committee.

that the long-term threat to Britain was the Soviet Union. With what were claimed to be pragmatic and objective observations the Chiefs concluded that the Soviet Union was the only obvious enemy for Britain once Japan and Germany were broken: and Foreign Office officials were putting their 'heads in the sand' and acting like appeasers if they could not understand this. The military realities of Europe were that

the north east of Germany will pass under Russian political and economic influence whether it is a Russian zone of occupation or a Prussian State in a dismembered Germany. The spread of this influence to the rest of Germany, however, could more easily be checked if the remainder of Germany comprised two separate states each under the control of a western democratic state.[23]

They advocated a divided Germany based on the zones of Allied occupation with Western and Eastern influence over these states. Each should look outwards, not inwards, for its political and economic links, which would thereby discourage German nationalism. The Chiefs thus favoured dismemberment both to stop a German revival and to provide in-depth defence for Britain against the Soviet Union. For if the 'USSR were eventually to develop hostile intentions towards us . . . we should require all the help we could get from any source open to us, including Germany'.[24] The Western powers had to accept that the Soviet Union would not give up her interest in her zone. The logic of this was that she would therefore never accept a rearmed Germany if it might be used against her. Britain needed and should hold on to the north-western zone, both to control Germany and, if necessary, to use that zone against the USSR. It was vital that a part of Germany was included as an area of major British strategic interest to help to preserve a balance against the overwhelming presence of the Soviet Union in Europe. This view was most cogently expressed by Field Marshal Alanbrooke. In his diary on 27 July 1944 he asked:

[23] PHP(44)15(0), 15 Nov. 1944, CAB 81/45; Secretary's minute, 1661/4, COS(44) 323rd, 2 Oct. 1944, CAB 21/957.
[24] COS(44)822(0), 9 Sept. 1944, CAB 21/957. Jebb recalls that several members of the Service Departments gave a 'whoop of joy' at the prospect of dismemberment; Gladwyn, *Memoirs*, 135.

should Germany be dismembered or gradually converted to an ally to meet the Russian threat of twenty years hence? I suggest . . . the latter and feel certain that we must from now onwards regard Germany in a very different light. Germany is no longer the dominating power in Europe—Russia is. . . . She . . . cannot fail to become the main threat in fifteen years from now. Therefore, foster Germany, gradually build her up and bring her into a Federation of Western Europe. Unfortunately this must all be done under the cloak of a holy alliance of Russia, England and America. Not an easy policy.[25]

The logic of a divided Germany also emerged in the practical work of the Allied planners, in particular that of the European Advisory Commission (EAC), which also advocated a zonal military occupation of Germany. In the EAC three occupation zones were suggested by Britain, corresponding to the existing strategic balance of Allied forces, and with Britain holding the north-west, Ruhr area. This would protect her, first, against any resurgence of German power based on the industrial wealth of the Ruhr, second, against Soviet bad faith in the war, and third, against any American withdrawal from Europe. After lengthy Anglo-American squabbling the zones were accepted in large measure at Yalta in February 1945, when, under pressure from the British, the French were also given a zone carved out of the two Western zones. At Yalta these occupation zones were also considered as a possible preliminary to a subsequent dismemberment of Germany, for the proposed surrender terms stated that the Allies should 'take such steps . . . as they deemed requisite' over dismemberment, and this decision was reinforced by the establishment of an Allied Dismemberment Committee, that sat in London during 1945.[26]

The Foreign Office files, however, reveal that until the last months of the war dismembering Germany into zones of occupation was an unwelcome option, although it was clear that any debate about the future of Germany would be incomplete if Germany were considered in a vacuum. The Foreign Office only grudgingly

[25] Arthur Bryant, *Triumph in the West, 1943–1946* (London: Collins, 1959), 242.
[26] Keith Sainsbury, *The Turning Point* (Oxford: Oxford University Press, 1985), 77 f.; Tony Sharp, *The Wartime Alliance and the Zonal Division of Germany* (Oxford: Clarendon Press, 1975), 65; Yalta Protocol, Article 12(a), CAB 21/957. For the few ineffectual meetings of the Allied Disarmament Committee, FO 371/46871–3.

came down in favour of breaking up Germany when they thought this was the option favoured by the Soviet Union, who might otherwise think that an Anglo-German combination was being planned. They did concede that dismemberment gave some advantages, as any German aggression would inevitably be preceded by attempts at reunification which would be a clear warning sign of future trouble. But they suspected that talk of breaking up Germany might encourage the Soviet Union to make a separate peace with Germany and to build her own sphere of influence in eastern Europe. This could have serious effects upon hopes for joint Allied control in Europe and therefore on relations with the United States.[27]

But Eden nevertheless found that he faced a strong demand for dismemberment, not only from sections of his own Department and the Service Departments, but also from the APW Committee and particularly from both the future Prime Minister and the future Foreign Secretary. Whilst planners were looking ahead beyond military occupation, it was not yet clear whether any central administrations should be retained or recreated when Germany surrendered. Bevin argued that *any* German central administrations would prepare the way to another war, and Attlee thought that the German machine had to be 'smashed'. Attlee produced a paper on German policy after a ferocious APW meeting, arguing that Britain and the United States would never be prepared to stay in Germany for a long occupation and that therefore both the State of Prussia and those who controlled heavy industry had to be destroyed, whatever the economic effects; for 'everything that brings home to the Germans the completeness and irrevocability of their defeat is worthwhile in the end'.[28]

Eden responded by asserting that the economic collapse in Germany would not help Europe to recover, and threatened to refer the whole question to the War Cabinet. Bevin continued to advocate a separate administration for the Ruhr and to insist that even a temporary central administration before dismemberment was unacceptable. Once established, 'we should never break it down at a later stage'. Eden silenced his critics

[27] Ross, 'Foreign Office Attitudes to the Soviet Union', 525.
[28] APW(44)43, 11 July 1944, CAB 87/67; APW(44)10th, 20 July 1944, CAB 87/66.

temporarily by claiming that both the United States and the
Soviet Union were planning on at least a short-term central
administration for Germany, although he did agree that such a
decision should not prejudice future decisions.[29]

The dispute over the future of Germany and Anglo-Soviet
relations continued to simmer throughout the summer and autumn
of 1944. Eden was particularly anxious not to explore any
hypothetical postwar scenario that involved breaking up Germany
as a measure of insurance against possible Soviet aggression. But
this was for strictly practical reasons. 'It seems to me essential
that any such connections should be avoided like the plague in
our consideration of German problems. If we prepare our post
war plans with the idea at the back of our minds that the Germans
may serve as part of an anti-Soviet block, we shall quickly destroy
any hope of preserving the Anglo-Soviet alliance.'[30] Eden was
genuinely anxious that COS and APW plans would fall into Soviet
hands, and Orme Sargent was convinced that the Russians already
knew of the doubts among military planners about Soviet
goodwill. The issue was left unresolved, and the APW were still
asking the Foreign Office for their views on the issue in early
1945.[31]

At the same time as these discussions were taking place Eden
had also asked for papers on the strategic implications of the
proposed world organization. The PHPS obligingly reiterated their
anxieties about a possible threat from the Soviet Union.[32] The
strongest emphasis was placed upon the need to develop good
relations with France and the United States in the postwar years.
The idea of a Western bloc based initially upon an Anglo-French
alliance was more acceptable to Eden and the Foreign Office as
it appeared ideologically less contentious than the construction
of an anti-Soviet front. The Soviets were consulted in December
1941 and again in November 1944 about such a bloc and
appeared to have no major objections. They themselves were

[29] APW(44)14th, 23 Aug. 1944, CAB 87/66; APW(44) 89, 5 Oct. 1944,
CAB 87/68.

[30] APW(44)90, 5 Oct. 1944, CAB 21/957: this paper was later withdrawn.

[31] Sargent minute, 18 Aug. 1944, FO 371/43306; Elisabeth Barker notes that
Donald Maclean had recently been transferred to Moscow and was receiving copies
of PHP papers, *The British Between the Superpowers*, 9.

[32] PHP(44)27(0) Final, 9 Nov. 1944, CAB 81/45.

building their own network of treaties with Czechoslovakia, Yugoslavia, and Poland. The Western grouping was also to be constructed under the umbrella of a world organization, with a view to protecting Europe from a German revival. The Chiefs further supported French proposals for the permanent military occupation of the Rhineland, a proposal also supported by Bevin, who had already advocated the separation of this region from the rest of Germany. However, the real charm of a Western bloc for the Chiefs was that it could, if necessary, be transformed into the basis of an anti-Soviet alliance. Ironically it was Churchill who now rejected a Western bloc, arguing that France was too weak to be a reliable ally, that the British would not want the commitment of a continental army, and that for Britain, as a power with global commitments, air and sea defences were of the greatest importance. Despite his reluctance, by the end of the war the Foreign Office had a draft treaty with France already prepared. This was drawn up on the basis of a Western group, a notion which presaged that of containing the power of the Soviet Union to the east, even though by now it was known that the Russians were beginning to change their mind about the acceptability of a Western bloc.[33]

These debates certainly did much to crystallize the trend of British thinking towards the postwar world, but other decisive influences resulted from the progress of the war itself. Officials in the Foreign Office became increasingly sceptical about the future as the Soviets advanced from the east, and their dominance in Europe, so feared by the Chiefs of Staff, seemed close to becoming a reality.

Ironically it is quite possible that one of the reasons that the Soviet Union appeared confident that her security interests in eastern Europe might be protected after the war was the informal agreement struck between Stalin and Churchill in Moscow in October 1944. The Percentages Agreement was accepted by President Roosevelt as a wartime expedient and a means of postponing Anglo-Soviet rivalry, but it is fair to assume that Stalin

---

[33] Brief for Potsdam Conference, Annex H, J, 12 July 1945, CAB 21/1614. The change of opinion in Moscow was evidenced by a hostile reaction to a series of articles in *The Economist*. Martin Gilbert, *Road to Victory: Winston Churchill 1941–1945* (London: Heinemann, 1986), 1070.

interpreted it as an acceptance of Soviet influence in eastern Europe on the principle of *cuius regio, eius religio*. This agreement gave an overwhelming predominance of influence to the Soviet Union in Rumania and Bulgaria and to Britain in Greece. The agreement has been criticized in many quarters and Churchill himself was anxious about how it might be received if it became public. Such naked power politics obviously sidestepped the interests of smaller powers, but it has to be said that it represented a simple acceptance of the security needs of the great powers without any of the overlying ideological claims and counterclaims that were to sour East–West relations. Churchill admired Stalin's consequent restraint in Greece, and the Soviets clearly saw the Percentages Agreement as the basis of at least a 'hands off' agreement.[34]

During the early months of 1945 the problem of what to do with Germany after the war raised itself in another guise. This concerned the old question of reparations. Once again the experience of the First World War settlement, when massive reparations were imposed upon Germany, was crucial. But Roosevelt's remarks at Yalta that the United States would leave Europe two years after the end of the war would make reparations, disarmament, de-nazification, and dismemberment a daunting task, and the Chancellor, Sir John Anderson, argued that if Germany was to pay reparations again after the Second World War, she must be rich enough to do so without European and American help. To be punished Germany could not simply be destroyed, although this would present the Allies with the dilemma of a prosperous Germany that might become a dangerous Germany.[35]

Despite doubts in the Foreign Office about dismemberment, the Yalta agreement of February 1945 had been generally well received in Britain. As Dixon, then Private Secretary to Eden, noted in his diary, 'the auguries are good'.[36] But over the following few months the international situation changed dramatically, for the Soviet advance west into Germany as far as the Oder and Western Neisse rivers caused considerable anxiety,

[34] Wheeler-Bennett, *Semblance of Peace*, 46 ff.; Elisabeth Barker, *Churchill and Eden at War* (London: Macmillan, 1978), 284.

[35] APW(45)40, 19 Mar. 1945, CAB 87/69.

[36] Dixon, *Double Diploma*, 148.

as the new frontiers of Poland had not yet been decided. It is well known that Churchill pressed very hard for a tougher military line during these last months of the war, suggesting in particular that Western troops should not withdraw from areas allocated to the Soviet Union until a settlement was reached over Poland's borders. This would have been in contravention of the zonal agreements, and Eisenhower refused, thereby allowing to slip away the last opportunity of using the military dispositions of Western troops in Europe to influence the postwar settlement more advantageously.[37]

Despite the fluctuations, disagreements, and differences of emphasis between postwar planners, one central trend is clearly discernible, and that is that by the end of the Second World War a general but private consensus had evolved, that the major threat to the peace of the postwar world would be the Soviet Union. It is traditionally held, however, that the Foreign Office retained a firm belief in four-power co-operation into the early postwar period. But amongst senior Foreign Office officials and certain diplomats there was a growing suspicion of Soviet postwar intentions. The major question seemed now to be whether Britain would once again sit staring like a mesmerized rabbit at preparations for war, afraid to take action lest it should produce 'the calamity we desired to avert'.[38] After the war Britain would have to act independently on the world stage, hopefully leading an Anglo-Saxon bloc and defending Europe against the predominance of Soviet power. Perhaps the most elaborate statement of this view was made by Deputy Under-Secretary of State Sir Orme Sargent on 11 July 1945, in his 'Stock Taking after VE day' memorandum. Sargent, known as 'Moley' to his colleagues, probably because of his firm stand against appeasement in the 1930s, sought to analyse trends in Soviet policy and the response Britain should take to these trends.

The memorandum is central to an understanding of the real agenda of the immediate postwar world. It is full of references to the nature of the threat that Hitler posed before the Second World War. In the same way that the Nazis demanded

[37] Chester Wilmot, *The Struggle for Europe* (London: Collins, 1952), 691 f.; Rothwell, *Britain and the Cold War*, 140 ff.
[38] Duff Cooper, *Old Men Forget*, 347.

Lebensraum in the 1930s, Sargent thought Stalin intended 'to obtain his security . . . by creating what might be termed an ideological Lebensraum in those countries which he considered strategically important'.[39] Hitler had explained in *Mein Kampf* both his objectives and his methods, but 'in the case of the Soviet Union Stalin is not likely to be so obliging. We shall have to try to find out for ourselves what is his plan of campaign.' British foreign policy makers had an obligation to stand firm in any diplomatic trial of strength that the Soviet Union might care to try. Sargent, unlike some of his other colleagues, still hoped to retain a Western influence in Eastern Europe by keeping 'our foot firmly in Finland, Poland, Czechoslovakia, Austria, Yugoslavia and Bulgaria, even though we may have to abandon perhaps for the moment Rumania and Hungary'. He further feared the capacity of the Soviet Union to 'exploit for their own ends the economic crises which in the coming months may well develop into a catastrophe capable of engulfing political institutions in many European countries' and knew that the struggle for Germany would be central to the overall pattern of the European balance of power. 'It is not', he argued, 'overstating the position to say that if Germany is won this may well decide the fate of liberalism throughout the world'.[40]

Equally pessimistic views were also being expressed by the influential Frank Roberts, Chargé d'Affaires in the British Embassy in Moscow, who argued that

the Soviet state was still run by orthodox Marxists and that there is a fundamental divergence between Soviet political philosophy and totalitarian practices and the way of life of the outside world. Given these facts we should be rash to base our policy upon the hope that in the foreseeable future the Soviet Union will settle down into a country with whom our relations can be normal and easy.[41]

Britain must also expect to be excluded from most of eastern Europe. 'Since Europe has been divided by Soviet action into two parts, we had better lose no time in ensuring that ours

[39] Rohan Butler and M. E. Pelly (eds.), *Documents on British Policy Overseas*, 1st ser., i. (London: HMSO, 1984), 181 ff. (Henceforth *DBPO* i).
[40] Ibid.   [41] Roberts to Warner, 25 Apr. 1945, FO 371/47882.

remains the better and—with the support of the outside world—
the stronger half'.[42]

In Paris the British Ambassador Duff Cooper was also sceptical
about the Soviet Union, although he did not emphasize the
ideological dimension of any future balance-of-power problem
in Europe. Duff Cooper produced his 'political testament' as part
of a campaign to draw Britain and France together as the core
members of a new Western bloc against German or Russian
power, and warned that 'the ineluctable logic of events compels
us to acknowledge that in the period that follows the war Great
Britain must beware of Russia' as well as Germany, not just
because of her ideology but because of the size of her army, and
that it would be foolish to eliminate the possibility of an alliance
between the two. Now they were only separated by mutual
hatred—and Poland. Whilst he supported a world organization,
he, like the Chiefs of Staff, asserted that political realism dictated
that solid foundations, instead of 'kind words and scraps of paper',
should form the basis of postwar foreign policy.[43]

The far-sighted and independently minded Gladwyn Jebb also
supported Sargent's stocktaking memorandum as well as the
general drift of Duff Cooper's analysis. He too realized that the
Soviet Union would almost certainly emerge from the war as the
principal land power in Europe. This power would have to be
balanced in some way, and Jebb was in favour of a Western bloc,
a tacit admission of defensive spheres of influence, and the creation
of an effective world organization.[44]

Given this realistic appraisal of the balance of power in postwar
Europe, it was imperative for Britain to continue to act as a great
power. Sargent thought that

in the minds of our big partners, especially in that of the United States,
there is a feeling that Great Britain is now a secondary power and can
be treated as such, and that in the long run all will be well if they—the
United States and the Soviet Union—as the two supreme world powers
of the future, understand one another. It is this misconception that it
must be our policy to combat.[45]

---

[42] Ibid.; Frank Roberts, 'Foreword' to Richard Crockatt and Steve Smith (eds.),
The Cold War Past and Present (London: Allen and Unwin, 1987), xv.
[43] Quoted in John Charmley, *Duff Cooper: The Authorized Biography* (London:
Weidenfeld & Nicolson, 1986), 185; Duff Cooper, *Old Men Forget*, 346 ff.
[44] 'Western Europe', 9 May 1944, CAB 21/1614.   [45] *DBPO* i. 181 ff.

Roberts echoed this view, writing that we 'must also show them [the Soviet Union] that we are not bankrupt in political and economic leadership and that the Western world, under our guidance and with the vast economic sources of the Anglo-Saxon world behind it, remains strong and healthy enough to resist Soviet pressure or infiltration tactics'.[46]

Dixon, both a well-placed participant and an astute observer of these years, agreed. He noted at Potsdam that once again the British team were debating 'the perennial question whether Russia was peaceful and wanted to join the Western Club but is suspicious of us, or whether she is out to dominate the world and is hoodwinking us'. And he added ominously, 'it always seems safer to go on the worst assumptions'.[47]

The analyses of these officials is particularly pertinent to any examination of postwar British foreign policy. These men, and others in the Foreign Office who agreed with their ideas, for example Assistant Under-Secretary Oliver Harvey, were all to hold posts of considerable influence under Bevin's Foreign Secretaryship, and were to be given a very free hand in evolving long-term policy towards Germany in the frantically busy months following the war. This was in spite of the fact that both Orme Sargent and Duff Cooper expected to be replaced if a Labour government came to power. Their views, and in particular their growing distrust of Soviet ideology and intentions and their reassertion of Britain's place at the top table of world conferences, were strongly echoed in Bevin's own thinking both during and after the war.

Expectations and Constraints: Potsdam

But as the war ended, how to play Britain's hand in Europe and Germany became less of a hypothetical question and more of a dilemma that would, at least in the short term, be determined by the international environment. Britain's options were necessarily restricted. Most of eastern Europe and much of Germany was militarily occupied by the Red Army; western

[46] Roberts to Warner, 25 Apr. 1945, FO 371/47882.
[47] Dixon, *Double Diploma*, 165.

Germany was occupied by British, American, and French forces. Practical problems of refugees, food, and transport were the first priority. Soviet policy was unclear, if not schizophrenic, as the conflict between their reparation demands and an apparent desire to seek a united pro-Soviet Germany seemed to reveal.[48] American policy was also unclear, and the Americans seemed to be more suspicious of British than of Soviet intentions. It was no moment to air worries about the Soviet Union, while the equilibrium of European and world forces still lay in the balance.

It was at Potsdam that a settlement was forged which set the framework for the next two years of negotiations over Germany between the wartime Allies. On 5 June the Allied Generals had met in Berlin to sign the Declaration of Defeat and Assumption of Supreme Authority over Germany. By the end of the month the Allied powers had agreed on the establishment of the Allied Control Council which would take unanimous decisions 'in matters affecting Germany as a whole', leaving the individual Commanders-in-Chief with ultimate authority in their own zones.[49]

Organizational difficulties apart, the British zone—coveted for the industrial wealth of the Ruhr and its strategic position—presented quite enormous administrative problems. The question of Germany's future role in European politics was overwhelmed by the urgent need to recover from the chaos of war, although Montgomery also asserted that it was hard to see how Germany could ever again become an economic whole under one supreme authority.[50] There existed no government, no effective currency. Bombing had disrupted transport, communications, and industry. Housing shortages, food shortages, and coal shortages prevailed.

[48] Shlaim, *The United States and the Berlin Blockade*, 19.
[49] *DBPO* i. 1265. The British Commander-in-Chief was Field Marshal Bernard Montgomery, the American, General Dwight Eisenhower, the Soviet, Marshal Zhukov, and the French Commander, General Koenig. Their Deputies were Brian Robertson, Lucius Clay, Vassily Sokolovsky, and Louis Koeltz respectively. The British Commander-in-Chief, his Deputy, and the Control Commission (CCG) were under the control of the War Office. The Political Adviser, William Strang, was, however, a Foreign Office official. In Oct. 1945 the British Control Commission was transferred from the War Office to the Control Office. John Hynd, Chancellor of the Duchy of Lancaster, was in charge of this department, but his post was not a Cabinet one, FO 941/1 *passim.*
[50] *DBPO* i. 69 ff., 1203. W. Krieger, 'The Interregnum in Germany: March to August, 1945', *Political Science Quarterly*, 64 (1949).

Seventy per cent of the zone's food had to be imported. There were roughly two million displaced persons there. The cost of administering the zone was estimated at £80 million for the first year, and the Foreign Office official Jack Troutbeck conceded that

the Control Commission is built on shifting sands and has had to scrap strategy in favour of tactics. But I do not think this is as much the result of our set-up in Germany as of the facts of the situation. Our authorities are faced with one dreadful problem after another, and can do nothing else but try to improvise some solution.

'The same complaint', he added, 'has often been made of this august office.'[51]

Given the grim realities of the situation on the ground, conceptual plans about holding Germany down to preserve Allied unity, or building her up to protect the West against Soviet encroachment, seemed of secondary importance to those most closely involved. It was more important to look forward to recreating a functioning organism than to look back to paying the debts of war or thinking of traditional strategic concerns. British wartime thinking had been a blend of vengeance and anxiety and had striven to resolve the contradictions of destroying the German state by dismemberment and not destroying it so that reparations could be taken, between eliminating German power and preserving something of Germany should her weight be needed against the Soviet Union. Now the considerations seemed more practical. To prevent starvation Germany required food from the east as much as coal and steel from the Ruhr. This was the only economic argument for German unity.

The Potsdam Protocol of 2 August 1945 laid down political and economic principles for the treatment of Germany. But it was unrealistic and unworkable unless all four occupying powers were in agreement, as the Allied Control Council was responsible for major decisions, yet had to rely on unanimity, while responsibility for administering each zone rested with its own Commander. This was to give each occupying power ultimate responsibility and freedom for the development of its own zone.[52]

---

[51] Troutbeck minute, 31 Aug. 1945, FO 371/46973.
[52] *DPBO* i. Protocol: 1263–77. Appendix A.

The first tasks of the military authorities were to ensure disarmament, demilitarization, denazification, decentralization, and democratization of Germany. These requirements sought both to eradicate any traces of the Nazi regime and to prevent a resurgence of militarism and industrial/military might. The political framework that the Potsdam Protocol advocated was one of preparation for an eventual return of the country to democracy. Decentralization and local responsibility, the gradual introduction of parties and trade unions, freedom of speech and of the press were all to be introduced within the constraints of ensuring military security. Although no German central government was yet envisaged, central administrations would be introduced in the fields of finance, transport, communications, foreign trade, and industry, under Control Council direction.[53] But the greatest difficulties of the Potsdam Protocol lay in the two separate sections that dealt with economic unity and reparations.

Paragraph 14 of the Economic Principles stated that 'during the period of occupation Germany shall be treated as a single economic unit. To this end common policies shall be established.'[54] The British hoped to be able to continue to feed their zone from the east, and one of the major themes of their subsequent talks with the Russians was that this clause took precedence over the clauses that dealt with reparations.

Reparations are an emotive issue, involving both retribution and compensation. Wartime and postwar thinking was guided by the experience of reparations after the First World War and in particular what amounted to the financing by the United States of the reparations programme. Soviet interest in reparations became evident at the Yalta Conference in February 1945. Maisky, in the Soviet Foreign Ministry, demanded reparations of $10 billion for the Soviet Union both from capital deliveries and current production. Churchill opposed naming a figure until it was known what Germany could pay, fearful that the Western powers would find themselves meeting the bills to sustain payments. However, the American delegation accepted the sum of $10 billion 'as a basis of discussion'. This was a decision that left

[53] Ibid.   [54] Ibid.

them constantly on the defensive in their subsequent negotiations
with the Soviet Union.[55]

The reparations issue was closely linked to the question of
dismemberment, as Germany's capacity to pay would obviously be
determined by her geographical boundaries. But reparations were
rarely discussed in Cabinet before Potsdam, Ministers of both
parties were not enthusiastic about them, and Churchill warned the
Cabinet that 'no opportunity should be lost of bringing home to the
Russian representatives the dangers and difficulties of reparations.
We should give the Russians the benefit of the experience which
we have gained in these matters after the last war.'[56]

Reparations at Potsdam were almost entirely a Soviet–
American affair, partly because of the British general election.
Byrnes wanted to link a quick reparations settlement that would
not produce endless wranglings, to a settlement of the Polish
question, which was of great psychological importance for the
United States. The British team knew that the Americans were
now anxious not to deindustrialize Germany too far and not to
name figures as they had done at Yalta. The Soviets too were
prepared to create a workable reparations settlement and even
to reduce their original demand because of what they had already
taken from their zone. But when Byrnes proposed a zonal solution
for the bulk of reparations payments, the Soviets made it clear
that current production was of vital importance to the recovery
of their economy and expressed fears that the Ruhr might be
virtually sealed off to them in any such reparations deal. They
therefore suggested a separate quadripartite control of the Ruhr,
which the British immediately rejected.[57]

During the last feverish days of the conference, Byrnes's wish
to construct a deal prevailed and the Protocol recorded what was
in essence a zonal solution for reparations.[58] This deal gave each

[55] Billion = 1,000 million. On Yalta conference, J. L. Snell (ed.), *The Meaning of
Yalta: Big Three Diplomacy and the New Balance of Power* (Louisiana: Louisiana
State University Press, 1956); Cairncross, *The Price of War*, 70 ff., 80 ff.

[56] CM(45)7, 11 June 1945, CAB 65/53. A Ministerial Committee on the subject
met only once: RM(45)1, 1 May 1945, CAB 98/59.

[57] *DBPO* i. 1013–4; Gaddis, *The United States and the Origins of the Cold
War*, 238.

[58] Cairncross, *The Price of War*, chap. 4; Edmonds, *Setting the Mould*, 59 ff.;
Llewellyn Woodward, *British Foreign Policy in the Second World War*, (London:
HMSO, 1976), chap. lxix. For relevant text see Appendix A.

occupying power what was effectively a free hand to take the reparations it wanted from its zone. However, this agreement did not in any way reduce Allied friction over Germany, which had been one of his express wishes. It simply postponed the debate. Since future deliveries were represented in percentages and not in figures, quadripartite agreement still had to be found over the level of industrial development to which Germany would be allowed to aspire. Although reparations from current production were not specifically mentioned as part of the deal, it must be noted that commodities were to be allowed to be shipped west in exchange for capital equipment (section III, 4(*a*)). Of greater importance, section III, 4(*a*) and (*b*) were not subject to the first charge principle, and it is on these clauses that the reparations argument subsequently turned.[59] The Protocol thus failed to link effectively the section on economic unity with that on reparations and thereby created two areas of conflict—how to share German resources and the relationship between reparation and rehabilitation.

The incompatibility of these two sections became the leitmotif of subsequent discussions at the Council of Foreign Ministers. Even at Potsdam it was obvious to the Russians, the Americans, and the British alike that the reparations settlement implied separate development within the zones. Molotov asked Byrnes if he interpreted the settlement to mean that 'each country would have a free hand in their own zones and would act entirely independently of the others?', and Jack Troutbeck commented that 'it is difficult to believe that such a system would not divide Germany completely into two parts'.[60] When Bevin asked what the position now was he was advised that 'the general trend of this Conference suggests that, whatever the *de facto* result of dividing Germany into zones of occupation will be, the idea of planned and deliberate dismemberment is dead'.[61]

Sir David Waley at the Treasury pointed out that the system of trading reparations, of swaps, was unworkable as 'the peasant in Brandenburg who sells his potatoes to Berlin has to be paid

[59] For the wording of these sections see Appendix A.
[60] *Foreign Relations of the United States, 1945, Conference of Berlin*, ii (Washington: United States Government Printing Office, 1960) (henceforth *FRUS*), 450; *DBPO* i. 920 n. 1.
[61] Harrison to Bevin, 30 July 1945, FO 371/46872.

by receiving boots and shoes from Berlin and cannot be paid by
Russia receiving steel plant'.[62] He thought the principle of
Germany as a single economic unit would effectively have to be
abandoned and knew that some in the American team were
thinking along the lines that 'however undesirable it may be to
draw a line across the middle of Germany, this is bound to happen
and it is unrealistic to make a bargain except on a basis which
assumes that it will happen'.[63] But this does not mean that these
Americans were thinking in grand strategic terms of dividing
Germany and building up the western area; the main influence
on the reparations decisions was a determination to settle the
Polish problem, at least temporarily, and to stall friction with
the Russians over Germany.[64]

What is interesting is that Bevin, despite his aggressive
determination to act as an equal to the Soviets and the Americans
at Potsdam, went along with this agreement, although with some
reluctance.[65] He did so particularly because a percentages rather
than a fixed-sum agreement would keep the Americans involved
in discussions on Germany. Moreover, it avoided a major
showdown between the Allies which would have been unthinkable
during the very first few days of the new Labour government.
But the reparations settlement at Potsdam reinforced the
subsequent division of Germany. The direction of economic
policy, of political development, and, of most immediate
importance, of rationing was decided on a zonal basis, and when
Bevin returned to make his first speech to the Commons as Foreign
Secretary, it was these practical questions that he addressed, rather
than the long-term implications of the Potsdam talks.[66] 'We
were', Attlee told Churchill after Potsdam, 'powerless to prevent
the course of events in the Russian zone'.[67] The façade of great
power unity was preserved, yet the Potsdam Protocol completely
failed to do more than give each occupying power freedom to

[62] *DBPO* i. 1050, 1053.
[63] Ibid. 1258. I am grateful to Robin Edmonds for drawing my attention to this
memorandum.
[64] Backer, *The Decision to Divide Germany*, 91.
[65] *DBPO* i. 1105.
[66] Robin Edmonds, 'Yalta and Potsdam: Forty Years Afterwards', *International
Affairs*, 62/2 (1986). House of Commons, *Debates*, 20 Aug. 1945, vol. 413.
[67] *DBPO* i. 1143.

develop its zone in the way it thought best. Bevin's long-standing dislike of central administrations was only tempered by the glaring need for more food supplies, which traditionally had come from the east. After the Potsdam conference the two faces of British policy gradually emerged, the one maintaining the appearance of unity and co-operation between the Allies, the other laying the ground for a programme of gradual preparation for a division of Germany, should genuine co-operation with the Soviet Union on Western terms, and in a way that would preserve British interests in Europe, become impossible.

2

EARLY DISCORD

DURING the early postwar months very little was achieved by way of implementing the Potsdam Agreement. Indeed, Bevin thought that the time had not yet come to 'take major political and economic decisions necessary to establish our long term policy' towards Germany; the dust had not yet settled after the war and European affairs were still in 'a state of flux'.[1] This was a view that seemed to be shared by the Russians and the Americans, who agreed that major German questions should still only be discussed through diplomatic channels.[2]

At the Potsdam Conference the Americans had formally proposed the establishment of a Council of Foreign Ministers (CFM) to carry out the preliminary work on the peace treaties with the defeated powers. This idea had been discussed in London and in Washington during the war, as the experience of the 1919 Versailles Conference was such that diplomats felt a smaller group should hammer out the details of a settlement before all the victorious powers gathered. It was intended that the French and the Chinese should join the Americans, the British, and the Russians on the Council. The Russians were happy to accommodate the presence of the French, but suggested at Potsdam that France should not participate in the preparation of peace treaties with countries with whom she had not signed an armistice agreement, clearly fearing that the presence of a third Western power might tip the balance against the Soviet Union. On 21 July it was agreed that the first meeting of the Council should take place not later than 1 September, and London was agreed upon as the meeting place.[3]

But it was not until 11 September that the first session of the

---

[1] ORC(45)27, 30 Aug. 1945, CAB 134/594; Sargent minute, 4 Mar. 1946, FO 371/57315.

[2] Roger Bullen and M. E. Pelly (eds.), *Documents on British Policy Overseas*, 1st ser., ii, 411. (Henceforth *DBPO* ii.)

[3] On the establishment of the Council see Patricia Dawson Ward, *The Threat of Peace: James Byrnes and the Council of Foreign Ministers, 1945–1946* (Kent: Kent State University Press, 1979). See also Appendix A.

Council was convened in London. The American, British, and Soviet Foreign Secretaries[4] were joined by the French Foreign Minister Georges Bidault. The immediate task of the Council, as defined in the Potsdam Protocol, was to draw up peace treaties for the so-called German 'satellite' states of Italy, Rumania, Bulgaria, Hungary, and Finland, while the German problem would be left for later discussion. However, the Council broke down amidst confusion and acrimony on 2 October.[5] The breakdown formally occurred over France's legal status at the Council. Because of the loose wording in the Potsdam Protocol, the assumption that France would participate in the preparation of the peace treaties for all the satellite states was not specifically mentioned. At the first meeting of the Council Molotov agreed to Bevin's suggestion that France should participate in discussion. However, he was then instructed by Stalin to reverse this agreement, which did technically contravene the Potsdam Protocol. But neither Bevin nor Byrnes would agree to such a humiliation for France and so the Council thus adjourned *sine die*, without a communiqué even being issued.[6]

The theme of the London Council was a mutual testing of the limits of the spheres of influence of each of the Great Powers in three areas: Eastern Europe, the Far East, and the Mediterranean. However, the reason for the collapse was in part that the Soviets felt that their justifiable sphere of interest in Europe was being threatened by Western non-recognition of the Rumanian and Bulgarian governments.[7] The session was a galling experience which left Bevin sceptical and disillusioned about the whole Potsdam peace process, Molotov gravely dispirited, and Byrnes acutely aware that he had failed to exploit American advantages and had been badly outmanœuvred.[8] No progress had been made over the Italian colonies, Eastern Europe, Japan, or Iran. The Council had immediately and publicly shown how very fragile any postwar international system might be. There had been no co-ordination of Western policies before the meeting,

---

[4] James Byrnes, Ernest Bevin, and Vyacheslav Molotov.
[5] Proceedings of the CFM: *DBPO* ii, 100 ff.
[6] *DBPO* ii, 103, 302, 467 ff. Appendix A, A(1)–(4).
[7] *FRUS 1945* ii, 194 ff.
[8] For Bevin's reaction, *DBPO* ii, 480. For Molotov's reaction, Roberts to FO, 31 Oct. 1945, FO 371/47883. For Byrnes's reaction, Ward, *The Threat of Peace*, 44 ff.; Bohlen, *Witness to History*, 247.

although Bevin had hoped to secure underlying principles for the Western powers that would determine the peace settlements, to give Britain a good chance to stand up for her vital interests. It was obvious that it would be imperative to be firm during the early postwar weeks, for as the pattern of the peace settlement became established it would be harder for Britain to assert herself and claim her place with the United States as one of the major Western actors.[9]

In Whitehall the failure of the Council also had a more significant impact, crystallizing general apprehensions about the intentions of the Soviet Union into fear about Soviet policy in clearly defined areas. Bevin told the Chinese delegation to the Council that he 'resented the way in which the Soviet delegation tended to attempt to place Great Britain in the dock in regard to political issues, and he would not stand for it. Nor did he think it was possible to make much progress with M Molotov.'[10] But the Council meetings made it very clear that Britain's great power status and her capacity to stand up to the Soviet Union would depend largely upon her relations with France and with the United States, and, in the weeks and months that followed, officials reassessed those relations in the light of changing circumstances, new information, and their own assumptions.

Bevin echoed wartime Chiefs of Staff and Foreign Office thinking when he announced, soon after taking office, that a French alliance was a first priority for Britain. This would help to shore up democratic government in France and eventually make her an economic and military ally, although 'both the Russians and, to a lesser extent, the Americans were unwilling to treat France as a first class power'. Britain's own status might also be reinforced by a treaty with France that would form the core of a Western grouping, or bloc. The course of events leading to the signing of the Treaty of Dunkirk in March 1947 was to be a tortuous one, and continuous efforts would not have been made to secure

[9] *DBPO* ii, 76 f. For British optimism before the Council, Bullock, *Ernest Bevin: Foreign Secretary*, 118; Walter Lipgens, *A History of European Integration*, i. *1945–1947: The Formation of the European Unity Movement* (Oxford: Clarendon Press, 1982), 170. However, for a more pessimistic analysis see Clark Kerr to Eden, 10 July 1945, FO 371/47883: Bevin thought this a 'good summary'.

[10] *DBPO* ii, 189.

the treaty if it had been conceived as being solely anti-German. Military planners well knew that one advantage of such a treaty was that it might be used for protection against the Soviet Union, should the need ever arise.[11]

France was seen as an unreliable yet essential ally to Britain. Anglo-French antagonism reached back into the war years and beyond. France's harsh treatment of Germany after the First World War culminated in her invasion of the Ruhr when the Germans failed to honour their reparations obligations, and drove Britain into the Locarno agreement to forestall a renewal of French aggression. In the spring of 1940 serious talks had resulted in a public commitment to close co-operation in the postwar world.[12] But France's defeat by Hitler in 1940 brought renewed doubts about her value as a military ally. In the Middle East the Levant raised the perennial issue of imperial rivalry, and Charles de Gaulle was to insist that the two powers could not reach accommodation in Europe until the Levant conflict was resolved. Doubts over French policy had been reinforced by a bitter personal wartime antagonism between Churchill and de Gaulle. As Churchill reminded de Gaulle, 'each time we must choose between Europe and the open sea, we shall always choose the open sea'.[13]

Anglo-French relations were therefore seldom easy, but were eventually to be cemented by a concealed but very real common interest in keeping Soviet power—especially Soviet power in Germany—at bay, although in public debate the French were to concentrate to an even greater extent than the British upon fears of a revival of German power. By the beginning of 1945 both British and American officials realized the important role that France would have to play in the postwar world, especially if the United States were to withdraw from Europe. At Yalta, a firmly pro-French line by Britain had secured France a zone in Western Germany. However, France was not invited to the meeting

---

[11] Brief for Bevin, 13 Aug. 1945, FO 371/49069; *DBPO* ii, 927, Confidential Annex. John W. Young, *Britain, France and the Unity of Europe, 1945–1951* (Leicester: Leicester University Press, 1984), chap. 3; Bert Zeeman, 'Britain and the Cold War; An Alternative Approach. The Treaty of Dunkirk Example', *European History Quarterly*, 16/3 (1986).

[12] Woodward, *British Foreign Policy in the Second World War*, 288.

[13] Charles de Gaulle, *War Memoirs*, iii. *Salvation* (London: Weidenfeld & Nicolson, 1960), 56.

at Potsdam and therefore did not consider herself bound by its Protocol. This was to leave her free to propose her own solutions for postwar Germany, adding to the already considerable difficulties politicians were to encounter over the German question.[14] These were first elaborated to British officials in August 1944 by the French Ambassador, René Massigli, and were repeated at the London Council in September 1945. Massigli rejected the idea of a German central government and proposed that the Ruhr should be separated and administered internationally, that the Rhineland should be separated from Germany and militarily occupied, that the Saar should be bound to France economically, and last that reparations were once again to be paid by Germany. These proposals were considered essential for the future security of both Europe and the world. The French also wanted a French-led Western bloc to keep Germany down. These plans for the future of Germany were in the tradition of France's hopes after the First World War when Georges Clemenceau commented that 'the Rhine . . . was the traditional frontier, a real frontier defining French territory . . . that is where we ought to have landed up'.[15] For the first six months after the war the British took France's proposals very seriously, and a lively debate took place about the consequences of separating the Ruhr, or Ruhr and Rhineland area from Germany.

To ensure France a role in the formulation of the Peace Treaties was an issue that was important enough for Bevin to allow the breakdown of the London Council in October. The British had acted in concert with the United States over the French question, but relations between the two English-speaking countries were not at all cordial in the immediate postwar months. This was a cause of continual British anxiety and irritation, as Anglo-American relations were the key to Britain's capacity to deal effectively with the Soviet Union.

[14] John Gimbel, in his *Origins of the Marshall Plan* (Stanford: Stanford University Press, 1976), reassesses France's place in the postwar settlement.

[15] De Gaulle, *Salvation*, 49 ff.; Young, *Britain, France and the Unity of Europe*, 6 f.; A. W. de Porte, *De Gaulle's Foreign Policy* (Harvard: Harvard University Press, 1968), 198 ff.; Clemenceau's remarks are quoted in Dorothy Pickles, *Government and Politics of France*, i. *Institutions and Parties* (London: Methuen, 1972), 218.

So if France was viewed as at once unreliable but essential to Britain, the same was true of the United States, though here the stakes were very much higher. Historically, a common ideology and language had served to forge a close, if sometimes awkward, relationship between the two. As the war drew to an end the first aim for British foreign policy makers was to secure a continued American presence in European affairs. But this was not viewed as an easy task.

As in the case of France, Britain looked back to the experience of the First World War, when the Americans retreated into isolation. America's part in European affairs has been well described as a 'fireman's role', only intervening in great emergencies to keep the European machine functioning properly.[16] The interests of the United States were not primarily in Europe but were world-wide and included Asia and the Pacific region. She had tended to see her role in international affairs in an idealistic and abstract way, in part because of the importance of projecting her policies to the American electorate and to Congress. And 'once engaged in a foreign enterprise, American purposes were proclaimed to be the building of a just and lasting peace, resisting aggression and change by force, assuring democracy and self-determination everywhere, building a new peace order'.[17]

The American governmental machine was more diffuse, fluctuating, and uncertain than the British, as British officials were frequently to remark. It was subject to influence from pressure-groups, from Congress, from public opinion, and from within different departments. Over the early postwar years departmental rivalry between the State and War Departments caused tremendous tensions in Anglo-American policy towards Germany. The American administrative machine was fragmented and not easy to comprehend; there was a lack of consultation before international conferences, and American policy appeared indecisive if not muddled. Lord Halifax, British Ambassador to Washington during the war, noted (in a most patronizing fashion) that 'American politics are conducted in an eighteenth century

---

[16] A. W. de Porte, *Europe Between the Superpowers: The Enduring Balance* (New Haven, Conn.: Yale University Press, 1979), 77.
[17] Ibid. 78.

atmosphere of violence and lack of coherent action which the Americans themselves deplore but are greatly surprised if we take seriously'. They were, however, well-intentioned 'if we can bear with their sometimes almost unbearable methods (from which we may educate them gradually but which we cannot hope to change quickly)'.[18]

During the early war years relations between Britain and the United States had been very close: indeed it has recently been argued that Churchill almost succeeded in his vision of an Anglo-American 'marriage'.[19] But relations were often difficult during the later war years, especially over matters of planning. However, if the British saw American planners as idealistic, often woolly and hard to pin down, they also knew that the Americans saw Britain as a potentially difficult ally as well. Americans were suspicious of Britain's imperial interests and her declining economic strength, some seeing her as 'prostrate economically, relatively impotent militarily'.[20] However, not all American opinion underestimated the United Kingdom's capacity to try to manage postwar diplomacy along the lines she traditionally favoured. British policy had always been to prevent any one state dominating the European Continent by throwing her support first to one power and then to another. It was not a characteristic of European politics to place sole reliance on untried methods of diplomacy, and therefore Britain would be expected to follow this course again, despite American hopes for an international security organization. She would not be an easy partner after the war.[21]

But for Britain the principal threat to postwar order was the Soviet Union, and an American partnership was essential whatever the problems involved. Britain did not have the resources alone— or even when joined with some Western European bloc—to withstand a Soviet onslaught. This the Chiefs of Staff had made abundantly clear: 'Our own forces and those of our European allies would be utterly inadequate to limit a Soviet advance through Poland and through a disarmed Germany into Western

---

[18] *DBPO* i, 185; FO to Washington, 20 Feb. 1944, CAB 122/1553; Thomas, *Armed Truce*, 129 ff. for a vivid description of Admiral Leahy, Truman's candid adviser.
[19] Ryan, *The Vision of Anglo-America*, 2.
[20] Quoted in Williams, *A Prime Minister Remembers*, 161.
[21] *FRUS 1945 Potsdam* i, 256 ff.

Europe. The United States is, therefore, the only country which possesses sufficient manpower and reserves to stabilize and restore the situation.'[22] As Attlee later remarked, 'what remained of Europe wasn't strong enough to stand up to Russia by itself. You had to have a world force because you were up against a world force. . . . Without the stopping power of the Americans the Russians might easily have tried sweeping right forward.'[23] The Americans were well aware that the British saw the major threat to the security of Europe as the Soviet Union and that everything possible would be done to elicit American support in Europe, but the British struggle to gain their support would not be an easy one. The American solution was to define Europe's security problem within the dimensions of the German problem and to try to carry the wartime alliance against Germany into the postwar world through a world organization and later the proposed Byrnes treaty, and to 'promote understanding between Great Britain and Russia on all matters of dispute . . . thereby fostering tripartite collaboration so necessary to lasting peace'.[24]

For Britain the main thrust of policy would be to bind the United States to Europe, and the United States had to be convinced that Britain would and could still act as a responsible world power and would not fail to act because of financial constraints. In his celebrated 'Stocktaking on VE day' memorandum Sargent had warned that Britain had to persuade the United States, as well as the Soviet Union, to treat her as an equal:

We must be prepared for the United States to falter from time to time when called upon to pull their weight in Europe, and to prefer the more agreeable and less arduous role of mediator in European affairs generally and in particular in any disputes between Great Britain and Russia. . . . We must have a policy of our own and try to persuade the United States to make it their own.[25]

Thus British policy had to 'avoid public confrontation; seek private influence. Propitiate openly; manipulate secretly.'[26]

[22] PHP(44)27(0) Final, 9 Nov. 1944, CAB 81/45.
[23] Williams, *A Prime Minister Remembers*, 171.
[24] *FRUS 1945 Potsdam* i, 264.   [25] *DBPO* i, 185.
[26] David Reynolds, 'A "Special Relationship?": America, Britain and the International Order since the Second World War', *International Affairs*, 62/1 Winter 1985/6, 2.

During the second half of 1945 Anglo-American relations went through what has aptly been called a period of 'American disengagement—British disenchantment'.[27] The British Government found it hard to assess the direction of American foreign policy and the omens did not look good. Many American troops had been either demobilized or sent to the Far East. Roosevelt had stated at Yalta that American troops would leave Europe during the first two years of the peace, although it was feared that this would seriously weaken the Western position in Europe. Indeed, between mid-1945 and 1947 American troop levels in Europe fell from over 3 million to 200,000. Wartime lend-lease had been rapidly and unceremoniously ended in August 1945, which shocked Whitehall. This threatened Britain's own economy as well as her capacity to underwrite her overseas liabilities—a financial Dunkirk, as Chancellor Dalton called it.[28] Furthermore, the negotiations for a loan of $5 billion—which Keynes had originally hoped would be interest-free for the first ten years—were proving tough and dispiriting for both negotiators and the Labour Government alike, and revealed very uncomfortably Britain's own financial weakness and her dependence upon American aid to retain her great power status.[29]

Although planning for the postwar world was intended to be based upon great-power co-operation, there were other substantial areas of Anglo-American conflict. These included Palestine, where the Americans' seemingly indiscriminate attachment to zionism undermined the strategic considerations that, for Britain, had to underpin any settlement of the Palestine problem. In the Far East the British still feared that the Americans would try to exclude other powers from the region. The atomic question deepened suspicions not only between the Soviet Union and the West, but also between Britain and the United States. Whitehall officals

[27] The phrase is Robert Hathaway's in *Ambiguous Partnership*, chap. 11 title.
[28] Dalton, *High Tide and After*, 73. Keynes also used the same phrase, Roger Bullen and M. E. Pelly (eds.), *Documents on British Policy Overseas* (London: HMSO, 1986), 1st ser., iii, 36.
[29] C. C. S. Newton, *Britain, the Dollar Shortage and European Integration 1945–50*, Ph.D. thesis (University of Birmingham, 1982), esp. chap. 5; Alec Cairncross, *Years of Recovery: British Economic Policy, 1945–51* (London: Methuen, 1985), chap. 5; on the loan negotiations, Pimlott, *Hugh Dalton*, 429 ff.

hoped that Britain could be an effective partner over atomic developments. But, despite the Attlee–Truman Agreements of December 1945, the MacMahon Act, passed through Congress in July 1946, made the passing of any atomic information to any country illegal.[30]

It also seemed that the advent to power of a new President and Secretary of State had moved the Americans to one of 'their more cockahoop moods'.[31] They underestimated the need for planned, co-operative action by the two major Western powers, instead regarding the UN as a 'deus ex machina which will relieve [her] . . . of some of the responsibilities arising from her position in the world, instead of thinking of it as an experimental structure, which must not be tested for strength before heavy burdens are laid upon it'.[32] Harry Truman's credibility did not run high in Whitehall, especially after the ending of lend-lease. Halifax found that Truman was 'frankly fogged as to what had apparently so soon and darkly clouded the atmosphere of Potsdam', a remark that reveals Truman's ignorance about the real implications of the Potsdam settlement.[33] After Truman had been in office for six months, Halifax still thought that 'the man at the helm is no longer master of the ship'.[34]

British officials were dismayed by American diplomacy at the London Council. Truman had told his Secretary of State to give the Soviets 'hell', and the Americans had managed to create a deadlock over eastern Europe, an area in which the British were ready for quiet diplomacy. Indeed, the minutes of the Cabinet meeting of 25 September record that HMG 'should make it clear to the United States Government that it was impossible for us to work with them if they constantly took action in

---

[30] Avi Shlaim, 'Britain and the Arab–Israeli war of 1948' in Michael Dockrill and John W. Young (eds.), *British Foreign Policy 1945–56* (London: Macmillan, 1989); *DBPO* ii, 542 ff., 675 ff.; Margaret Gowing, 'Nuclear weapons and the Special Relationship', in William Roger Louis and Hedley Bull (eds.), *The Special Relationship: Anglo-American Relations since 1945* (Oxford: Clarendon Press, 1986). The best analysis of Anglo-American relations during these difficult months is in Hathaway, *Ambiguous Partnership*.

[31] Gage minute, 21 Aug. 1945, FO 371/44538.

[32] Logan minute, 7 Jan. 1946, FO 371/51606.

[33] Washington to FO, 25 Sept. 1945, FO 800/512.

[34] Quoted in Peter Boyle, 'The British Foreign Office View of Soviet–American Relations, 1945–6', *Diplomatic History*, 3 (1979).

the international sphere affecting our interests, without prior consultation'.[35]

Bevin did not care for Byrnes's approach to diplomacy, and the antagonism between these two flared up when the American suggested a three-power meeting to ease the deadlock of the London Council. Then on 23 November Byrnes suggested to Molotov, without informing Bevin first, that the three Foreign Secretaries alone should meet in Moscow the next month. Clark Kerr was correct in thinking that such a suggestion would not be welcomed in London.[36] Bevin was furous. When, four days later, he discussed the proposal in a teletype conference with Byrnes he immediately went on to the offensive. Such a meeting could only fail and what he wanted was a clear statement of American policy, to 'see how far it fits in with ours'.[37] There were no doubts about Bevin's perceptions of Britain's status in this last remark. It took nearly two weeks to persuade Bevin to accept the invitation, and to be persuaded that, despite the humiliation, Britain would be even less well served by a bilateral than by a trilateral meeting. The incident served to show Whitehall that the Americans, and Byrnes in particular, had 'much experience to gain' and needed 'experienced British guidance' in diplomacy.[38]

Experienced British guidance is precisely what the British hoped to give to the Americans. Once treaties were signed and old scores settled, Britain's negotiating skills would not be as useful as they could be during the first fluid months when the world was readjusting to peace. This was no easy task. The chilling of Anglo–American relations was not just a matter of specific disagreements, but was measured by a marked decline in American perceptions of Britain's great-power status, fuelled by the loan negotiations of the autumn of 1945. Moreover, as Soviet–American relations warmed, as they did towards the end of 1945, Anglo–American relations suffered.

Worst of all, Britain was in a desperately weak negotiating position at the end of the war, as her economic problems began

[35] *DBPO* ii, 358 ff.   [36] *DBPO* ii, 636.
[37] Bevin to Washington, 4 Dec. 1945, FO 800/466.
[38] Gage minute, 28 Aug. 1945, FO 371/51609. Lascelles thought Byrnes 'very shifty': BEVN II/9/3, 30 Dec. 1945 (Churchill College, Cambridge).

to be assessed. There were few illusions about Britain's parlous financial state. Financial and economic talks had been continuing during the war and Britain relied heavily on lend-lease. It was clear even during the war that another loan would be needed from the Americans in the postwar period, for the war had taken a heavy toll on the British economy. Exports were at 30 per cent of their prewar level, and Britain now had the largest external debt in her history, as well as high gold and dollar liabilities.[39] But, as Lord Franks later remarked, Britain's financial position was seen as a temporary embarrassment rather than as symptomatic of long-term economic decline.[40] It is clear to us now that Britain's economic decline was to act, over the long term, as a major determinant of her foreign policy. However, immediately after the war, concern to create a viable new balance of power when the European and global system had been destroyed was an immensely powerful motivation within the Foreign Office, in spite of the competing pressures of economic reconstruction and, indeed, of economic survival.

British attitudes towards the Russians stiffened noticeably during the post-Council period. One factor that contributed to this was the personal antagonism Bevin felt towards Molotov. He continually, and presumably quite deliberately, mispronounced his name, was frequently personally offensive, declaring openly that the 'philosophy and attitude' of the Soviets made progress at the Council impossible.[41] The two Foreign Ministers had two private meetings during the course of the London Council. The records for the meetings reveal the defensive attitudes they both held. 'If His Majesty's Government knew', Bevin chided Molotov, 'what the USSR wanted, the Russians would be told frankly whether or not it was acceptable to us and we would do our best to fit our policy into it.' But Bevin had already started the meeting off on the wrong foot by bemoaning that 'the whole European problem was drifting into the same condition as that which we had found ourselves in with Hitler'. The tactless Hitler analogy was one

---

[39] Cairncross, *Years of Recovery*, chap. 1.
[40] Oliver S. Franks, *Britain and the Tide of World Affairs* (London: Oxford University Press, 1955), 6.
[41] *DBPO* ii, 293.

which Bevin was to repeat, although it obviously caused the Soviet Foreign Minister the deepest resentment. Bevin tried temporarily to recover from his initial abrasiveness by assuring Molotov, without much conviction, that neither he nor any of his colleagues approached the Soviet Union with any sense of superiority.[42] At the plenary session of 30 September Bevin again attacked Molotov personally, claiming that his attitude 'was reminiscent of Hitler. As this was being translated, Molotov went pale and blotchy and got up and walked to the door, saying that he had been insulted. E. B. apologized and Molotov resumed his place; but after the incident it was clearer than ever that no agreement was possible.'[43]

The British record of the Bevin–Molotov meeting of 1 October paints Molotov in a most unflattering light. The meeting began by Bevin claiming that he did wish to have a better understanding with the Soviets. The two men covered the principal topics discussed in the Council, but Molotov 'harped on' about being patient. No progress was made over the recognition of Rumania and Bulgaria, or over the former Italian colony, Tripolitania, which the Soviets hoped to have as a base in the Mediterranean. Molotov accused Bevin, with some justification, of trying to create a monopoly in the Mediterranean and then pleaded whether it was not possible for the Foreign Secretary to meet him in something. Bevin simply retorted that Molotov had met the British in nothing. The meeting ended with Bevin regretting so little progress had been made: Molotov, the record states, 'made some incomprehensible noise in reply'.[44]

John Foster Dulles, who was in London with the American delegation, tellingly describes how Molotov provoked the 'bluff and hearty' Bevin, treating him 'as a banderillo treats a bull, planting darts that would arouse him to an outburst', until, before one Council meeting, Bevin exploded that 'now, I'll get 'im'.[45] Bevin also held Molotov, rather than Stalin, responsible for the murder of millions of Russian citizens and this personal dislike was compounded by his long-standing distrust of the Soviet Union

---

[42] CP(45)218, 11 Oct. 1945, CAB 129/3.
[43] Dixon, *Double Diploma*, 192.
[44] CP(45)202, 4 Oct. 1945, CAB 129/3.
[45] John Foster Dulles, *War or Peace* (New York: Macmillan, 1950), 28.

that stretched back into his trade-union days, and also by the instinctive distaste of the social democrat for the communist. It was also a mutual feeling, as 'Bevin's vaunting of his own working-class background was to irritate Molotov who, for all his revolutionary past, was very much a bourgeois in his background and demeanour. Snobbery is not a negligible factor, even in international relations, even in this century.'[46]

But this deterioration in Anglo-Soviet relations was not simply a matter of personalities. Evidence of Soviet intransigence accumulated during the postwar months: intransigence over Iran, eastern Europe, and the Straits. Indeed, Bevin remarked that just 'as a British admiral, when he saw an island, instinctively wanted to grab it, so the Soviet Government, when they saw a piece of land, wanted to acquire it'.[47]

The explosions over Hiroshima and Nagasaki in August 1945 had also had a detrimental effect on East–West relations, as the Soviet Union had not been consulted or informed. Roberts, in Moscow, also felt that the atom bomb intensified Soviet fears, leading them to consolidate their defence area in Eastern Europe and to avoid concessions which might be interpreted as yielding to the threat of the bomb, for 'their pride makes them unnecessarily self assertive lest they be thought to be afraid'. But he was not yet totally gloomy about the Soviets, in spite of their apparently obstreperous diplomatic behaviour. They still had limited objectives in the short term and were uncertain about the long term. Their confidence had been shaken at the Council with talk of a Western bloc and the refusal of a corner of the Mediterranean for them, as well as by developments in the Far East, the disorderly demobilization of the Red Army, economic difficulties, and the early onset of a hard winter.[48]

But Warner, in the Northern Department, noted more pessimistically that

Russia attaches great importance to maintaining the appearance, at any rate, of collaboration in postwar consultative arrangements. I think it is valuable for the Government to appear . . . as a benevolent and enlightened Great Power striving for the general betterment of the world

---

[46] Adam B. Ulam, *Expansion and Coexistence: Soviet Foreign Policy, 1917–73* (New York: Praeger, 1974), 394 n. 25.

[47] *DBPO* ii, 735.   [48] Roberts to FO, 31 Oct. 1945, FO 371/47883.

and it would not do for her from this point of view to sabotage the machinery for consultation and co-operation.

He thought that the Soviet Union would co-operate only 'where it pays', as she did not value long-term collaboration but only short-term interests.[49] Thomas Brimelow, also in the Northern Department, could see little ground for optimism either. 'I think we must reconcile ourselves', he noted after the Council, 'to the fact that the Russians look upon international co-operation of any kind solely as a means to the achievement of the ends of the Soviet Government.'[50] This mutual hostility was, however, healthier than the situation that had existed in the 1930s, Orme Sargent thought. Then the complacence of the Western powers in the face of the 'self-confident and ambitious Germany' gave rise to the moral cowardice of appeasement with its disastrous consequences. At least now both sides were afraid as well as suspicious.[51]

The distinction between legitimate Soviet security needs and aggressive expansionism had never been clearly defined in Britain, although it lay at the heart of the strategy to contain Soviet power in Europe after the war. Many senior Foreign Office officials, if not Bevin himself, saw very quickly that to hope to drive the Russians out of eastern Europe was quite unrealistic, given the military disposition of troops there. Before the London Council the British had tried to secure a joint Anglo-American approach over eastern Europe, arguing to the Americans that it was essential to decide whether those eastern European countries now under Soviet military control should remain within the Soviet sphere of influence. Economic assistance might persuade them to look to the west, but it had to be recognized that, even then, some of the countries might 'not be sufficiently advanced to make a success of democratic government on western lines'. The Western powers were not on firm ground, as eastern Europe was militarily occupied by the Red Army and to challenge Soviet predominance would require 'the most careful navigation'. But if this delicate conflict was not quickly resolved, Bevin thought, there was a grave risk that Soviet–Western relations

[49] Warner minute, 29 Oct. 1945, FO 371/47883.
[50] Brimelow minute, 31 Oct. 1945, Ibid.
[51] Sargent minute, 24 Sept. 1945, FO 371/47861.

would be poisoned.[52] It seemed clear that it was impracticable to try to do more than exert gentle pressure on the Soviets about their flouting of the Yalta Protocol, and secure a mutually face-saving arrangement for Rumania and Bulgaria. Roberts warned that otherwise Britain would be meddling in the affairs of a part of Europe where she had no major interests. She should be happy to work to Soviet drafts over eastern Europe, provided that 'the Russians tacitly or otherwise agree that we and the Americans are accorded comparable priority in the preparation of the Treaty with Italy'.[53] This attitude reveals a healthy respect for a Soviet bloc in the tradition of the Percentages Agreement. It did not interfere with the primary aim of securing an American presence in Europe, but sought to work within the *de facto* situation of eastern Europe. The British continued to adhere to this position.

This does not mean that the very nature of marxism–leninism was not a cause for British concern, quite apart from the Soviet Union's possible strategic interests. For if ideology was a prime factor in determining policy, then the Western powers had reason to fear and to try to stem any westward drift of communist influence, although it could not hope seriously to influence events in the east. Such beliefs came to dominate the Foreign Office, and the debate was sustained by the stream of provocative and well-penned telegrams sent by Frank Roberts from Moscow. With a broad historical viewpoint, Roberts sought to show how the uncertain qualities of Soviet foreign policy were a blend of ideology and strategic interests. Roberts stressed the fundamentally hostile nature of the Soviet Union, as well as its opportunistic approach to foreign policy. He drew parallels between the domestic and foreign policy of the Soviet Union, which threw a more sinister light on the broad intentions of her foreign policy. It was perhaps inevitable that observers should extrapolate from domestic policy, as information on Soviety foreign-policy intentions was so scarce. Roberts's dispatches, though less well known, deserve the same kind of attention given to those written by his very much more celebrated friend and opposite number at the American Embassy, George Kennan. Indeed, the two used to quip that their views

---

[52] *FRUS 1945* ii, 102 ff.; Barker, *The British Between the Superpowers*, 34.
[53] Roberts to FO, 13 Oct. 1945, FO 371/47883; *DBPO* ii, 110.

were so close that to have two Embassies in Moscow was an
unnecessary duplication.[54]

Ironically, Whitehall also had plenty of evidence that the Soviet
Union was still genuinely interested in great power co-operation,
was not yet clear about her own strategy, and was very fearful
about the British and Americans 'ganging up'. Although Molotov
had agreed that the Soviet Union could accept the formation of
an anti-German Western group, he was also worried about the
place Britain and the United States were trying to create for France.
He believed correctly that the British were trying to extend, rather
than consolidate their influence in the Mediterranean and Bevin
reported that Molotov thought the British were treating the Soviets
in a way that was far worse than the treatment given to the Tsar
during the First World War. Britain 'wanted the Turks to hold
Russia by the throat and when the Russians had asked for one
trusteeship in the Mediterranean we had felt that she [the Soviet
Union] was encroaching on our rights. But we could not go on
holding a monopoly in the Mediterranean. . . . It was very hard
to understand.'[55] Molotov was at pains to tell Bevin about Soviet
insecurity, how hurtful Hitler's views on the racial inferiority of
the Russians were, and how the West seemed prepared to support
the Soviet Union only when she was useful to their own ends,
exactly the same comment as Warner had made about the
Russians. But he could not resist coupling this with a veiled threat
as to the 'serious trouble' that failure to co-operate would
bring.[56]

There were plenty of strong arguments put forward within
Britain that the Soviet Union should not be dismissed as an ally.
E. H. Carr, whose columns in *The Times* caused the Government
considerable dismay, rebuked commentators for concentrating
on East–West differences, for the Soviet Union's passionate
preoccupation was with her own security. Her historical
experience of Europe was as a place from which unprovoked
aggression had once again been launched.[57] The *Manchester
Guardian* reflected this view and commented that the Soviets were
still trying to understand the events of 1941. They played cards

[54] Interview with Sir Frank Roberts, London, 20 Nov. 1985.
[55] CP(45)218, 11 Oct. 1945, CAB 129/3.   [56] Ibid.
[57] *The Times*, 29 Oct. 1945.

with different rules from the West, and owed 'nothing to the missionaries of Rome'. The Western powers should be making a greater effort to understand these fundamental differences.[58]

So, although the eastern perimeter of Europe appeared lost, it was also obvious that the future of at least the western zones of Germany was not yet secure, as Russian ambitions might well extend this far west. It might then be possible for the western zones, with their economic resources, and under a democratic rule, to provide a means of containing Russian power in Europe. But to develop a bastion for Western influence in Germany would require not only the support of a coalition of Western European powers including France, but also American support, as her dollars, military might, and common ideology were indispensable to Britain. The task for Britain was to convince her Atlantic ally of the nature of Soviet foreign policy and in particular the threat that it posed. This meant a close re-examination of Britain's options in Germany, which became the focus of extensive evaluation in the weeks and months that led up to the second meeting of the Council of Foreign Ministers in Paris in April 1946.

[58] *Manchester Guardian*, 20 Dec. 1945.

3

TOWARDS A 'WESTERN' STRATEGY

THE Potsdam settlement had indeed established a 'strange and precarious framework' for the settlement of the postwar German problem.[1] Declaring in favour of Germany's economic and, in the long term, political unity, the Allies had mapped out a vague and largely zonal reparations settlement which was dependent on continued co-operation. But there was no trust upon which this enterprise could be based. In the months following Potsdam doubts about the Soviet Union crystallized into a perception of a coherent Soviet policy towards Germany, and fear of the Soviet Union was to become the first and major determinant of British policy towards Germany. Indeed, even as early as September 1945 officials thought that Soviet action might eventually force Britain away from economic unity, although this would mean a drastic revision of Potsdam.[2]

In February and March of 1946 a combination of events in Germany were to transform this long-term problem into a dangerous situation that required decisive action. On 7 February Otto Grotewohl, the German Social Democratic leader in the Soviet zone, agreed, under strong Soviet pressure, to a fusion of the Social Democratic Party (SPD) with the Communist Party (KPD), forming the new Unity Party (SED). Even before Churchill's celebrated 'iron curtain' speech Grotewohl feared 'the "iron curtain" had come to stay': he had been 'tickled by Russian bayonets' and now the Eastern zone and the Soviet sector in Berlin had no Social Democratic Party.[3] This was a most serious development, for officials proceeded 'on the assumption that the Soviet Government will continue to do all it can to ensure that the future German government will be Communist and Soviet-

---

[1] Hynd 5/3. (Churchill College, Cambridge).
[2] 'Review of Discussion of the Berlin Conference on German Affairs', 10 Sept. 1945, CAB 21/957; Robertson to Street, 21 Feb. 1946, FO 942/475.
[3] Steel to FO, 7 Feb. 1946, FO 371/55586; Draft Cabinet Paper, undated, FO 945/16.

controlled. This is the attitude they have adopted in other border countries; their methods in Germany are true to type.'[4] Not only could the Western powers 'kiss goodbye to democracy on the Western pattern for what is practically half of pre-war Germany which politically is now being reduced to a Balkan level. . . . A German puppet regime for the Soviet Zone will now soon be an accomplished fact', but the Soviets had embarked upon a campaign to attract the whole of Germany into their sphere of influence by destroying its social structure.[5]

Tension about Germany's future was also heightened by an important meeting that Bevin held with Bidault on 18 February. In this meeting Bidault revealed his real preoccupations over Germany. 'The Ruhr', he argued, 'was the key to Germany, we could either leave it to Germany and therefore to the Soviet Government, or cut it off and keep it for the west.' Bevin agreed with this very significant admission, but his prescription was rather different and he told Bidault that 'if we were to take away the Ruhr it would probably mean that the Russians would colonise the rest of Germany'.[6]

Britain's £80 million bill for the zone was now also becoming a worrying burden in a country so badly overstretched, and Dalton was particularly anxious to decrease management costs and reduce commitments, as the total employed by the Control Commission was 54,000, which included nearly 29,000 in the British zone.[7] The population of the zone was swollen by displaced persons, but even before the war Germany had not been self-sufficient in agricultural produce. Reports were now coming in to London from the Control Commission confirming that it was impossible to ignore the need for economic and political rehabilitation for much longer as the majority of Germans were already alienated by 'the present regime of misery'.[8] It was anachronistic to base British policy upon fear of a revival of German military power, indeed it now seemed that 'there is not much point in leaving in

[4] GEN 121/1, 11 Mar. 1946, CAB 130/9.
[5] Franklin minute, 8 Feb. 1946, FO 371/55586.
[6] Bevin–Bidault meeting, 18 Feb. 1946, CAB 21/1872.
[7] CM16(46), 18 Feb. 1946, CAB 128/5; Robert W. Carden, 'Before Bizonia: Britain's Economic Dilemma in Germany, 1945–6', *Journal of Contemporary History*, 4/3 (1979).
[8] Report by Montgomery, 1 Feb. 1946, PREM 8/219.

Germany the kind of vacuum in which Nazi influences are bound
to flourish and . . . we must make some attempt to see what kind
of workable economy can be evolved'.[9] Despite the enormous
financial expenditure, economic life in the zone was still
deteriorating, a harsh winter had only exacerbated the problems,
and the food ration had to be lowered to 1,000 calories, although
extra supplies of wheat were imported, which in turn had meant
spending more precious dollars.[10] Therefore, for those on the
ground, and in the Treasury, some prospect of economic recovery
in the British zone was axiomatic for both economic and
humanitarian reasons.

But during the early months of 1946 the Allied Control Council
discussions on the level of industry that Germany was to be
allowed were proceeding very badly for Britain. The Potsdam
Agreement had stated that Germany was to make the maximum
reparation consistent with being left enough resources to subsist,
without external assistance, at an average living standard not
exceeding that of European countries other than the United
Kingdom and the Soviet Union. This level had to be fixed before
the amount of plant ultimately available for reparations was
decided, and, obviously, the lower the level of industry, the more
would be available for reparation. The British team found
themselves in a minority of one as they favoured the highest
levels of production in Germany. This isolation increased the
sense of panic in London and Berlin. Alec Cairncross, who
was in Berlin working on the Plan, wrote at the time that
at the

end of the last war, Lord Keynes familiarized us with the truth, which
experience is now reiterating, that Germany was the hub of the entire
European economy and that upon her prosperity the prosperity of
Europe in large measure depends. . . . The lower the level of industrial
activity, the less rapidly will Germany gravitate either towards the west,
with which her industrial links will be feebler, or towards democracy,
which will appear more of a luxury.

Germany had lost 25 per cent of her farm land, and he
estimated that it would take ten years to return to her prewar

---

[9] Cairncross to Sharpston, 22 Oct. 1945, private collection of letters of Professor
Sir Alec Cairncross.
   [10] Waley paper, Dalton comments, 5 Mar. 1946, T 236/970.

agricultural output, bringing an inevitable delay for industrial recovery.[11]

The Potsdam Agreement was attacked by Harvey as a 'restrictive and dangerous policy for Germany, Europe and ourselves', and by Hynd, who argued that the dilemma was now whether 'either to accept a penal reparation plan for the purpose of maintaining the principle of unity in the Control Council or . . . insist on retaining in our own zone of occupation, which contains the major part of industry of Western Germany, enough plant to achieve for the Germans a standard of living and ensure a balance of payments'.[12] This was not simply a question of resources, for

if . . . Germany is completely beggared there is no point in wasting effort on democratization. We should soon give up the task of attempting to finance and police her . . . Germany would undoubtedly become a Russian sphere of influence. This combination of Russian resource and German organization and industry would indeed be formidable.[13]

But on 15 March ministers had to concede that they had no option but to succumb to international pressure to settle a level of industry. However, they insisted upon conditions, the only occupying power to do so. If the population rose above 66.5 million, Britain would be free to revise levels upwards. If the western frontier was altered, the plan would have to be altered. Most important of all, economic unity for Germany had to be achieved before the plan was brought into operation in the zone. With these crucial provisions, that were also to underpin the implementation of the 'Western' option, the British accepted the four-power Level of Industry Agreement.[14]

The creation of the SED, the privately expressed fears of the French, the economic difficulties of the zone, and the Level of Industry talks, coupled with Byrnes's suggestion that another session of the Council of Foreign Ministers be convened in April, all acted as stimuli to the debate within the Foreign Office about

[11] Quoted from his own records in Cairncross, *The Price of War*, 138 f. Chaps. 5 and 6 give the most penetrating account available of these discussions. Letter from Cairncross to Turner, 11 Feb. 1946, Cairncross letters, private collection.
[12] Harvey note, 2 Aug. 1945, FO 371/55400; Hynd to Bevin, 7 Mar. 1946, FO 942/475.
[13] CCG to FO, 15 Jan. 1946, FO 942/530.
[14] GEN 121/1st, 15 Mar. 1946, CAB 130/9.

the next move to make over Germany.[15] Two fundamental assumptions underpinned this debate. One was that, because of the aggressive and expansionist nature of marxism–leninism, the Soviet Union sought more than a security zone in eastern Europe. The containment of this expansionism would lie at the heart of British analyses, despite the financial cost. The second assumption was that hunger, poverty, and unemployment were ideal breeding grounds for political extremism, both nazism and now communism. Economic recovery would in itself make extremism less attractive as well as reducing the burden on the Treasury.

Having established herself securely in her zone, it seemed that the Soviet Union was now 'preparing to launch out on a more forward policy in the West' with a policy that consisted of three elements:

(i) to prevent at all costs the revival of a strong and independent Germany;

(ii) to prevent western Germany with the Ruhr, or even the Ruhr alone, being brought into any close grouping of the Western democracies;

(iii) to ensure that Germany eventually looks east and remains under strong and, if possible, exclusive Russian influence.[16]

She was seeking to create a united Germany that was not prosperous enough to be independent, and which would therefore have to look to the Soviet Union. This might be achieved through the machinery of government, by establishing and then dominating central administrations and eventually a strong central government. It might be achieved through the economic control of Germany's economic heartland, the Ruhr. And it might be edged along by a propaganda effort to win over to communism the hearts and minds of depressed and undernourished Germans. For 'Russia can absorb countries without spending money on them, but we cannot. The western way of life depends upon a minimum of material wellbeing.'[17]

From Moscow Roberts advocated a strong policy that would nevertheless not openly raise East–West tension still further, and

---

[15] Washington to FO, 6 Mar. 1946, FO 371/57265.
[16] CP(46)186, 3 May 1946, CAB 129/9.   [17] Ibid.

his flood of telegrams over these weeks continued to make a comprehensive contribution to official thinking about the nature and aims of Soviet policy. The Western powers had to retain sufficient strength to stop Soviet adventures, and Britain should indeed develop the resources of her zone rather than worry about a centralized Germany. But it was essential to retain the public 'façade of German unity' to stop Soviet fears that the three Western zones were being built up into a solid unit which could be integrated into a Western bloc. He thus advised strength with caution, blocking the Soviet Union's expansionism while not overtly threatening her keen sense of insecurity, or overestimating the certainty of her long-term policy.[18] For it was agreed

that the long term aim of Russian leaders is to consolidate around her boundaries a belt of states subservient to Russia so that she may build up strength without fear of attack. It is considered, however, that such an aim implies the gradual but continual broadening of the belt . . . such expansion will be sought by all means short of war until she has enough strength to embark on agressive [*sic*] action.[19]

'Appeasement won't pay', Hankey, head of the Northern Department warned, the 'more Russia gets the more she will want'. The Soviet Union was flexible and would not consciously provoke a major clash on any single issue in the short term. However, in the long term, her interests were dynamic and expansionist as 'she thinks she is bound to win out and can afford to be patient'.[20] Ambassador Duff Cooper thought that although the German menace was still more threatening to France than the Soviet one, Germany as a satellite of the Soviet Union would create the most formidable power the world had ever seen. But he still felt that building up a strong, unified Germany to fight the Soviet Union hardly merited examination, as 'Frankenstein learned it does not pay to manufacture monsters'.[21]

Strang, in Berlin, argued that although Britain should still keep her options open for a unitary Germany that would be harmless, reasonably prosperous, and certainly not communist, he realized that the situation was 'deteriorating to the advantage of the

---

[18] Roberts to FO, 29 Mar. 1946, 27 Apr. 1946, CAB 21/1872.
[19] Roberts to FO, 20 Mar. 1946, FO 371/56831.
[20] Hankey minute, 25 Mar. 1946, FO 371/56831.
[21] Duff Cooper to FO, 1 Mar. 1946, FO 371/55400.

Russians and to the disadvantage of ourselves', in part because of the obstructive attitude of the French over the Ruhr. It was necessary to speed up the political rehabilitation of the British zone, as the Soviets were clearly trying to extend their influence all over Germany, while following an 'iron curtain' policy in their own zone. Indeed, now there was something to be said for the argument that, if the Soviets actually thought they could achieve a united eastward-looking Germany, this might in itself be a good argument for opting for a divided Germany. But he was at pains to point out that such a 'Western' policy would require the full support of the Americans. Simply detaching the Ruhr/Rhineland area would not, however, provide an adequate defence, and a viable division would have to include a broader area of western Germany, perhaps extending to the eastern boundaries of the British and American zones.[22] This, of course, was a very different proposition from detaching the Ruhr/Rhineland. Hall-Patch, seconded to the Foreign Office from the Treasury, joined the debate, agreeing with the need to bring in the Americans, and that, if Germany was to be broken up, then at the very least the whole of the Rhineland should be detached; while the Francophile Assistant Under-Secretary Harvey was less guarded, arguing that 'it is only through zonal government that the rot has not gone further . . . we should hold the Ruhr securely by removal and occupation and then await developments'. It might, he agreed, eventually 'come to dividing Germany on the Elbe'.[23]

But Troutbeck feared that to think in terms of a bloc against the Soviet Union would be to play a dangerous game, although, if the British were now thinking of the German problem in terms not of guarding against the German danger but of rivalry against the Soviet Union, then as Strang suggested, an enlarged Germany—the 'whole of Western Germany'—was preferable.[24] Brimelow summed up the drift of official thinking, minuting that 'the odds are on their side, and will remain on their side unless we build up an equally efficient organisation with an equal or

[22] Strang to FO, 26 Feb. 1946, ibid.; Minutes of Control Commission Conference, 12–13 Oct. 1945, FO 371/46736.

[23] Hall-Patch minute, 8 Mar. 1946; Harvey minute (initialled by Sargent), 28 Feb. 1946, FO 371/55400.

[24] Troutbeck minute, 28 Feb. 1946, ibid.

greater counter-appeal to the inhabitants of the countries where an expansion of Soviet influence is expected'.[25]

Roberts suggested that a body be set up to examine Soviet overseas policy. It would be essential to formulate a strategy for Germany within the context of a comprehensive analysis of Anglo-Soviet relations throughout the world, rather than simply responding to economic circumstances. For

the first essential is to treat the problem of Anglo-Soviet relations in the same way as major military problems were treated during the war. It calls for the closest co-ordination of political strategy, for a very thorough staff study embracing every aspect of Soviet policy—not forgetting the ubiquitous activities of the communist parties directed, if not controlled in detail, from Moscow.[26]

So on 2 April the Russia Committee, a Foreign Office committee, held its first meeting. Its brief was to analyse

the development of all aspects of Soviet policy and propaganda and Soviet activities throughout the world . . . to ensure a unified inter-pretation thereof throughout the political and economic departments of the Foreign Office. . . . The committee will maintain close contact with the Joint Intelligence Committee with a view to co-ordinating intelligence and policy at every stage

and, if necessary, would report back directly to Sargent. By establishing this committee the Foreign Office was acting in response to what was perceived as the homogeneous character of Soviet policy, to 'this Russian aggressive policy as a whole in all its different manifestations' which might require a 'defensive-offensive policy' by the British.[27] Propaganda as well as firm diplomacy were clearly essential. In western Germany the battle over the future of the Social Democratic Party must not be lost, although this would involve greater expenditure there. It was also argued in the Russia Committee that Britain alone could not hope to stave off the communist threat. She needed as much support as could be looked for from the United States and to a lesser degree from France.

[25] Brimelow minute, 24 Mar. 1946, FO 371/56831.
[26] Roberts to FO, 18 Mar. 1946, FO 371/56763.
[27] Terms of reference of the Russia Committee, 12 Apr. 1946, FO 371/56885; Warner note, 2 Apr. 1946, FO 371/56832. Ray Merrick, 'The Russia Committee of the British Foreign Office and the Cold War, 1946-7', *Journal of Contemporary History*, 20/3 (1985).

The Gordian knot of Potsdam—central administrations and zonal autonomy, economic unity and decentralized government, self-sufficiency and reparations—had been concealed when the Allies still had Germany as a common enemy, but could now no longer be ignored. 'The big German questions', one official despairingly noted, 'are in fact tied up together—western frontier, central administration, level of industry and reparation.'[28] In these months a divided Germany was widely and openly discussed in British government circles. Of course Germany had already been temporarily divided with the annexation of some territory to Poland, and there were many possible ways of further dividing it to protect the Western zones from communism. The British zone could be administered independently, at least in the short term. Alternatively, a new Western German administration might be created, composed of the British and American or the British, American, and French zones. Not only was every issue inter-related, but German policy had to await the tide of international diplomacy, and particularly of American diplomacy. The German peace settlement thus increasingly became an object of international politics. As Bevin told the Cabinet in May 1946, until

recent months we have thought of the German problem solely in terms of Germany itself, our purpose having been to devise the best means of preventing the revival of a strong aggressive Germany. . . . But it can no longer be regarded as our sole purpose, or, indeed, perhaps as our primary one. For the danger of Russia has become certainly as great as, and possibly even greater than, that of a revived Germany.[29]

During these months there were shifts, hesitations, arguments, and counter-arguments, as officials tried to steer a course among conflicting aims and policies in Germany. Policy discussions fell into two broad categories—how to ensure economic recovery of a westward-looking Ruhr region, and how to secure a future western German political system against communism. Considered as a strategic or as an economic question, by May 1946 a divided Germany presented the best hope for British success.

---

[28] Troutbeck minute, 7 Mar. 1946, FO 371/55779.
[29] CP(46)186, 3 May 1946, CAB 129/9.

The Ruhr Valley in the British zone lay at the heart of proposals for deindustrialization and of Germany's capacity to pay reparations. When the zones had been allocated during the war, Britain had been determined even then not to allow Soviet control in this area, for it had enormous economic and strategic significance, and Bevin rightly saw it as at the heart of German aggression, and the most important single problem in Germany. He took a serious and informed interest in economic questions, and particularly in the future of the Ruhr because of its wealth-creating potential for Europe. Whether the Ruhr was to be held down, redeveloped, politically separated, socialized, or internationally controlled would also affect the kind of Germany that would exist in the postwar world. As early as 22 August 1945 Bevin asked the interdepartmental Economic and Industrial Planning Staff (EIPS) for studies on the Ruhr industries. He was inclined to favour public ownership of major industries with an international body set up to run them, hoping, nevertheless, that this might help to incline the trade of the area towards the west.[30] The EIPS, which had been considering the French proposal during the war, had, however, come to the conclusion that political separation was the inevitable corollary of economic separation of the region, otherwise there would be untold resentment amongst Germans, who would see their national wealth managed by foreign powers and flowing away from Germany.[31]

In December Bevin took a fresh look at the EIPS scheme. He knew all too well that the issue was both an economic and a security one. The political security that was fundamental to industrial recovery would not, he realized, be guaranteed by territorial annexations, and he hoped that an international socialist concern would be established in the Ruhr with shares held by participating governments, including the Soviet Union, and run on a day-to-day basis by a mainly German management committee. The Ruhr, after the reparations period, would concentrate on partially manufactured commodities that would then be finished elsewhere. This might, he hoped, create the 'first

[30] Hall-Patch to Turner, 22 Aug. 1945, FO 942/515. House of Commons, *Debates*, 21 Feb. 1946, vol. 419.
[31] EIPS/P(45)1, 8 Jan. 1945, EIPS/P(45)27, 7 Sept. 1945, FO 942/515.

foundation . . . of something like the Economic United States of Europe'.[32] With this new brief from the Foreign Secretary the EIPS set to work once again, and produced another report in February 1946. This time they assumed a united Germany which had paid reparations. A larger industrial area comprising the Ruhr and the Rhineland would function under an International Holding Company, with profits going to the Germans.[33]

This report therefore reflected Bevin's personal ideas about European reconstruction, and it is interesting that, despite his personal antagonism to the Soviet Union, he thought that practical four-power co-operation might still be possible. The most revealing aspect of this scheme, however, was the almost universally hostile reaction it received, particularly from the pro-French group in the Foreign Office. Duff Cooper elaborated France's fears that it would be safer 'that the might arsenal of the Ruhr should never fall into German hands', and he was formally backed by Harvey and Sargent.[34]

Bevin then presented his plan to the especially constructed Cabinet Committee on Germany Industry on 15 March, along with an extremely gloomy analysis of the subject. The Soviets were 'deeply interested in the Ruhr', and had been since their request at Potsdam for a special four-power regime for the area, although then they had wanted to keep its industries depressed. Bevin wanted economic recovery in the region in order to reduce the financial burden for Britain, for the benefit of Europe, and to aid democracy in Germany. To do this it would be necessary to establish a much higher standard of living than that proposed in the Level of Industry Agreement. Potsdam was a policy of negation and would need to be modified to secure a positive policy for the Ruhr.

Bevin showed that the French plan of political separation of the Ruhr and the Rhineland had some merit, for if Germany was likely to be under Soviet control it would be better that the Ruhr

[32] Bevin memorandum, 16 Dec. 1945, FO 942/515; Meeting of 5 Jan. 1946, FO 942/516.
[33] EIPS Report, 4 Feb. 1946, FO 942/516; GEN 121/1, 11 Mar. 1946, CAB 130/9.
[34] Duff Cooper to FO, 1 Mar. 1946, FO 371/55400; Bidault to FO, 15 Jan. 1946, FO 942/516; Sargent minute, 13 Feb. 1946, FO 371/55586; Harvey minute, 28 Feb. 1946, FO 371/55400.

should be separated. But imposing political separation would be unpopular in Germany itself, and a small, densely populated Ruhr region would be economically vulnerable and open to communist infiltration, especially during an economic slump. He therefore favoured retaining the Ruhr and Rhineland in Germany and pursuing the EIPS Plan—his 'industrial' instinct—although it meant Soviet participation. Bevin had clearly hoped to use this meeting to brief his colleagues on Germany before a Cabinet meeting, but although they accepted that the western frontier should remain intact, they criticized some economic aspects of the EIPS plan. Cripps argued that the idea of finishing industrial processes in areas other than the Ruhr could lead to the build-up of new industrial centres. Attlee disliked the idea of a higher standard of living for the Ruhr than for the rest of Germany, and feared industrial action against an international concern in the area. Bevin was asked to revise the scheme before it went to the Cabinet.[35]

After the Cabinet Committee had met, officials, as well as the Chiefs of Staff, looked at the EIPS scheme again, bearing in mind the security aspects of the question. The Chiefs of Staff obligingly took their consistently hard line that the Soviet Union appeared to be the most likely potential enemy. They cast the Ruhr question entirely within a strategic framework, dismissing the Bevin/EIPS plan out of hand because it depended on Soviet participation. The iron curtain had long since fallen and, from the security point of view, the Ruhr was by far the most important area of Germany, and would largely determine the future of the country. But deprived of both the Ruhr and the Silesian area in the east, Germany could hardly count as an independent actor in Europe and would fall into the arms of the Soviet Union. Planners should strive to isolate the Soviet Union as far to the east as possible, and remember that British interests would be best served by the creation of a Western democratic Germany: 'Our policy towards Germany should be such as would not prevent us from building her up again if this becomes necessary. In addition, so that we could count on effective German assistance in the event of conflict

---

[35] GEN 121/1st, 15 Mar. 1946, CAB 130/9. Brook note, 19 Feb. 1946, CAB 21/1872. On Bevin's 'industrial' instinct, House of Commons, *Debates*, 21 Feb. 1946, vol. 419.

with Russia, we should try to avoid arousing permanent German antagonism towards us.'[36] Nothing had fundamentally changed from the COS debates of 1944–5.

Other Foreign Office and Treasury officials were also sceptical about the plan and Geoffrey Vickers, a senior industrialist, was asked to draw up a charter to give the EIPS scheme more shape. Instead, with Sargent and Hall-Patch, he thoroughly revised the scheme, suggesting instead a new province for the Ruhr region. A socialized German corporation would be set up with an international control organization to supervise the operation. Control of the major industries concerned would be vested temporarily in the Commander-in-Chief of the zone, with an announcement that they would not be returned to their former owners. The Western powers most closely affected and the United States would be associated in the project, but the Soviet Union would not now be included.[37] Bevin, who by mid-April had realized the impracticality of his own scheme, agreed that a new province should be created and that the Soviet Union should be offered participation in a socialized German corporation only on a *quid pro quo* basis with Western involvement in Saxony, although it was made clear that this should not appear to be flouting the Potsdam Agreement. In reality Western participation in Saxony would be as unacceptable to the Soviet Union as Soviet participation in the Ruhr was to the Chiefs of Staff.[38] On 17 April the Cabinet approved the new scheme, which broke the spirit, if not the letter, of Potsdam, but realistically

faced the fact that Europe was now being divided into two spheres of influence, and it would give us an opportunity to prove that we could build up in Western Germany, under a democratic system, an efficient industrial organisation which challenged comparison with that which was being created under a different system in Eastern Germany.[39]

---

[36] COS(46)105, 5 Apr. 1946, CAB 84/80. See also JP(46)65(Final), 4 Apr. 1946, ibid.; COS(46)93(0), 4 Apr. 1946, CAB 79/47.

[37] FO 942/417 *passim*; Report of 10 Apr. 1946, FO 371/55401; for Treasury opposition, Annex 2, GEN 121/1, CAB 130/9.

[38] Meeting of 12 Apr. 1946, FO 371/55402; CP(46)139, 15 Apr. 1946, CAB 129/8.

[39] CM36(46), 17 Apr. 1946, CAB 128/5.

The Potsdam Agreement had envisaged central four-power administrations for finance, transport, communications, foreign trade, and industry in Germany, acting under the direction of the Allied Control Council, although their character and scope would inevitably have some bearing upon the future political orientation of Germany. During the earlier postwar months neither the British, the French, nor the Soviets were very enthusiastic on the subject of these bodies, being fearful of their possible consequences. From October 1945 onwards the French blocked discussions on central administrations in the Control Council until a decision was reached on Germany's western frontier. With some reason they argued that, once central administrations were agreed to, it would be impossible to redefine Germany's borders; moreover, central administrations would lead to a strong, and therefore dangerous, Germany once again. For they already considered that any central adminstration tending towards a unified Germany would result in communist influence spreading westwards through German channels.[40]

As for the Soviet Union, one early view in the Foreign Office was that she was still undecided. She might favour central administrations when they could be used to penetrate the Western zones and was now simply being difficult over providing information about the Soviet zone, glad to shelter behind the strong French stand until she had made up her own mind; for the French were being 'so obstructive on the Control Commission that Russian obstructiveness was superfluous'.[41]

It was only the Americans who were openly pressing for central administrations. Their position was greatly influenced by General Lucius Clay, the Deputy Military Governor for the American zone, as was so much of the United States's German policy immediately after the war. Clay wielded great power partly because of his autocratic and sometimes hysterical style, and partly because of the division between his department—the War Department—and the State Department, which only developed an active interest in German affairs when their significance for

[40] BAOR to War Office, 10 Oct. 1945, FO 945/17.
[41] Brimelow note, 20 Nov. 1946, FO 371/47861. Oct. 1945 Report on ACC, FO 1030/317; Steel to FO, 7 Apr. 1946, FO 371/46736; John W. Young, 'The Foreign Office, the French and the Post-War Division of Germany, 1945–6', *Review of International Studies*, 12/3 (1986).

the future of Europe became more obvious.[42] With his military background Clay was perhaps unsuited to the major administrative task he was given: to cope with the complexities of the situation on the ground and the considerable pressures upon him, he interpreted literally his brief, the Potsdam Protocol, and the American policy document JCS 1067.[43] Clay continually repeated the view that the Americans should withdraw their troops if central administrations were not introduced, and then frequently suggested that joint administrations for the other zones be established without the French if they would not co-operate, although it does not appear that he was in any way spearheading moves in favour of a divided Germany or playing cold-war politics.[44]

Whitehall had never been enthusiastic about central administrations, or about any future central German government that would not be federal and very decentralized in character, because of fears both of the Soviet Union and of a revival of German nationalism. Indeed Bevin admitted to the French Ambassador Massigli that the only advantage of central administrations was that they could be a means of 'enabling us to penetrate to some extent the Russian zone of occupation' and to keep a toehold in Berlin.[45] There was also some hope that they would establish a structure whereby the British zone might receive food from the Eastern zone. But there had also been a massive and not immediately successful land reform there, and much of eastern Germany's agricultural land had been transferred to Poland. This raised doubts among British officials as to whether a surplus did in fact exist at all.[46] In practice the British were as happy as the Russians to hide behind the French in the Control Council on this issue. Harvey argued that Britain would not be able to exploit all-German administrations to penetrate the Soviet zone although

[42] There is a rich seam of literature on this theme, e.g. Backer, *The Decision to Divide Germany*; Schmitt, *The US Occupation in Europe*; Gimbel, *The American Occupation of Germany*.

[43] More is known about Clay than about his British counterpart, Brian Robertson. See his *Decision in Germany* (London: Heinemann, 1950), and papers, edited by Jean Edward Smith, *The Papers of General Lucius Clay: Germany 1945–1949*, 2 vols. (Bloomington: Indiana University Press, 1974) (henceforth *Clay Papers*).

[44] Montgomery to Street, 18 Nov. 1945, FO 945/517.

[45] Bevin–Massigli conversation, 23 Oct. 1945, FO 371/46989.

[46] Waley to Bridges, 24 July 1946, T 236/959.

the Russians might use them against the Western zones, but this could not yet be said openly, as it would give the Soviets an opportunity to claim that it was Britain who was flouting a Potsdam decision. However, British officials declined to exert pressure on the French over this issue, as the Americans were doing.[47]

But not to advance with central administrations had serious implications for the whole Potsdam process. A political and administrative stalemate was quickly reached in Germany, which threatened to have disastrous consequences for the restoration of the British zone. Therefore the zone itself had to be reorganized. Once again it was Montgomery who warned that if the 'difficulty of working with them [the Soviets] in practice prevents the formation of the centralised ministries, the next best alternative is for central administrations to be formed for the West of Germany', and who suggested to the Cabinet that an economic plan for the British zone should be secured if inter-Allied agreement could not be secured.[48]

At a Control Commission conference in October 1945 William Strang advocated that zonal political development must be speeded up and Brian Robertson produced a report that was but the start of a series of protracted debates about the nature of democratic reform for Germany.[49] It was not until 1949 that the results of these discussions came to fruition with the creation of the Federal Republic. In 1945–6 they simply underscored the gap between the professed ideals of Potsdam and the political realities with which officials had to contend. How was it possible to have central administrations and a future central government that did not subject the Western zones to Soviet influence? But how was it possible to have economic unity in Germany without central administrations to organize that unified economy? 'There is no Potsdam doctrine', a German Department official despairingly declared, 'for the simple reason that its authors had not thought the problem out. . . . If the centre is to be responsible for economic administration, it must also hold the power.'[50]

[47] Harvey minute, 12 Nov. 1945, FO 371/46736.
[48] Montgomery Report, June 1945, CAB 120/561; CM2(46), 3 Jan. 1946, CAB 128/5.
[49] Report of DMG, 20 Dec. 1945, FO 371/55586.
[50] Troutbeck report, 8 Jan. 1946, FO 371/55586.

For the time being there was no hurry to proceed with constitutional changes in Germany, which would anyway eventually require the participation of the Germans themselves, but no effort should be made to agree, 'for the sake of peace and quiet in the Control Council in Berlin, to measures which will unnecessarily increase the disintegration of the economic life and social structure of our zone'.[51] A Zonal Advisory Council was being established for the British zone, and Control Commission official Harold Ingrams was instructed to draw up plans on the assumption that

in view of the French opposition to central administration, Russian intransigence and growing American clamour to withdraw from Europe, quadripartite arrangements will break down and that the central administration at Berlin proposed to be set up by the Potsdam agreement will not materialise. The result of this would be that we should be responsible solely for the government of the existing British Zone. . . . In other words the British Zone would be treated as a separate country.[52]

Interestingly, Ingrams decided to work within the political principles of Potsdam, but applying them to the British zone alone, including treating the zone as a single economic unit. This tactic was to be used again and again by the British.

It was not hard to convince Bevin that the only value of pursuing discussions on central administrations was that the Americans valued such talks. During the War Bevin's own scepticism stemmed from a desire to break up the German Reich entirely, and then from his anxiety lest the Soviets penetrate the Western zones. As he told the Cabinet Committee on German Industry, communists, aided by the Soviet authorities, were at present busy forcing through fusion with the Social Democrats in their zone with the further intention of extending this fusion to the Western zones.

So long as the present zonal occupation continues and Germany is not centralised, our presence and that of the Americans in the West affords some protection to the democratic German parties against Communist

---

[51] Troutbeck report, 8 Jan. 1946, FO 371/55586.
[52] 'German Administration for the British Zone', IGMS 4/3. (Churchill College, Cambridge).

pressure from the Eastern Zone. . . . Once Berlin again becomes the seat of a German Government, [local elections] will be exposed to strong Communist and Soviet pressure. The Communists will be entrenched in the East and will proceed to the offensive against the parties in the West. . . . [So] we should be wise, I think, to prolong the present system of administration and government by zones and delay the setting up of a single German Government operating from Berlin.[53]

Central administrations would be too vulnerable to commmunist take-over. If they were ever eventually created, this should only be after the Western powers had gained time for economic recovery to begin and for democratic parties to become established.

Thus, by the spring of 1946 economic and political arguments both pointed in the same direction: Germany had to remain divided, at least in the short term, for if

we can get Western Germany past the world food and economic crisis and put her on the way to economic recovery and readjustment before we withdraw our military government, we might effect lasting work. If we go, leaving only the army of occupation in strategic areas, or if we allow premature centralisation while famine and economic chaos remain, I doubt if the German democratic parties can stand for one moment against totalitarianism.[54]

In the 15 March Cabinet Committee meeting Bevin had come out against central administrations, at least in the short term. This meeting was also presented with a summary of British interests in Europe, which were listed as being:

(1) Security from the revival of German aggression.
(2) Reasonable economic well-being in Germany and Europe.
(3) Reduction of the British costs of occupation of Germany and feeding of Germans.
(4) A democratic and Western-minded Germany.
(5) The restriction of the predominating Soviet influence as far East as possible.
(6) The recovery of France as a solid member of the Western democracies.[55]

[53] GEN 121/1, 11 Mar. 1946, CAB 130/9.
[54] Harvey report, 25 Mar. 1946, FO 371/55612.
[55] GEN 121/1, 11 Mar. 1946, CAB 130/9.

This summary also raised the crucial issues of keeping American troops in Europe, of alternatives open to Britain if she also had to withdraw, of separation of the Ruhr from Germany, and of the role of France.

The implications of the summary were more fully discussed by Bevin and his own senior officials three weeks later in the context of possible troop reductions in Germany. According to the two accounts available to us it was at this meeting that Bevin agreed to let his officials outline the realistic alternatives now available to Britain in Germany, given her rejection of the French proposal. This was to lead to the elaboration of a 'Western' strategy of containing Russian power in Europe at the Elbe. This strategy was to remain unchanged until the Americans backed it with their superior resources and the shape of the new Germany and Europe started to become clearer during 1947.

On 3 April it was the Chancellor of the Duchy of Lancaster, John Hynd, Minister in charge of the Control Office, who again posed Britain's dilemma. He reminded the meeting that the Russians were bringing great pressure to bear on the Social Democrats in the Western zones. Financial pressures were also taking their toll on British occupation policies. Decisions had to be made and Britain was 'faced with the question whether we are to go ahead with setting up central administrations or whether we shall give up all interest in Eastern Germany and settle down to develop Western Germany', for currently 'our policy was purely negative as was that of the Americans'. The German Social Democrats and Christian Democrats had to know what the British intended to do in Germany, for they were 'rapidly losing their grip on Western Germany and the Communists are going ahead'. Hynd wanted to regenerate industry, nationalize key industries, and set up works councils. Britain was legally free to go ahead with her own plans in the zone, pending quadripartite agreement.[56]

Bevin commented that 'he had never understood why we could not proceed with our own policy in our own zone in the same way as the Russians were proceeding with their policy in their zone'.[57]

---

[56] Interdepartmental meeting with Bevin in attendance, 3 Apr. 1946, FO 945/16. I am grateful to Professor Geoffrey Warner for discussion on this document.
[57] Ibid.

Mr Hynd then resumed his statement and said that the question must be faced whether we should now proceed to establish a German Government in our zone with full powers of Government including economic powers. Mr Arthur Street remarked that this amounted to a partition of Germany and Sir Orme Sargent said that such a step would be irrevocable. Mr Bevin said this meant a policy of a Western Bloc and that meant war. Sir Orme Sargent said that the alternative to this was Communism on the Rhine.[58]

It is clear that the intervention of Sargent, a senior official with an unblemished track record as an opponent of appeasement, was critical. His theme was that Britain's economic weakness and the vulnerability of her position in Germany actually increased the obligation upon her to act decisively and with speed towards her own zone, for 'we might, by failing to take a decision now, merely drift along until we found ourselves obliged, under American pressure added to our own manpower and financial difficulties, to hand over suddenly to a German Government which would be under Communist influence'.[59] But in Germany officials had replied to questions posed by the Foreign Office on German organization, in particular 'some form of unified administration for the Western Zones', that this would produce a 'first class row with the Russians', and would be 'quite impossible without clear US Government directions and it can be taken as quite certain that present US representative would recommend against a unified administration for Western Zones'. Bevin thus concluded that the Americans clearly had to be 'carried with us' in whatever future policy was conducted in Germany, and it was hoped that Byrnes would be in a position to come to some general agreement with the British in the future.[60]

Before then he wanted to see the 'alternatives now before us clearly and starkly set out with all their realistic implications for the Cabinet to face up to them', including the problems associated with creating a government for the British zone. Because of the welter of Labour Party legislation and reforms, Cabinet and Party interest in Germany had hitherto been sporadic

[58] Ibid. The meeting is also recorded in FO 371/55586.
[59] Meeting, 3 Apr. 1946, FO 371/55586.
[60] Sugra 489, 25 Mar. 1946, Argus 444, 30 Mar. 1946, FO 371/55779; Meeting, 3 Apr. 1946, FO 371/55586.

and had mainly consisted of requests by Dalton and the Treasury to reduce expenditure, although there is no evidence that officials had been anxious to take these questions up to Cabinet level before this date. Bevin now wanted to introduce a paper to the Cabinet and have it discussed, without asking for immediate decisions. The paper should cover the contradictions between zonal organization and the Potsdam formula, the state of affairs in the Soviet zone, and 'an estimate of ultimate Russian aims; the effect on Russian policy of our taking a firm line', and the possible long-term financial obligations to which Britain might be committed with a separate British zone.[61]

Taken in conjunction with the papers on the Ruhr, the very long, full, and sometimes contradictory Cabinet paper of 3 May was the first major paper the Cabinet had before them on the long-term prospects for Germany since the end of the War, and the first serious opportunity for Bevin's colleagues to discuss the gamut of crucial issues it posed. In many respects it can be considered as the primary source of Britain's containment policy for Europe. It set out to consider whether 'we should continue to work towards a unified (though federalised) Germany or whether, in view of the Russian attitude and the danger of Communist domination of Western Germany, we should regard this as dangerous and work towards a Western German State or States which would be more amenable to our influence'.[62] The Potsdam formula had not been a success, for four-power government at the centre 'is beginning to creak and the burden of government to flow to the zones which are tending to become quasi-independent'.[63] The two options Bevin had discussed on 3 April were then fully rehearsed. The 'Western' option meant the organization of either the British or the Western zones as a separate unit, a division which was envisaged as being permanent. The consequences of the 'Western' option would therefore be profound for Germany and Europe as a whole. The iron curtain would be rung down for good as the Soviet zone, Berlin, and eastern Europe would be 'irretrievably' lost to the Soviet Union. It would mean a separate

---

[61] Sugra 489, 25 Mar. 1946, Argus 444, 30 Mar. 1946, FO 371/55779; Meeting, 3 Apr. 1946, FO 371/55586.
[62] CP(46)186, 3 May 1946, CAB 129/9.   [63] Ibid.

currency and separate nationality, and possibly even the eventual establishment of a Western German army, for she would have to become part of an anti-Soviet bloc. The expected Russian reaction to this 'Western' strategy might also bring about the end of the United Nations Organization and the support of France would be essential. Opposition from the German people might be contained initially but 'the conception of German unity is a basic fact which has survived many centuries and is unlikely to be destroyed by any artificial creation established today'.[64]

On the other hand a 'Western' policy would be a significant display of firmness by the West. It would signal an intent to contain communism at the Elbe and to stall the dual threat of the expansion of Russian influence and of communism. The great majority of Germans would probably welcome this (despite the anathema of dismemberment), if coupled with a renunciation of the Level of Industry Agreement and reparations. As they became more contented 'by seeing our determination to save them from the Russians' they would increasingly be involved again in running their own country.[65]

Two conditions would be crucial to the success of a 'Western' policy. One would be that 'we should give an immediate fillip to the population by raising the food ration and maintaining it at a satisfactory level, although it would take 2–3 years to render Western Germany self-supporting', and the second would be to be assured of the full and continued financial and military support of the United States.

The Cabinet was also asked to discuss immediate questions which flowed from the broader issues. The most important of these was what line to take on central administrations. The Americans thought them 'one of the most urgent requirements for Allied policy', and in theory their establishment might bring more food to the Western zones. But the Soviets would probably 'merely try to use them to infiltrate into western Germany, while taking good care they were not used by the western powers to infiltrate into the east'. He was not sure whether the Western democracies or the Soviet Union would exercise the stronger pull over Germany and feared 'the balance of advantage seems to lie with the Russians. . . . Communism already has its addicts in

---

[64] Ibid.   [65] Ibid.

western Germany and the liberal attitudes of the occupying authorities in the west would allow them a free hand'.[66] He suggested that 'such German administrations as may be found absolutely essential for the purpose of treating Germany as an economic whole' should be referred to the Allied Control Council for study. (They had, of course, been trying to study central administrations since October.) Central administrations should, however, only co-ordinate the activities of regional units and their activities in each zone would be subject to the control of the respective zone Commanders. This would not interfere with the proposed introduction of the new province of the Ruhr/Rhineland area, so it was at best a tepid endorsement, and was, rather, a diplomatic manœuvre to reconcile American and French opinion, which was totally divided on the subject. If central administrations were established, they would, as John Hynd described them, be 'purely co-ordinating bodies without effective control'. It was the half-way house option which 'might permit of central administrations, but not of effective ones, which indeed it would be one of its chief purposes to prevent'.[67] They could, on the other hand, form a useful basis for long-term Western co-operation, if Germany was split.

Bevin and his officials furthermore knew that any move towards a 'Western' policy was not the cheapest option for the British in Germany. If decisions were to be formulated solely upon financial criteria, it would have been easiest simply to abandon responsibility for the zone as quickly as possible. But the security of western Europe, and Britain's role as a world power, were of overriding importance. Publicly Bevin was to base his arguments upon the need for economic unity, which would relieve British taxpayers of the enormous costs of the zone by bringing food from the east. But the cost of the zone was a simple and appealing argument for use at Council meetings and in the House of Commons.

The reality was more complex. Bevin explained to the Cabinet that there was no suggestion that Britain should withdraw from her responsibilities as a great power, for 'it is easy', he warned his colleagues,

---

[66] CP(46)186, 3 May 1946, CAB 129/9.
[67] Draft Cabinet Paper, undated, FO 942/549.

to over-simplify the issue and regard it as one between continuing our occupation and control with all the expense that is involved in that responsibility and withdrawing from Germany and so saving our pockets. . . . By withdrawing from Germany we could no doubt save ourselves some expense, but not the whole bill, and we should have little control over . . . what type of authority in Germany e.g. Nazi or Communist, had the use of it . . . we are not prepared to leave the field to Russia.[68]

£80 million was a small reinsurance to pay to keep communism beyond the Elbe.[69] The Cabinet discussion on Germany took place during a continuing and painful reassessment of Britain's defence expenditure. Dalton had long argued that expenditure could not continue at its present level without bringing economic disaster. However, Britain's responsibilities as a great power could not be avoided, and Bevin had been concerned since January to educate the Cabinet as to the nature and extent of Britain's problems in Germany.[70]

In the Cabinet discussion over this paper Dalton disagreed with Bevin's general analysis, thinking as he had always done that 'we should avoid drifting into an anti-Soviet policy', and should hand over more responsibilities to the Germans to put their own country right and thereby save expenditure. On financial grounds he favoured the creation of the new Ruhr province to encourage economic recovery. Aneurin Bevan, Minister of Health, and Emmanuel Shinwell, Minister of Food and Power, both attacked Bevin for exaggerating the Soviet threat. They argued that Soviet influence weakened as it penetrated further west, and that Britain should leave the Germans to evolve their own political structure.[71]

Herbert Morrison was Bevin's long-time sparring partner (when informed that Morrison had been told that he was his own worst enemy, Bevin replied 'not while I'm alive, he ain't'). Morrison criticized Bevin's style and advocated a livelier leadership to keep the way clear to more harmonious relations with the Soviet Union,

---

[68] CP(46)183, 3 May 1946, CAB 129/9.
[69] Harvey minute, Feb. 1946, FO 371/55586.
[70] DO(46)1, 11 Jan. 1946, CAB 131/1; Montgomery to Robertson, 23 Jan. 1946, FO 1030/323. Montgomery gave the Cabinet 'straight facts' about Germany on 3 Jan., CM2(46), CAB 128/5.
[71] Confidential Annex, CM43(46), 7 May 1946, CAB 128/7.

although she had been at fault in her behaviour.[72] Only Attlee backed Bevin's position, but wondered if the British zone alone could be a 'stable separate unit'. It is possible that these clear indications of Cabinet disagreement reflect the fact that the discussion took place without Bevin, who was already in Paris.[73]

Bevin's colleagues maintained this higher level of interest in the future of Germany during the Paris Council, although they accepted his paper on 3 May. It is abundantly clear that the influence of Harvey, of Roberts in Moscow, and in particular of Orme Sargent were decisive in convincing their political master that the moment had arrived to take a firm stand and to act as a great power to defend Britain's interests on the continent, in spite of her financial problems. They, in their turn, were deeply influenced by the appeasement analogy. Bevin had not yet come down openly in favour of a change of policy, but the thrust of the argument was clear.

Both the Potsdam policy and the 'Western' policy presented great dangers. To follow Potsdam would mean losing Germany to communism. The 'Western' option would ring down the iron curtain and would require an Anglo-American partnership to sustain it within the framework of a Western bloc. Bevin told the Cabinet that he thought 'the general dangers of splitting Germany now are greater than those of continuing our present policy', but the reason for this was that the Americans were not yet ready for a 'Western' policy. American support thus became the most vital ingredient of any new policy initiative towards Germany, as no 'Western' policy could hope to succeed, even if France were to throw her weight behind Britain.

The volatile Americans still posed enormous problems for Britain, although during February and March they too hardened their general attitude to the Soviet Union. On 22 February 1946 Kennan had sent his famous telegram to the State Department, reporting on Soviet foreign policy. As he said in his memoirs, the timing was exactly right: six months earlier and he would have been ignored, six months later and the report would have been merely confirming the obvious. As it was, the telegram was sent 'all over the town' and Roberts sent a précis of it to the Foreign

---

[72] Confidential Annex, CM43(46), 7 May 1946, CAB 128/7.
[73] Ibid.

Office. If it were to be accepted in Washington as more than an intellectual argument, it would signal an important shift in American perceptions of Soviet intentions: and Soviet–American hostility could only benefit Anglo-American relations.[74]

The Americans did begin to follow an obviously tougher line. They complained over Soviet refusals to withdraw their troops in time from Iran, and the battleship *Missouri* was sent to the Mediterranean as a warning. On 28 February Byrnes made a speech attacking those who challenged the United States's role as a world power, demanding a shift away from appeasement and that Americans stand up to aggression. This speech was similar in tone to one made by Senator Vandenberg, who was to have great influence on American diplomacy in Paris.[75] The so-called 'Riga axiom', the hard American line that perceived the Soviet Union as an expansionist power, was beginning to dominate American foreign policy circles.[76] Churchill's 'iron curtain' speech at Fulton was read by Truman, who privately approved it (as did Bevin and Attlee). However, Truman had to denounce the speech publicly as public opinion in the United States was still clamouring for a reduction of occupation forces in Europe.[77] Thus British officials had good reason to feel that the Americans were becoming more aware of the Soviet threat. However, this by no means meant that they understood the specific urgency of the German problem. Until the Americans could be convinced of the dangers that communism presented to Western Europe, Bevin's best option was to show them publicly that he was still trying to work within the Potsdam formula. For he feared that the 'Western' option would be resisted 'tooth and nail' and in 'any case one could not count on continued American support even if they came to agree to it. But full American support would be essential.'[78]

[74] Kennan, *Memoirs*, 295; Yergin, *Shattered Peace*, 171; Roberts to FO, 2 Mar. 1946, FO 371/56840.

[75] Gaddis, *The United States and the Origins of the Cold War*, 304 ff.

[76] On the 'Riga axiom' see Yergin, *Shattered Peace*, 11.

[77] Anderson, *The United States, Great Britain and the Cold War*, 113 ff.; Francis Williams, *Nothing So Strange* (London: Cassell, 1970), 245; for reaction of the Cabinet see CM23(46), 11 Mar. 1946, CAB 128/5.

[78] CP(46)186, 3 May 1946, CAB 129/9.

Meanwhile, while working for American support, Britain would concentrate upon initiating constitutional changes through the unilateral introduction of the new province, by speeding up the return to German participation in government, as well as by encouraging economic regeneration which would strengthen hopes for social democracy in the zone. This dual approach would also allay criticisms at home from Cabinet colleagues, from the rank and file of the Labour Party, whose conference was due to take place during the Council meeting, and from public opinion at large. It would show that the Government was acting positively as a great power to convince the Americans, French, Germans, and British alike that they were 'the champions of a dynamic and progressive faith and a way of life with an appeal to the world at least as great as those of the communist system of the Kremlin'.[79] Caution was vital, for, if there was a breakdown in the wartime alliance, it would be 'most important to ensure that responsibility for the break was put squarely on the Russians'.[80]

[79] Roberts to FO, 18 Mar. 1946, FO 371/56763.
[80] CP(46)186, 3 May 1946, CAB 129/9; Roberts to FO, 29 Mar. 1946, CAB 21/1872.

4

THE PARIS COUNCIL
April–July 1946

The Opening Rounds

ON 25 April 1946 *The Times* reported that the Paris Council was 'the last chance which the allies will have of working together to set up a new world order. If they do not agree, they will inevitably be inclined to divide the world into spheres of influences and eventually into hostile blocs'.[1] However, Germany, the litmus test of great-power relations, was not the central question on the agenda. Bevin was reluctant to commit himself to formal talks while international policy towards Germany was so unsettled and while he was still trying to probe American and Soviet thinking. But before the Council opened he was forced to concede that German questions should be raised after the proposed satellite treaties had been discussed.[2]

The Council discussions on Germany were on 29 April and 15–16 May in the first session, and then on 9–12 July after the Council had recessed for a month. These meetings were described by Bidault as a number of soliloquies instead of concrete discussions, but they were to culminate in a decision by Britain and the United States to begin to frame policy within the 'Western' option, while still publicly proclaiming a desire for quadripartite agreement over Germany.[3]

Britain's principal task in Paris was to apprise the Americans of Soviet intentions, and then to evolve a practical policy that would continue to involve the United States in Europe and keep the smaller Western powers and the French amenable. The Defence Committee assessment was that

there are two realities in Europe, the 'Eastern Bloc' created and dominated by Russia and the 'Mediterranean Zone' controlled by Great Britain. . . . We are entitled to construct a 'Western Zone' if we can. . . .

[1] *The Times*, 25 Apr. 1946.
[2] Paris to FO, 26 Apr. 1946, FO 371/57266.
[3] *FRUS 1946* ii, 909 ff. For CFM see FO 371/57265–83.

It has been denounced by Russia as a 'Western Bloc' directed against her, but we are entitled to build up good neighbours and a defensive core.[4]

The key to external policy was the closest possible co-operation with the Americans, even at the expense of France, but if Britain were to be the first to give up the Potsdam process, her standing in the United States would be gravely damaged and the already uneasy Anglo–American relationship would suffer.[5] So if the Potsdam decisions were to be cast aside, it must not seem to be because of a lack of British enthusiasm to try to make the system work. Bevin had therefore to use 'tactics of exposing the Soviet attitude' to show the Americans how hard it would be to work constructively with the Russians.[6]

The British did not want to concentrate solely on trying to create a partnership with the Americans, and had several talks with the French about coal and in particular about the Ruhr while the Council was in progress. Bevin now had to inform Bidault that the British had rejected the French idea of a political separation of the Ruhr and the Rhineland from Germany and that the Ruhr issue must not be isolated from the broader question of Germany as a whole.[7] For both knew that, while appearing to deal merely with provisional situations, they were in fact taking decisions which could be final. Bidault did try to bring pressure to bear on Bevin by offering to reconsider the levels of industry for the Ruhr if it were separated, but for the British this put the price of French friendship too high.[8]

Byrnes, it seems, came to Paris intent on achieving some kind of breakthrough, in particular over the satellite treaties. He was a politician who clearly reflected American attitudes—tough when the United States was tough and flexible when she was. By April he was in a mood of 'grim determination, not unmixed with despair'.[9] He brought with him a large and respected team, the most formidable of whom was Senator Vandenberg, who was determined to ensure a non-partisan foreign policy. Clay and

[4] DO(46)40, 13 Mar. 1946, CAB 131/2.
[5] Soviet Policy Co-ordination Committee, 9 Apr. 1946, FO 371/56885.
[6] Ibid., 14 May 1946.
[7] Bevin–Bidault meeting, 26 Apr. 1946, CAB 21/1872.
[8] Bevin–Bidault meeting, 9 May 1946, FO 371/55842.
[9] *New York Herald Tribune*, 24 Apr. 1946.

his Political Advisor, Robert Murphy, also spent much of the period in Paris.

Anglo-American relations were still beset by friction and misunderstanding, although Bevin and Byrnes discussed strategic questions and Byrnes had declared himself ready for a show-down with the Soviet Union.[10] But it seems that Byrnes was still probing Soviet attitudes, informing Molotov that 'there were many people in the United States who were unable to understand the exact aim of the Soviet Union'.[11] He also asked Bidault what the French thought the Soviets were trying to achieve in Europe. Bidault replied that he thought the Soviet Union sought security through expansion, and graphically rehearsed his anxieties about the dangers of a Soviet occupation of France with, as he said, 'Cossacks on the Place de la Concorde'.[12]

Over Germany Bevin needed clarification about American views on the internationalization of the Ruhr, and fretted that they still had not understood that to press for central administrations for Germany now might mean that communists would dominate them because of the economic weakness of the Western zones. In his meetings with Byrnes there had been little substantive discussion about German questions.[13] Indeed, Byrnes had earlier indicated that 'the occupation of Germany under the prevailing agreements is expected to continue for an indefinite period', and that he did not intend to break up Germany. He wished to establish central administrations, which the French were still blocking, and told his Ambassador to France 'orally and discreetly' to inject the thought that 'any steps which the French Government may publicly take at this time in the way of co-operating with American aims should help to create a more favourable atmosphere for the important economic and financial talks which they are about to initiate'.[14] James Riddleberger, the American Chief of Division of Central European Affairs, explained to British officials in Paris that the Americans were anxious to have another try with a 'limited programme of centralisation'. This suggestion had a frosty reception, as the British were 'still extremely doubtful about central

---

[10] 'Anglo-American Discussions', undated, FO 800/513; Bevin–Byrnes meeting, 26 Apr. 1946, FO 800/446.
[11] *FRUS 1946* ii, 146.   [12] Ibid. 204 f.
[13] 'Anglo-American Discussions', undated, FO 800/513.
[14] Halifax to FO, 28 Feb. 1946, FO 371/55579.

administrations' and wanted to convince the Americans that the emphasis should be on building up regional units in each zone to prevent communist domination during a period of economic debilitation.[15]

On 3 May Clay, who was trying as always to force the pace in Germany and to show that those on the ground could achieve results, suspended the dismantling and delivery of reparations from the American zone until central administrations had been agreed upon by the four powers. He felt that he was having to operate within a policy vacuum as the French were not prepared to end their veto on central administrations until the fate of the Rhineland was decided, and Britain had not been putting pressure on the French to shift their ground.[16] Indeed, the Soviets thought that France would not have taken such a strong line against central administrations if she had not had the backing, or at least the acquiescence, of Britain and the United States.[17] The British did not formally join the reparations stop, although no deliveries were being made from the British zone, and Bevin was cheered to hear of a terrific row Molotov and Byrnes then had in which Molotov accused Byrnes of a policy of imperialist expansion and of a British–American 'gang-up' after the reparations suspension. He thought this would be a useful part of Byrnes's education about Soviet behaviour, and that there was 'some advantage, for once, in letting the United States and Soviet Governments have a row by themselves', for Anglo–American relations could only benefit from Soviet–American tension.[18]

Although the 3 May Cabinet Paper had rehearsed the options for Britain over Germany, there was little the British could do publicly in Paris until the American position became clearer. The problems concerning Germany which were discussed at Paris fell into two categories: the American proposals for demilitarization and then the territorial questions that would need to be resolved before a peace treaty with Germany could even be drafted.

---

[15] Burrows report, 5 May 1946, FO 371/55842; Brief 43 for CFM, FO 371/55404.
[16] *Clay Papers* 1, 204.
[17] *FRUS 1946* v, 506; John Backer, *Priming the German Economy: American Occupational Policies, 1945–1948* (Durham, NC: Duke University Press, 1971), 110 f.; Gimbel, *Origins of the Marshall Plan*, 97.
[18] Delegation meeting, 7 May 1946, FO 371/57270.

One major initiative that the Americans had made over Germany was to propose a four-power treaty of disarmament and demilitarization. In January 1945 Senator Vandenberg submitted a proposal for the permanent demilitarization of Germany and Japan. This was mentioned at the London Council to Molotov, who thought it a very interesting idea, and Stalin then asked for further details about it in December. So a draft treaty was sent out in February 1946 which now aroused 'serious objections' from Molotov.[19] It provided for quadripartite inspection in Germany after the period of Allied occupation, to ensure Germany remained demilitarized. Although the draft clearly merited Allied discussion, some British officials feared that the Americans simply wanted to withdraw their troops from the ground and substitute inspection for a military presence. The Chiefs of Staff, on the other hand, argued that the advantages to Britain's strategic position would be enormous if the Americans did intend to keep a military presence in Europe.[20]

By the time of the Paris Council the draft treaty was welcomed in Whitehall, both as a sign that American foreign policy-makers were prepared to try and move policy forward over Germany, and to test whether the Soviet Union really wanted security, or simply expansion—that is, as an opportunity for calling their bluff. This was an interesting interpretation of the proposed treaty, which was undoubtedly originally conceived in the United States as a means of containing Germany collectively within the framework of Rooseveltian aspirations for the postwar world.[21] Bevin was briefed to try and firm up the exact implications of the treaty, to press the Americans to agree that the treaty would mean that American troops would stay in Europe, and to advise that, if this were not the case, the provisions of the treaty could run counter to British proposals for the Rhineland, which included a proposed long-term military occupation by Western European troops.[22]

On 29 April Byrnes submitted his draft to the Council without consultation or any prior warning to the British. Publicly, Bevin

[19] *FRUS 1946* ii, 82 f.
[20] COS(46)105(0), CP(46)139, 15 Apr. 1946, CAB 129/8.
[21] Ward, *The Threat of Peace*, 119 f.
[22] Halifax to FO, 1 May 1946, FO 371/55842; *FRUS 1946* ii, 82 f., draft text 190 ff.; Brief for Paris, undated, PREM 8/520; Yergin, *Shattered Peace*, 225.

welcomed the proposals—a welcome that was echoed in the House
of Commons on 4 June—but he was in fact surprised and irritated
that he had had no warning that these secret proposals were about
to be made public.[23] It is likely that Byrnes had hoped to bounce
the British into a quick response and thereby impress American
public opinion, for the treaty created a sensation in Washington,
but in fact it gave the Russians a chance to deflect discussions
away from the long-term issues, and to turn the discussion
round into an attack on Bevin and on British policy in
Germany.[24]

Molotov argued, and not without reason, that there was
perfectly adequate provision for Germany's disarmament and
demilitarization under the Potsdam Agreement. What he,
Molotov, wanted to know, was whether reports of large
concentrations of troops still in the British zone were accurate.
This was to be echoed in complaints by the American journalist
Walter Lippmann when he wrote of the 'silken curtain' in
the British zone, behind which were concealed large German
military contingents.[25] Bevin was hastily recalled to a meeting
at Chequers and there informed an anxious Attlee that Byrnes
also was not at all sure that this was not true.[26] After a certain
amount of sparring the Foreign Ministers agreed that the Control
Council should establish a mission of investigation for all four
zones. Meanwhile, Attlee favoured sending an independent British
mission to investigate the British zone. Bevin had been forced to
defend British zonal administration against both Soviet and
American criticisms instead of being able to exploit the possible
benefits of the draft treaty.[27] The Russians had also successfully
prevented Byrnes from seizing the stage with the draft, and he

[23] Paris to Washington, 5 May 1946, FO 371/55842; House of Commons,
Debates, 4 June 1946, vol. 423.
[24] Halifax to FO, 1 May 1946, FO 371/55842.
[25] *Washington Post*, 4 May 1946.
[26] Chequers meeting, 12 May 1946, FO 371/57272.
[27] There was cause for Attlee's concern, as the British were behind with their
programme of destruction of armaments factories. There were 41,000 prisoners of
war and over 100,000 in labour units—including the Dienstgruppen—helping with
transport, quarrying work, and mine-sweeping operations. The Military Governor
also reported that research was still going on in the British zone on underwater
explosions, guided missiles, and radar. See Delegation brief, 14 May 1946,
FO 371/55381.

found when he brought up this ill-fated document again that the initiative had effectively been lost for that Council session.[28]

By the time that the Council came to discuss the territorial questions that needed to be resolved before a peace treaty could be drafted, the climate was quite unsuitable for positive and practical talks. There had been little progress over the satellite treaties, and what progress had been made had been slow and difficult. Nor do these weeks seem to have brought the British and Americans much closer together. Talks with the French had completely failed to break the deadlock over policy for Germany, although Bidault had told Byrnes privately that the French position in regard to the Ruhr was an inflated one, sustained partly because of its popularity in the country and the effect that this could have for him in the June elections.[29] France would probably 'come to some agreement on less than its current demands', as she really took a much less dogmatic view than it appeared in her official policy on separation.[30]

It is hardly surprising that the Council meetings on Germany on 15 and 16 May were bad-tempered. Bevin was tired and irritated by Soviet attempts to stonewall, but determined not to be out-manœuvred on German questions again. Attlee was urging him not to let the Council collapse, which it had looked on several occasions as if it might do. Furthermore, Sargent had warned Bevin that Byrnes might well have 'one of his sudden brainwaves' and either 'go soft' on the Soviets, or opt for bilateral treaties if the Council did collapse.[31] As the discussions turned to the Ruhr, Bevin, who was in the chair, pointed out that nothing could be done about the Ruhr until the question of Germany as a whole was settled. Molotov countered by saying that the Soviets had been told at Potsdam that Britain did not want to discuss the Ruhr because the French were not there, but now the French were present; he added that the Soviets had also heard 'rumours of

---

[28] Bevin report, 16 May 1946, FO 371/55842. Murphy thought the Americans still naïvely believed that they could maintain a weak Germany in the centre of Europe, *Diplomat Among Warriors*, 359.
[29] Riddleberger–Hall-Patch talks, 10 May 1946, FO 371/55404.
[30] *FRUS 1946* ii, 205 f.; *FRUS 1946* v, 566 f.
[31] Attlee to Bevin, 13 May 1946, CAB 120/204; Sargent to Bevin, 13 May 1946, FO 371/57270.

plans for the establishment of an administration in the Ruhr as well as of economic corporations'. Bevin retaliated sharply, ignoring the comment and saying he would like 'to know what was happening in Saxony, Thuringia and the Eastern Zone'.[32]

At this Byrnes intervened to change the subject. He wanted the talks to move ahead in a more practical way and suggested that Special Deputies should be appointed to consider five questions: the internationalization of the Ruhr, the import–export question, administrative machinery for Germany, zonal borders, and Germany's western frontiers. If the Deputies could come to some arrangement on these matters within a 60–90-day period, then the suspension of reparation dismantling could be ended, which should please the Soviets. He also agreed that the economic wealth of the Saar region should be transferred to France to persuade her to co-operate too. Byrnes's proposal was based upon a hard-hitting telegram from Under-Secretary of State Dean Acheson, who, however, laid most of the blame for the delays in the Control Council with the Soviets.[33]

Bevin concurred with Byrnes's proposal but thought it premature for discussion. He clearly had no foreknowledge of the proposal and argued that he could not yet reach any conclusions. He would prefer Deputies to examine 'the whole problem of Germany, to study the implementation of the decisions of Berlin [and] to study proposals to lead up to the preparation of a Peace Treaty and the fixing of frontiers'.[34]

Bevin cabled Attlee with Byrnes's proposals, and the next day, after a hurried Cabinet meeting, he explained to the Council that they were not acceptable to the British in their present form. Byrnes's first proposal, that Special Deputies should consider the Ruhr, ran counter to British insistence that the moment for 'trading' negotiations had not arrived. He would not yet be able to give a direct answer at this meeting about the Saar, again because that would be to discuss specific rather than broad issues. He then delivered his most aggressive attack on the Soviets, determined to force them onto the defensive and to deflect any

[32] *FRUS 1946* ii, 399 f.

[33] *FRUS 1946* v, 550 ff.; CFM(46)6th, 15 May 1946, FO 371/57272. For Byrnes's five points, *FRUS 1946* ii, 400 ff.

[34] Ibid., 412; Paris to FO, 8 May 1946, FO 371/57270.

more embarrassing questioning about the British zone. He reminded Molotov that he was prepared to work on the basis of 'complete reciprocity without reservation' and that they should remember that it was not just the Ruhr that warranted attention but that Silesia was also of great economic importance for Europe. He added threateningly that 'it had only been agreed that Poland should occupy certain areas pending final settlement . . . the United Kingdom Government had not yet committed themselves as to the eastern frontiers except as an occupational zone and they would have something to say in view of their experience when the time came to fix them'.[35]

Clearly, the very last thing that Molotov would want was to open up a discussion on the eastern frontiers of Germany. Molotov retaliated that the Special Deputies were being asked to discuss matters of too great importance to be delegated, and that the proposals should be discussed later by the Foreign Ministers themselves. The Special Deputies proposal was still unresolved when the Ministers adjourned on 16 May.

The Council Adjourned

Britain had not put up a good performance in Paris over German questions, and Bevin now had little over a month to refine his strategy. Fears about long-term Soviet intentions remained, and the British team still had little confidence in American diplomacy. Although the four-power treaty proposal and the European food crisis had heightened American interest in Europe this interest could well decline with pressure to bring troops home. Anglo-American relations were also extremely delicate over Palestine, and over the proposed American loan which was still going through Congress. Bevin had to show the Americans, and convince British public opinion, that it was Soviet intransigence that was making the task of administering the British zone impossible. The experience of the Paris meeting made the 'Western' option seem increasingly desirable, he told Attlee gloomily, 'but any such arrangements would . . . have to be concerted carefully with the Americans and French and it is clearly impossible to

[35] *FRUS 1946* ii, 426 ff.; Bevin to FO, 16 May 1946, FO 371/55842.

open discussions with them while the Paris Conference is still proceeding'.[36]

Bevin was pleased that Byrnes had pinpointed the issues over which the Americans thought that implementation of the Potsdam Protocol would succeed or fail. But speed was now essential and Britain should take action in concert with the Americans to show the Russians how seriously their attitude was viewed. The Soviets were now known to be taking reparation from current production from 200 firms in the Soviet zone. Robertson reported that Sokolovsky had told him that the Soviets were importing cotton, wool, chemicals, and raw materials into their zone for the manufacturing process. The goods were then being returned to the Soviet Union and the Soviet interpretation of Potsdam did not preclude this. Bevin explained to the Ministerial Overseas Reconstruction Committee that the Soviet Union would

now try and defer a decision on Germany for as long as possible. . . . [She had] gone far towards consolidating her political position in her own zone and is looking to the new Socialist Unity Party . . . to infiltrate into western Germany while maintaining at the same time a rigid economic barrier between the eastern and western zones. . . . In these circumstances, delay in reaching a settlement is to Russia's advantage, but it is to our serious disadvantage, and, the sooner we take positive action, the better.[37]

Three considerations dominated the refinement of Britain's strategy for the next discussions on Germany. First, Molotov had to be told that economic unity and the import–export plan must take precedence over securing reparations from the Western zones. This was absolutely fundamental to Britain's interpretation of the Potsdam formula. Second, planning now had to take into account the aspirations of the German people themselves, who could not be ignored much longer. Third, whatever happened in Paris, for both political and economic reasons Britain now had to go ahead with a more positive policy in the British zone, by establishing the new province and taking direct control of the industries there.

Economic unity was in theory expected to enable food to be imported from the Soviet zone into the Western zones, and stop

---

[36] Brief for Attlee, 21 June 1946, FO 371/55405.
[37] ORC(46)51, 17 June 1946, CAB 134/596; Robertson–Sokolovsky conversation, 14 May 1946, FO 371/55614.

the Soviet Union—and France—taking reparations from current production until the German economy was self-sufficient. But although it was generally known that calorie rations were higher in the east than the west—in itself no contravention of Potsdam— there was no direct evidence of food surpluses in the east, and David Waley in the Treasury thought that the Russian zone had practically no surplus food at all. The massive land reorganization programme in the east was done very rapidly after September 1945 to be completed in time for the spring sowing, but output sank to about 35 per cent of prewar levels (and was still about 30 per cent below prewar levels as late as 1957). Moreover, wartime destruction had also taken its toll and, for example, Poland asked the United Nations Relief and Rehabilitation Agency (UNRRA) for 350,000 tons of wheat in 1945, although she had been a net exporter of wheat before the war.[38] It is clear that to focus upon economic unity as a pre-condition for any further developments over Germany would have the primary effect of convincing public opinion that it was the Soviet Union that was breaching Potsdam and Britain that was holding fast to agreed principles, however unrealistic those principles might now have become.

It was now also becoming clear that the interests of the German people could not be ignored for very much longer. The Joint Planning Staff anticipated a complete breakdown of law and order in the British zone if food rations were cut again.[39] Montgomery reported, as he left his post in May 1946, that

the whole country is in such a mess that the only way to put it right is to get the Germans 'in on it' themselves. We must tell the German people what is going to happen to them and their country. If we do not do these things, we shall drift towards possible failure. That 'drift' will take the form of an increasingly hostile population, which will eventually begin to look east. Such a Germany would be a menace to the security of the British Empire.[40]

Most Germans wanted to live at peace with their fellows, Hynd thought, and the 'decent, constructive elements' should be

---

[38] Waley to Bridges, 24 July 1946, T 236/959; Robertson–Sokolovsky conversation, 14 May 1946, FO 371/55614.
[39] JP(46)107, Final, 28 June 1946, CAB 84/82.
[40] Montgomery memo, 1 May 1946, PREM 8/216.

encouraged.[41] Or, to put it another way, if the zone was not positively organized by the British, 'social democracy, which is identified in German eyes with the form of government in Great Britain, will be gravely weakened and the working classes will look to communism and Soviet Russia as their only saviour'.[42] Social Democracy therefore had to go on to the offensive, armed with the promise of reorganization and rehabilitation, for the Soviets were undoubtedly planning a 'bid for German confidence in a united Germany' at the next Council session.[43]

The third consideration for the next session of the Paris Council stemmed from the other two. A new province with socialized industries represented a path forward when, as was expected, the Soviets refused to interpret the Potsdam Protocol in a way acceptable to the West. It would eventually involve more Germans in the administration of their country through public ownership of the major industries, and would encourage local patriotism; Western influence would be maintained by Western international control and this would 'keep Communism beyond the Elbe'.[44]

The Ruhr area would be part of a large province of North Rhineland and Westphalia, and discussions also took place about moving the capital away from the 'frontier town' of Berlin.[45] Bevin had been persuaded by Strang and Robertson that a large province would be more acceptable to the Germans themselves, and would be acceptable to the French, as 'a province with considerable autonomous powers and containing the seat of an international control would be the next best thing to political separation'.[46] But these decisions on the zone had to be kept private until the end of the Council as they would inevitably receive a hostile Soviet reception, and would convey the impression that the British were not taking the Paris talks seriously.

The intensive discussions between the Council sessions resulted in a decision that in Paris Bevin should bring matters to a head

[41] Draft speech by Hynd, 3 May 1946, FO 371/55588.
[42] CP(46)192, 9 May 1946, CAB 129/9.
[43] Strang to FO, 21 June 1946, FO 371/55588.
[44] Harvey note, 24 May 1946, FO 371/55843; ORC(46)49, 15 June 1946, CAB 134/596.
[45] Report of Economic Sub-Commission of the CCG, FO 1039/158.
[46] ORC(46)41, 11 June 1946, CAB 134/596; AHQ/3106, 27 May 1946, FO 1039/158.

by asking whether the Soviet Government seriously intended to carry out the Potsdam provisions about treating Germany as an economic whole. An ultimatum to the Soviet Union would be framed in the form of three conditions. If these were rejected, 'the present system cannot go on much longer . . . we may be faced with the necessity of dealing with Germany in two halves . . . which would no doubt be far more satisfactory from the point of view of making it economically viable and politically sound'. The conditions were:

that there should be equitable distribution of indigenous resources throughout Germany;
that procedure should be established for ensuring that any surplus of indigenous resources in one zone is made available to meet a deficit in the approved requirements of other zones;
that if, after this equitable distribution has taken place, there is still a surplus in any zone, and if there is a deficit in the balance of payments of Germany as a whole, the surplus may only be exported in return for acceptable currency (i.e. dollars), the proceeds being used towards meeting the said deficit.[47]

Reparations were not the first priority and current reparations had to be paid for in dollars as imports until economic unity was secured. If the Soviet Union were to refuse to agree, then the British would, as they had threatened when agreeing to the Level of Industry decisions in March, reserve their position generally in regard to Potsdam and to the Level of Industry Agreement.

A Bizone is Suggested

From 9 to 12 July five discussions were held on Germany during the second session of the Council of Foreign Ministers in Paris. Each was long, averaging about four hours, acrimonious, and disjointed. Formal prepared statements were interspersed with debate. All the Foreign Ministers had already spent three busy weeks in tense, technical debate on the satellite peace treaties; Byrnes was reported to be working under considerable nervous tension and Bevin had a heart attack on his return to London.

---

[47] ORC(46)56, Revise, 19 June 1946, CAB 134/596; Brief for Attlee, 21 June 1946, FO 371/55405; CM56(46), 6 June 1946, CAB 128/6.

However, Bevin had been fully briefed for these meetings, and knew that they could well turn upon detailed analysis of the Potsdam Protocol. He now intended, as he phrased it, to bring matters to a head, and had the three challenges prepared in London with which he would confront the Russians. They closely mirrored three of the five proposals that Byrnes had put forward for discussion by the Special Deputies on 15 May, but it would not be easy to prove that common policies should precede reparations, not vice versa. Bevin's major anxiety was that a suitable moment would not arise to present the three British challenges.

The first meeting on 9 July showed how impossible it was for the Foreign Ministers to agree on their interpretations of the Potsdam Protocol. Molotov accused Clay of an unlawful action in his suspension of reparations deliveries. Bevin left the running to Byrnes and Molotov on the first day: both stated their positions on reparations, the four-power treaty, and the Special Deputies proposal.[48]

On 10 July it was the turn of the British and the French. Bidault made a long statement which rehearsed his all too well-known public views on the Ruhr and Rhineland. He gave strong support to the Americans' Special Deputies proposal and to the proposed four-power treaty, but still pleaded for more coal from the Ruhr for France. Bidault had reason to think that some dramatic move was about to take place as Maurice Thorez, the leader of the French Communist Party had asked him unsuccessfully the previous evening to try to secure the postponment of this session.[49]

Bevin then read his own formal statement. Advocating the four-power treaty and a revised Special Deputies scheme, he went on to say that some action over Germany now had to be taken. Europe could move towards either a balance of power between states of equal strength, or domination by one power or two blocs of powers, or united control of Germany by four powers. In principle he favoured, he said, the last option, but at the moment the most pressing problem for Britain was the economic condition of the British zone. The Soviets were taking current reparations from their zone, resources were not being shared, and they had

---

[48] *FRUS 1946* ii, 843 ff. [49] Ibid. 860 ff.; *FRUS 1946* v, 577.

failed to co-operate in the establishment of a common import–export programme. The effect of this was to burden the British taxpayer. It seemed as though Europe was heading towards domination by one power. He concluded:

I must formally state that the United Kingdom will co-operate on a fully reciprocal basis with the other zones, but in so far as there is no reciprocity from any particular zone or agreement to carry out the whole of the Potsdam Protocol, my Government will be compelled to organise the British Zone of Occupation in Germany in such a manner that no further liability shall fall on the British taxpayer.[50]

Bevin had indeed thrown down the gauntlet. In response Molotov made an impassioned appeal over the heads of the Foreign Ministers to the Germans themselves. He knew that it was 'incorrect to identify Hitler with the German people': the Soviet Union's purpose was 'not to destroy Germany but to transform Germany into a democratic and peace loving state'. If four-power control of the Ruhr was achieved, he would be prepared to see the levels of industrial production rise above those arrived at in the Level of Industry Agreement, as Germany's military potential would then have been harnessed by the Allies. He wished to see a unified, not a dismembered Germany, but he did not want to impose a constitutional settlement upon the Germans, as any such solution would be most precarious. Instead, he surprised his fellow Foreign Ministers by suggesting plebiscites to determine the constitutional wishes of the German people.[51] Molotov had done exactly what Bevin hoped he would not do; first he had upstaged Bevin's own dramatic challenge, and then he had addressed himself directly to the Germans. Moreover, Molotov had committed himself to maintaining Germany's western frontiers, and had thereby ditched the French and neatly stalled Bevin's earlier threat to bring up the subject of Germany's eastern frontier with Poland.

No doubt because of the lack of contact between the British and the Americans, Byrnes did not immediately respond to Bevin's ultimatum, but again tried to get his five proposals referred to the Special Deputies and thereby take the steam out of the debate. Bevin had, rather lamely, to present his own three prepared

---

[50] *FRUS 1946* ii, 860 ff.   [51] Ibid.

challenges right at the end of the meeting with the tart request that the Foreign Ministers study the paper and 'come back tomorrow and agree to it'.[52]

Study it is clearly what Byrnes did, and the next day he made his own prepared statement. He also appealed to the Germans, denying that the Americans sought to impose a peace of vengeance on Germany. The economic revival of Germany was essential to the well-being of Europe, but the Allies must not lose sight of the interests of those countries devastated in the war. Once again he asked that Special Deputies be established to consider his five proposals.

Molotov then intervened and now threw away much of the psychological gain of the previous day. He reverted to reparations, a topic hardly guaranteed to sustain the support of the Germans, and claimed that Bevin's three proposals were 'calculated to hinder the delivery of reparations'. The Soviet Union did not like the Special Deputies proposal either and would prefer another meeting of the Foreign Ministers in the autumn to discuss Germany. He then laid out the Soviet Union's own priorities in the interpretation of Potsdam. He claimed

that the Soviet Government maintained its claim to reparations from Germany to the value of 10 billion dollars; that these reparations would be obtained not only from deliveries of capital plant and equipment, but also from commodities out of Germany's current production; that indigenous resources could not be sent from the Russian zone of Germany to other zones because . . . industrial capital equipment delivered as reparation from the Western Zones to Russia . . . had hardly begun to take place.[53]

Bevin once again retorted that he refused to delay further. He repeated that the British zone would be organized, regarding 'coal and in every other way', if economic unity was not agreed to, and promised the French the economic control of the Saar when the borders of Germany had been finally decided.[54]

It was at this moment that Byrnes made his now celebrated offer to join the American zone with any other individual zone. He opened his speech by saying that he hoped that 'we can avoid the situation outlined by Mr Bevin'. He still wished to refer the

---

[52] *FRUS 1946* ii, 860 ff.   [53] Ibid. 881 ff.   [54] Ibid.

German question to Special Deputies and hoped to be able to establish central administrations, but

pending agreement among the Four Powers to implement the Potsdam Agreement requiring the administration of Germany as an economic unit, the United States will join with any other occupying government or governments in Germany for the treatment of our respective zones as an economic unit.[55]

On 12 July the Foreign Ministers held their last meetings on Germany at this Council and examined the specific clauses in the Potsdam Protocol concerned with economic unity. Bevin attached the greatest importance to paragraphs 15 and 19—the economic sections—as they were the main pillars of the British Government's case. He now confessed to Molotov that he placed less value on the importance of setting up central administrations than on the urgency of economic unity, and reminded his fellow Foreign Ministers that it was he who had first suggested some form of co-operation between two or more zones.[56] His speech of 10 July was not the unpremeditated outburst of a tired and irritable man, but was clearly calculated to show the Soviets—and the Americans—that the British were serious and purposeful in their ultimatum. But Byrnes was still trying to secure a constructive agreement over central administrations before the Council closed, and, on the evening of 12 July, suggested that the four powers set up central administrations, excluding the Saar from their ambit to satisfy France. Molotov was clearly not briefed to discuss such a proposal and asked for more time. Bevin dismissed the proposal, and Dixon noted with some trepidation that the British team feared that Byrnes was already hedging on his bizonal proposals.[57] But the meeting, and with it the Council, closed with this proposal, the Special Deputies, and the draft treaty proposals seemingly lost, and with only the promise of another meeting in the autumn.

These last two days of the Paris Council set in train an incremental process that was to lead to the division of Germany and a diplomatic revolution in the global alliance system. Bevin and his officials were well aware of the significance of what had happened. They had not given way to the Soviet Union and had

[55] Ibid.; Clay, *Decision in Germany*, 165.   [56] *FRUS 1946* ii, 909 f.
[57] Ibid.; Dixon papers, 12 July 1946.

shown that the British and Americans meant business, one of the principal arguments for the 'Western' policy as stated to the Cabinet.[58]

The option of taking an independent policy in the British zone had been high on the British agenda since the end of February and was not in any sense an empty threat. Officials knew that Clay's enthusiasm for any change that would end the impasse in Germany was an insufficient guide as to how the State Department was thinking, and that any 'Western' policy would create a 'first class row with the Russians'.[59] But they themselves were not prepared to take the security risks perceived to be associated with an enthusiastic implementation of the Potsdam Protocol, or even to consider any positive proposals put forward by the Soviet Union. Once they had decided that gestures of Soviet goodwill simply masked a long-term hostile strategy against the West, any opportunity for compromise was lost. Hints at Soviet concessions over implementing an import–export programme on a year-by-year basis, and an offer that the whole Level of Industry Agreement could be re-examined if the British zone was in real difficulties, were not taken up. Robertson told Bevin that the Soviets could never agree to pay for imports from their zone in an acceptable currency, that is dollars, but Bevin still insisted on including this as a pre-condition to economic unity. Robertson also

reckoned that Molotov would accept the principle of economic unity, but would add that German economy was at the moment in such a bad state that each zone Commander must, for the time being, be responsible for his own economy. . . . Molotov could not agree to make a cash payment to meet deficits in other zones.[60]

British officials insisted that the Ruhr should not be singled out for special agreement, although it was the industrial powerhouse of Europe and British policy there had not yet brought an appreciable measure of rehabilitation. Both American and British officials in Germany agreed that it was not easy to find major

---

[58] Bevin to FO, 10 July 1946, FO 371/55844. Vandenberg thought Bevin was determined not to make a single concession in Paris, A. H. Vandenberg (ed.), *Private Papers of Senator Vandenberg* (Boston: Houghton Mifflin 1952). Departmental meeting with Bevin, 23 July 1946, FO 371/55589; Morgan, *Labour in Power*, 266.

[59] Troutbeck–Street correspondence, 23 and 30 Mar. 1946, FO 371/55779.

[60] Russia Committee, 16 July 1946, FO 371/56885.

breaches of Potsdam by the Soviet Union, but the reaction of Bevin and his officials to this was merely to comment that 'the manner in which . . . [the Soviets] have used the Potsdam Agreement as an aid to their policy is worthy of note, and indeed, of respect'.[61] Indeed, the same could be said of Britain. In Paris diplomats exploited those clauses on economic unity where the British had the strongest case, and played down those on reparations and central administrations, neither of which could offer so much to British interests.

All this raises the question whether the events of the last few days in Paris were the results of secret Anglo–American co-operation, a collusion between the two. The Paris Council has been marked out by revisionist historians as one of the moments when the United States made a bid for the control of Germany.[62] This would indicate that the outcome was planned in advance, although this assessment has clearly been overstated, and there appears to be no evidence either of a joint initiative over the bizone. It has also been argued that the American role in the events of 10–12 July was 'tactical rather than strategic . . . hastily conceived rather than planned as a last resort . . . reflect[ing] past failures rather than plans for the future'.[63] Indeed, John Gimbel concludes that Byrnes was acting as much defensively in reaction to Bevin's threat as offensively against the Soviet Union.

The pattern of American behaviour towards Germany was neither coherent nor consistent during these months. Clay's reparations stop was as much an expression of his frustration with the French as an opening shot in the cold war. He was determined to secure the implementation of the Potsdam Protocol and thought—and he admitted this—in terms of fulfilling his orders, not of the broader strategic implications of each action. His actions during the early postwar years were characterized by continual threats to act with those zones that would co-operate in very specific areas and threats to resign when he felt he was not getting State Department backing for trying to implement the Potsdam

[61] Delegation meeting, 1 July 1946, FO 371/57843; *Clay Papers* 1, 243.
[62] For example Kolko, *The Limits of Power*, 138 ff.; Kuklick, *American Policy and the Division of Germany*, 220; Freeland, *The Truman Doctrine and the Origins of McCarthyism*, 54.
[63] Gimbel, *Origins of the Marshall Plan*, 109 ff.

Protocol. He saw economic fusion as an interim solution for dealing with a particular problem, not a part of a more decisive shift in policy, and commented that the political structure of the American zone should be preserved and that 'political unification [as opposed to economic unification] is undesirable until the eventual success or failure of quadripartite government has been determined'.[64]

Clay's reparations stop of 3 May was interpreted in an anti-Soviet light by Acheson, who also suggested testing out Soviet goodwill with the Special Deputies proposal. However, Acheson thought that the main problem was 'how to devise a practicable plan which would provide strong support for Clay's stand on integral execution of Potsdam'. He perceived Soviet aims as being to create a divided Germany, at least temporarily, and does not appear to have yet thought of a Western-inspired divided Germany to deal with this threat.[65] It was George Kennan who was already thinking, like his fellow Moscow-based diplomat Frank Roberts and other senior British Foreign Office officials, of building up western Germany as a defensive barrier against the Soviet Union. But the Paris Council is particularly revealing about the fragmentation of American policy. For, in general terms, there is strong evidence provided both in David Yergin's important book, and more recently in Fraser Harbutt's work, that American policy-makers and American public opinion had moved into a confrontational phase by the spring of 1946.[66] However, there appears to be little evidence that this shift towards a harder public

---

[64] *Clay Papers* 1, 236 ff.; Ingrams records Anglo-American discussions in Germany on greater zonal co-ordination during the early summer of 1946, 2 July 1946, IGMS 5/8. He thought that if four-power control collapsed, however, the Americans would want to involve the United Nations in the administration of Germany, 28 June 1946, IGMS/6/1 (Churchill College, Cambridge).

[65] *FRUS 1946* v, 551; on reparations stop see *Clay Papers* 1, 203 f., 234; Gimbel, *The American Occupation of Germany*, 57 ff.; Gimbel, 'Cold War Historians', in Schmitt (ed.), *US Occupation in Europe*, 89 ff. Per contra, see Thomas G. Paterson, *Soviet American Confrontation: Post-War Reconstruction and the Origins of the Cold War* (Baltimore: Johns Hopkins University Press, 1973), 254; Wolfgang Krieger, 'Was General Clay a Revisionist? Strategic Aspects of the United States Occupation of Germany', *Journal of Contemporary History*, 18/2 (1983).

[66] Yergin, *Shattered Peace*; Fraser J. Harbutt, *The Iron Curtain: Churchill, America, and the Origins of the Cold War* (New York: Oxford University Press, 1986). Both books reflect a strong preoccupation with American policy, and take less account of British Government policy.

line towards the Soviet Union after the Kennan telegram was translated into a specific and deliberate American decision at the Paris Council to jettison the Potsdam formula and move towards dividing Germany.

Indeed, the general character of Anglo–American relations does not suggest that a collusion over Germany was probable, or even possible, in mid-1946. One of the most persistent threads running through Anglo-American relations was their mutual distrust and an American dislike of British–Soviet antagonism. If Britain was to be able to prove to Byrnes that American support in Europe was essential, she still had to show that she was trying to work with the Soviet Union in implementing the Potsdam Protocol, despite the political and economic dangers. To try to plan a 'Western' policy with the Americans at this stage could only be counter-productive. Indeed, the strongest argument Bevin used in Cabinet against a 'Western' policy had been that the Americans were not yet ready for this, and Robertson told Mark Turner that he was sure there was no specific Anglo–American plan for Germany.[67]

However, Bevin was heartened by the reparations stop as an indication of American willingness to stand firm, and he knew as the Council drew to a close, that the Americans were becoming increasingly frustrated by Soviet intransigence and refusal to consider their demilitarization treaty.[68] By threatening to organize the British zone, he was testing the Americans as well as the Soviet Union. Murphy acknowledges that the 'British decided very soon after Potsdam that Germany probably was permanently divided between East and West, and they proposed then that the United States and France co-operate with them in the three Western Zones', but, although he was Clay's Political Advisor, he categorically states that he did not at the time realize the significance of the bizonal proposals for the future of Germany and the European balance of power.[69]

The United States's positive response to the Bevin challenge was to help to seal a peacetime Anglo–American relationship,

[67] Robertson to Turner, 13 July 1946, T 236/959.
[68] Boyle, 'The British Foreign Office View of Soviet–American Relations'; Yergin, *Shattered Peace*, 222 ff.
[69] Murphy, *Diplomat Among Warriors*, 371 f.

and it gave Bevin the best way forward that could be hoped for to contain the spread of communism without yet openly declaring the breakdown of four-power unity. Ironically, it was an American commentator who neatly summed up the real direction of British foreign policy, observing that what British strategic interests required was 'the retention of Germany as the dominating force in central Europe. . . . They now wish the defeated Germany of today to be strengthened as a future buffer against a too powerful Soviet Union'.[70]

[70] Sumner Wells in the *Washington Post*, 18 July 1946.

PART II
From Paris to Moscow
July 1946–April 1947

5

THE BIZONE AND
THE BEVIN PLAN

Creating the Bizone

BYRNES'S offer to create an economic unit out of two or more
zones was thus a response to Bevin's initiative—or threat—to
organize the British zone independently. The offer was repeated
by the American General MacNarney to the Allied Control
Council on 20 July. He reiterated that the Americans' objective
was to arrest the economic paralysis in the zones and to abolish
the division of Germany into airtight compartments, and that their
offer was open to all the occupying powers.[1] It appears that at
this stage the offer was welcomed more enthusiastically by Bevin's
own officials than by Bevin himself.

Bevin was tired and ill during these weeks and vacillated
between insisting that American support in Europe had to be
secured at any price and fearing—as did some of his fellow
ministers—that Britain could no longer afford high expenditure
on Germany. He also admitted later that he did not fully
understand the complexities of the venture.[2] He was fully aware
of the implications of zonal fusion, and knew that, if the Russians
refused to join, the bizone would represent 'a measure which
implied a clear division between Eastern and Western Germany'.[3]
He was still very much afraid the Americans might 'leave him in
the lurch' in Europe and wondered if it might not be better to
organize the British zone independently by raising coal prices and
charging the other zones in dollars—not Reichsmarks—for coal.[4]
Some Treasury officials remained as sceptical as Bevin, for the
cost of a bizone was estimated at $500 million between 1947 and

---

[1] CP(46)292, 23 July 1946, CAB 129/11.
[2] Bevin note, 3 Oct. 1946, FO 800/466. Dalton recorded that Bevin 'seemed tired
and gave a sense of being generally baffled . . . he . . . is still not at all the man he
was', *High Tide and After*, 158.
[3] CM68(46), 15 July 1946, CAB 128/6.
[4] Interdepartmental meeting, 22 July 1946, meeting with Bevin and Hynd, 23 July
1946, FO 371/55589.

1949, whereas the cost of running the zone independently would be $350 million. It could therefore be argued that 'it would pay us to go back on the decision to fuse the zones, and charge the US in dollars for coal instead'. To do so would give Britain a chance 'to integrate the British zone with our general ideas of Western European economy, with the whole lot based on sterling', and would also give Britain political control over her own zone.[5] But Robertson and Foreign Office officials strongly resisted this kind of argument, as backing out might encourage the Americans not only to stop providing food, but possibly to retreat from Germany altogether and thus destroy the more important political and security benefits that the bizone might one day bring. Indeed Strang had argued that expenditure in Germany amounted to a contribution to Britain's defence policy. Britain was, moreover, 'morally committed to the Byrnes proposal'; no further progress could be expected with Anglo–American talks on Germany if the offer was rejected, and co-operation in other parts of the world could be prejudiced if this project failed. In the Treasury Playfair realized that, while 'going it alone' in Germany might ease Britain's financial problems more quickly, 'the political consequences were disastrous', and Waley added his voice that the American offer had strong political attractions but was 'certainly not the way to reduce the burden on the British taxpayer'.[6]

Bevin was persuaded to emphasize these political consequences to the Cabinet and to remind them that the Americans put this idea forward and that if Britain turned it down, 'it will certainly seem that we are leaving them in the lurch'. The financial arguments for organizing the British zone independently and charging dollars for coal, would not 'be practical politics. . . . The only contrary argument of importance is that we would appear, by joining our two zones, to be ganging up against the Russians, and dividing Europe into two. But it will probably be quite salutary for the Russians to feel that we can if we wish do this, and that we mean business.'[7] Thus the bizone would be a

[5] Brief for Dalton, 25 Nov. 1946, T 236/996; *FRUS 1946* v, 635 f.
[6] Robertson to Turner, 13 July 1946, T 236/959, who welcomed the end of 'hesitation and half-measures'; Turner minute, 23 July 1946, FO 371/55844; meeting with Bevin and Hynd, 23 July 1946, FO 371/55589; for Strang's comments, see Berlin to FO, 20 Oct. 1946, PREM 8/1210; Waley to Bridges, 24 July 1946, T 236/959.
[7] CP(46)292, 23 July 1946, CAB 129/11.

symbol of Anglo–American unity and strength as well as the primary means of containing Soviet power in Europe, despite its possible short-term economic disadvantages.

The paper that Bevin presented to the Cabinet on 25 July represented the clearest exposition to date of British priorities. Germany had to be a self-sufficient economic unit before there was any question of reparations. 'This provision', the paper stated, 'is unqualified, unconditional and unambiguous.' Furthermore, the Potsdam Agreement 'supersedes all previous Agreements and discussions about reparations'. This meant that the $20 billion reparation figure discussed at Yalta, as well as the discussions on reparations from current production, were now considered outside the terms of reference of the occupying powers.[8]

Although the Cabinet Paper had this positive and unequivocable ring to it, in reality the Potsdam Agreement was extremely ambiguous.[9] Mark Turner, one of the brightest of Bevin's advisers, thought that there was 'something in Molotov's case' that not all reparation should be subjected to the first-charge principle. He did not, moreover, think that Britain's three challenges, or principles, were 'a strictly accurate interpretation of Potsdam'.[10] But once the premiss of economic unity over reparations was firmly stated, the British would be free to raise the level of industry in their zone as they had only given their consent to the Level of Industry Agreement in March on the condition that economic unity was achieved. The legal argument that legitimized the bizone was that the Soviets had not agreed to British pre-conditions on economic unity.

Whatever the legal niceties of the Potsdam Protocol, the British position by mid-1946 was to put an end to any negotiation over Germany that was not conducted on British terms, although it was already not anticipated that the Soviet Union could agree to British conditions, either at Paris or later.[11] As long as American support was forthcoming, Britain could afford to hold to this position.

[8] Ibid.
[9] Ibid.; Edmonds, 'Yalta and Potsdam: Forty Years Afterwards', 212.
[10] Turner to Jenkins, 13 July 1946, FO 371/55844.
[11] CO(46)292, 23 July 1946, CAB 129/11.

Molotov's Paris speech rejecting German dismemberment had caused alarm amongst British officials who knew that they too would eventually have to secure the backing of the German people. Two further considerations therefore flowed from taking the bizonal route. One was that a continued public posture of attempting to secure a four-power settlement for the whole of Germany would serve to calm German fears that a deliberate division of their country was being planned over their heads. There was continued resentment in the British zone about British policy, and a 'complete lack of trust in all "official" explanations', which could only damage long-term prospects of carrying the German people with the reforms.[12] The second consideration was that it was now even more important to realize the prospect of economic recovery, which had so patently failed to materialize during the first year of Allied occupation.

For the first time since the end of the war Foreign Office officials were therefore able to see a way forward that was not apparently blocked at every turn by the Potsdam Protocol. The bizone was accepted primarily as a political weapon with which to show the Soviet Union that Britain and the United States could act jointly in Europe for the economic recovery of Germany. It was thus an expression of the very 'ganging-up' of which the Soviet Union was so afraid, and was to set in train the economic and then the political division of Germany. But officials now wished to carry on with practical developments rather than make any rash public formulation of policy, to develop the western areas in partnership with the United States without Soviet interference or procrastination.[13] For '[t]he division of Germany cannot be the ostensible object of our policy in Germany since we have to make the Russians appear to the German public as the saboteurs of German unity. This is however a tactical consideration which need not affect our main policy.'[14] Members of the Russia Committee felt much the same way and argued that 'we should do what we can to prepare for a united Western Germany should the next talks on Germany break down. At the same time, however, we

[12] Steel minute, 26 Nov. 1946, FO 945/41.
[13] Joseph Foschepoth, 'British Interest in the Division of Germany after the Second World War', *Journal of Contemporary History*, 21/3 (1986).
[14] Hankey note, 25 Oct. 1946, FO 371/55592.

should not give the Russians any excuse for alleging that we have been the first to break the Potsdam Agreement.'[15]

Officials were determined to press ahead with the bizone and with effecting constitutional changes in the British zone that would parallel those in the American zone. Speed was essential so that Britain would be in as strong a position as possible to secure the best basis for negotiation at the next Council meeting. For then it was likely that 'there would be a definite decision as to whether Germany would be one whole or in two parts'.[16]

For economic reasons, too, speed was needed. Britain had had to introduce bread-rationing herself in July and the Foreign Office was under continual pressure to reduce overseas expenditure, despite arguments that expenditure in Germany should not be regarded wholly as 'reparations' to Germany. Bevin reminded the Cabinet that the high level of British expenditure had been caused by a deliberate policy to limit Germany's revival in the interests of security and the protection of British industry and exports, and that, in the short term, the British zone could be made economically viable if all exports were paid for in dollars. But the sufferers would be the Western European powers and the Americans. Within the framework of the bizone, although an unfavourable balance of payments would remain for longer, Britain's expenditure in the zone might be reduced from £80 million to £25 million within a year.[17]

The Cabinet was much preoccupied by the bombing of the King David Hotel in Jerusalem and accepted Byrnes's offer on 25 July without much debate. Joint German administrations were to be set up for finance, transport, communications, industry, and foreign trade, supervised by the occupying powers involved. The bizone would be, for economic affairs, a single area.[18] Because of the pressure of work and Bevin's illness, planning was left almost entirely to officials until developments required Bevin to take a personal hand again when he was in the United States in November.

[15] Russia Committee, 16 July 1946, FO 371/56885.
[16] Working Party on German Directive, 8 Oct. 1946, FO 371/55593; Robertson and Clay also thought this, DMG to COGA, 23 Aug. 1946, FO 371/55591.
[17] CM73(46), 25 July 1946, CAB 128/6.   [18] Ibid.

The two Deputy Military Governors together planned the bizonal machinery. Clay proposed two administrative head-quarters in Minden and Stuttgart to avoid any accusations of the creation of a Western capital and the two devised a temporary bizonal structure, deliberately modelling their scheme on the Potsdam formula except that majority voting was allowed. They also postponed a decision on what to do about Berlin, as it seemed too provocative. By the early autumn a common ration of 1,500 calories was established for the bizone.[19]

But the problem of the external deficit of the two zones was too great for the Deputies to negotiate. Clay argued that the deficit should be financed on a population basis of 57 : 43, with Britain bearing the greater burden. The British had not really decided what they wanted, as the Control Council were pressing for a 50 : 50 split at the same time that Dalton was hoping the Americans would bear three-quarters of the burden. The Bipartite board—consisting of the DMGs—then accepted a compromise of 53 : 47, with Britain still bearing the heavier burden. But this was not acceptable in Whitehall, and so the matter had to be referred upwards. Bevin decided that a high-level party should visit Washington in November for financial talks on the bizone.[20] The British team was briefed to try to get the Americans to share the financial burden on a ratio of 4 : 1—the Treasury formula—as it was felt that the Americans would eventually agree to take the greater financial burden in Germany because of the power this might give them to control events there.[21]

But the Americans were anxious to play down the significance of the talks. Congressional elections were due and the Republicans had signalled their intention of trying to cut the budget by 20 per cent. It was only in Stuttgart in September 1946 that Byrnes made a public commitment to a continued American military presence in Europe, and the Americans were clearly

---

[19] Interdepartmental meeting, 31 July 1946, T 236/994; Bipartite Board minutes, 4 Sept. 1946, FO 944/736; *Clay Papers* 1, 248 f.; DMGs meeting, 4 Sept. 1946, FO 371/55592.

[20] Meetings of 10 Aug. 1946, 17 Sept. 1946, T 236/996; *FRUS 1946* v, 613 ff.

[21] CP(46)383, 17 Oct. 1946, CAB 129/13.

not yet ready to reinforce this by an open-ended commitment to the financial recovery of Western Germany.[22]

In other words, the Americans were still taking a short-term and hesitant view of the bizonal discussions and certainly their officials did not appear to conceive of it in grand strategic terms. Clayton looked with a 'very critical eye upon any further demands for funds for a common enterprise with us in Germany', and Clay, it was thought, was primarily after his 'pound of flesh' for the American zone. But Foreign Office officials appreciated the full significance a joint Anglo-American venture in Germany could have, and intended to try to extract maximum political benefit from the talks by drawing the Americans further into a commitment in Germany before the next Foreign Ministers' meeting, even hoping to secure a 'hefty' loan for Germany if necessary. This they had to do from a desperately weak negotiating position, with no real cards to play, with a dollar shortage, and, most seriously, with the prospect of a severe and long-term food crisis in the zone that could only become worse without access to American wheat.[23]

Bevin decided to try to bluff his way round this dilemma. He explained that Britain did not have the resources to split bizonal costs equally, and threatened that she would have to consider withdrawing completely from her zone. Troutbeck applauded this stand, thinking it would make the Americans 'hysterical'.[24] But the British knew that to pull out from Germany would in fact be a 'total abdication of our position as a European power', would give the Americans the upper hand, would end their own plans for the socialization of the Ruhr, and might also create a situation in which the Ruhr industries themselves could in time become a threat to British industry. The United States might also follow suit, thus leaving north-west Europe open to Soviet control.[25] Byrnes was not impressed by this threat, and archly volunteered to swap zones altogether with the British, adding bitingly that with

[22] GEN 155/1, 29 Oct. 1946, FO 371/55938; for Byrnes's Stuttgart speech, *Department of State Bulletin 15*; Murphy, *Diplomat Among Warriors*, 371.
[23] FO to Washington, 23 Oct. 1946, FO 371/55938; Washington to NYC, 14 Nov. 1946, 23 Nov. 1946, FO 944/889; *FRUS 1946* v, 637; 'Reconstruction Loan for Germany', 4 Nov. 1946, FO 944/736.
[24] Bevin to Attlee, 20 Nov. 1946, FO 944/889; Troutbeck minute, 22 Nov. 1946, FO 371/55539.
[25] Brief for Cabinet meeting, 25 Nov. 1946, FO 371/55941.

American 'organisation and the potentiality of the [British] zone they could make it a success in a very short time'.[26] He knew very well that Britain would never seriously contemplate abandoning her occupation of Germany and the great power status it conferred, or swapping zones. Bevin's bluff had been called.

The Cabinet looked at the bizone proposals and realized the same thing. They rejected the idea of 'going it alone' in the British zone, as there would then be no guarantee of food for the zone, and the collapse of the Anglo-American talks would quickly be exploited by the Soviet Union at the next Council of Foreign Ministers. So they agreed to accept the 50 : 50 offer, but with conditions. They stipulated that Bevin should secure a dollar ceiling of $300 million for expenditure on the zone, that the situation should be reviewed after 1947 'so that we are not fully committed beyond one year', and that the Americans should undertake not to block proceedings for the socialization of the Ruhr industries.[27] However, Bevin was by now thoroughly boxed in. Despite a personal appeal by Dalton to the Secretary of the American Treasury, John Snyder, the only concessions were to be that the agreement would be looked at again if Britain's dollar position deteriorated dramatically.[28] The Cabinet then reluctantly agreed to these harsh terms. The Americans had driven a very hard bargain and had in no way made the bizone an immediately attractive economic proposition.[29] Moreover, the negotiators had failed to agree a bizonal level of industry, the British had to pay $29 million under a former Pooling Agreement between the British and the American zones, and American officials had been reluctant even to discuss broader matters of common concern in Germany.[30]

But Bevin and the Foreign Office had drawn the Americans further into the web of Europe and Germany's reconstruction. Now 'we and the Americans became partners in the rehabilitation of Germany and thereby Europe. It is at this juncture of great political importance that we should join wholeheartedly in this

---

[26] Bevin to FO, 22 Nov. 1946, PREM 8/1210.
[27] CM100(46), 25 Nov. 1946, CAB 128/6.
[28] Bevin to FO, 30 Nov. 1946, PREM 8/1210.
[29] CM102(46), 2 Dec. 1946, CAB 128/6.
[30] Pooling Agreement negotiations, T 236/994, *passim*.

partnership.'[31] The economic costs seemed terrifyingly high, at least in the short term, but the political benefits for Britain's strategy in Western Europe could be immeasurable.

The negotiations for the bizone mark an important, if rather unsatisfactory, episode in British relations with the United States over Germany. The agreement itself quickly proved to be inadequate, and the operation of the joint system devised by Clay and Robertson was totally inappropriate, lacking a geographic centre and any built-in mechanisms to encourage the Germans to produce and export more. The agreement was not a cheap option, and was provisionally estimated to cost the British $500 million over three years. Bevin, who insisted on converting this to sterling prices despite the fact that it was payable in dollars, estimated that it represented one-seventh of the total value of the American loan. It provided, moreover, no financial limit of joint commitment to Germany—'we are tied unless the Americans agree to a divorce'— and consequently a dollar commitment of unknown proportions.[32]

British officials had not yet convinced the Americans that bizonia was not necessarily a stage on the road towards economic and political unity for all Germany. But the bizonal agreement marks a crucial change in British foreign policy, and shows the strength of the Foreign Office in driving through a policy which was, on the surface, partial and flexible, but which had as its hidden agenda the welding of American interests into Europe. The Americans now had an unlimited agreement to share bizonal deficits and therefore to ensure that the two zones would eventually become financially viable and strong. It was a 'formal and unequivocal partnership in the rehabilitation of Germany and thereby of Europe', completed at a favourable moment before the New York Council planned future discussions on Germany. It would also show the Germans themselves that their Western allies intended to take action that would improve the German economy, and not just to strip the country for reparations, as appeared to be happening in the east. And, despite the terrible anxieties about the cost, a 50 : 50 partnership could be retrospectively justified as giving Britain 'equal partnership' with

[31] NYC to FO, 30 Nov. 1946, FO 371/55942. The bizone was formally operational from 1 Jan. 1947.
[32] Eady note to Dalton, 1 Dec. 1946, T 236/997.

the United States as 'HMG will be free to press for acceptance of their views on policy on equal terms'.[33]

From July 1946 onwards British officials also sought to devise a constitutional structure for their zone that was federal and as close to that in the American zone as could sensibly be arranged, and that would function effectively whether Germany was treated as a political unit or as a divided country. Speed was again necessary as it was essential to create a *fait accompli* before the Council met, so that the application of these measures would not be held up by disagreements there.[34] Economic fusion alone would not resolve the problems the zones faced, and it was doubtful whether this area could be turned into a going concern without the establishment of central political as well as economic administrations and perhaps without the establishment of a separate currency.[35] Political fusion in the bizone was 'the logical outcome of economic fusion, and though we are avoiding it at the moment, we could not continue to do so indefinitely'.[36]

By September the Foreign Office had drawn up a new draft directive on policy in Germany that fitted in with the American zonal constitution, and allowed for the creation of weak central agencies for the Western zones alone, when it became clear that no all-German central administration would be created. Power—including control over industry through custodians—would rest with the *Länder*, which would protect Germany against both communism and a revival of German nationalism, in a framework which was as close as possible to the Americans'.[37] Bevin outlined his constitutional proposals for the zone in a major House of Commons review of foreign policy on 22 October. In a 'subdued and monotonous voice' he outlined the Potsdam Agreement and the economic conditions that needed to be fulfilled before economic or political unity could be achieved, emphasizing the financial rather than the political context of the British proposals,

[33] CP(46)438, 1 Dec. 1946, CAB 129/15.
[34] Draft Directive, 9 Sept. 1946, FO 371/55592.
[35] CP(46)383, 17 Oct. 1946, CAB 129/13.
[36] Working party on German directive, 8 Oct. 1946, FO 371/55593; brief for Sargent, 28 Aug. 1946, FO 800/466.
[37] Draft Directive, 9 Sept. 1946, FO 371/55592; CP(46)383, 17 Oct. 1946, CAB 129/13.

both because of the criticisms that had been mounting about the management of the British zone, and because the real agenda of British policy could not yet be revealed.[38] The new political arrangements were accepted by the Cabinet in spite of protests from the Control Office, who felt that it sacrificed chances for German economic recovery and effective socialization of industry under zonal governmental control to the Foreign Office's priorities.[39] The constitutional arrangements would, with the bizone, provide a westward-looking, decentralized environment, within which the zones could be rebuilt to withstand communist penetration or take-over.

The Bevin Plan

Both formal and informal Anglo-American discussions on the bizone and the future of Western policy in Germany were to reinforce the intense interest which the German problem inspired between the Paris and the Moscow Councils of Foreign Ministers. By mid-1946 Germany had become the

largest and most difficult political question in Europe, and British policy towards the Soviet Union largely depended upon their relations in Germany. . . . The German questions with which we are now faced are fraught with the greatest dangers to the whole of our future position, not merely in Germany, but in Europe generally.[40]

She now clearly lay at the centre of Britain's policy to halt what was seen within the Foreign Office as the desire of the Soviet Union to expand to the west.

Germany was not formally and comprehensively discussed by the Foreign Ministers until March 1947 in Moscow, but at the Paris Peace Conference (July to September 1946) seven informal meetings were held, which established that Germany should be brought up for discussion by the Foreign Ministers in

---

[38] Bullock, *Ernest Bevin: Foreign Secretary*, 321; House of Commons, *Debates*, 22 Oct. 1946, vol. 427.
[39] Hynd minute, 10 Oct. 1946, FO 945/17; Bevin minute, 6 Nov. 1946, FO 800/466; CM98(46), 19 Nov. 1946, CM105(46), 12 Dec. 1946, CAB 128/6; Bevin–Hynd meeting, 8 Jan. 1947, FO 371/64362; CP(47)26, 19 Jan. 1947, CAB 129/16. For decision, CM26(47), 6 Mar. 1947, CAB 128/7.
[40] Sargent to Jenkins, 3 Sept. 1946, FO 371/55572.

New York after the United Nations Assembly had finished its deliberations.[41] Byrnes had been more anxious than his fellow Foreign Ministers to have further discussions, but the British really wanted to secure the bizonal agreement before Germany was discussed again by the Council.[42] In fact Germany was on the agenda in New York, just one week after the bizone arrangements were secured on 1 December, when it was decided to have a full session devoted to Germany in March.[43]

The New York Council talks on Germany primarily turned on evolving machinery for the peace treaty and securing a progress report from the ACC, and set in motion a charade of four-power diplomacy that lasted well into the following year. While the Soviet Union wanted to confine the peace process largely to the great powers and seemed genuinely more concerned to secure an agreement, Bevin argued that the smaller powers, including the Dominions, should be involved in a more active way in the peace-making process, as they were complaining that the 'Big Four had cornered the subject'.[44] In reality he knew that the smaller powers would now slow down progress towards a general settlement, would publicize the issues at stake, and would thereby improve Britain's bargaining position *vis-à-vis* the Soviet Government, while the bizonal machinery had time to improve conditions in Germany.[45] But it seemed that 'the Russians do not yet seem aware of the fact that the result of the fusion agreement, if it is successful, may be that it will be we and not they who can best afford to deal with the German problem slowly'.[46]

Two reports were produced during early 1947, from the ACC and from the Special Deputies. The former report did no more than show that four-power control had failed. Containing a 'vast amount of material often irrelevant and usually contentious',

[41] For informal meetings, *FRUS 1946* ii, 313, 364, 383, 398, 538, 654, 856; FO 371/55927–9.

[42] Washington to FO, 23 Oct. 1946, FO 371/55927.

[43] The New York Council sat between 4 Nov. and 12 Dec., *FRUS 1946* ii, 1469 ff., FO 371/55928–9. These weeks were remembered as a 'nightmare' by Dixon, *Double Diploma*, 244.

[44] Deputies meeting with Dominion powers, 20 Jan. 1947, FO 371/64180.

[45] CFM(D)(47)(6)56, 12 Feb. 1947, FO 371/64185.

[46] Dean minute, 4 Jan. 1947, FO 371/64176.

it was considered to be unreadable on account of its length.[47] It simply highlighted different interpretations of the Potsdam Protocol and showed that the British position that 'it is impossible to fulfil the reparations plan in the absence of economic unity' was irreconcilable with the Soviet argument that 'the economic unity of Germany contains as its primary and most important element the implementation of the agreement on reparations'.[48] The Special Deputies report on a peace treaty was not a unanimous one, and the British insisted that even those agreed sections of the report were themselves subject to later agreement on the complete document.[49] Thus preliminary four-power agreement on the control of Germany had again failed to emerge.

Parallel to this public parody of serious diplomacy that was taking place at ACC and Special Deputy level, British officials were now working hard to consolidate the progress achieved on Germany. Whilst the Washington economic talks were being concluded, the British also had bilateral secret talks on more general German problems. These took place to clarify those general principles 'that the British felt were an essential corollary to increased American participation in Europe'. Bevin came to the United States armed with a paper to which the Cabinet had agreed before he left for the New York Council of Foreign Ministers. He had secured the authority to discuss long-term questions about Germany privately with the Americans, including agreement that the cost of any concessions that the Americans might intend to make with the Soviets could not be borne by the British. The paper was based upon the three conditions on economic unity and reparations that Bevin had presented to the Paris Council.[50] To the three Paris conditions were added two new conditions which were considered necessary 'to preserve a basis of equality between Russia and the Western powers'. They were:

---

[47] Berlin to FO, 24 Feb. 1947, FO 371/64410. There is a great deal of truth in this—the unbound report weighed over 6 lbs.

[48] Report of ACC to CFM, 25 Feb. 1947, FO 371/64559.

[49] The Special Deputies sat in London between 14 Jan. and 25 Feb. 1947. Report, FO 371/64176.

[50] See Chapter 4 n. 47.

(iv) that Russia should make a payment towards the accumulated deficits of the British and American Zones of an amount to be determined representing the value of continuing reparation deliveries taken by Russia to date;

(v) that the four Occupying Powers should share in the deficit from financing Germany in agreed proportions.[51]

Bevin warned his colleagues that the 'Russians would never accept (iv), were very unlikely to accept (v)', and, judging from conversations with them in Berlin, he thought they would probably not accept the earlier condition that zonal surpluses should only be exported for dollars until the whole German economy was self-sufficient.

The secret meetings mark an important stage in the welding-together of British and American policy. But they also show that Clay still had a powerful role in making American policy towards Germany, and that there were wide differences between the British and the Americans over the general thrust of Western policy towards Germany. Clay still argued that if the dismantling of war plants were properly carried out, considerable deliveries of reparation could be made from this source alone. He estimated that $60 million could be raised from the American zone alone, which could have eased Western–Soviet tensions considerably and which was also a substantial admission of Western dilatoriness over dismantling.[52]

Clay also told Bevin and Byrnes that, on the basis of informal talks, he thought that the Soviets would agree to raise the level of industry to help rehabilitate Europe, if they could secure some reparation from current production. He estimated that $7 billion could be forthcoming from this source without prejudicing Germany's exports, if the level of industry was raised by only 15 per cent. Indeed, evidence was available to the British that the Soviet position was also shifting over constitutional proposals, and that 'it seems possible that Soviet policy is moving in the direction of a weak though united Germany, not necessarily under Communist control, and away from a Communist-controlled state which might prove incoeniently [*sic*]

[51] CP(46)383, 17 Oct. 1946, CAB 129/13.
[52] Record of Discussions, Dec. 1946, FO 371/64234.

strong'.[53] But the startling implications of such a shift were never seriously considered within Whitehall, as there the five conditions were considered as absolute prerequisites to any settlement that was not simply a 'paper' agreement which would inevitably give the Soviet Union access to Western Germany. So Robertson emphasized that the level of industry had to be raised immediately by the British and the Americans, without waiting for quadripartite talks, an argument that was to be repeated privately by the British team in Moscow. Moreover, a separate currency was an issue that could not be ignored for much longer. While the British could not yet guarantee that a 'Western' option found general favour amongst American policy-makers, Robertson and Clay drew up an agreement on the pre-conditions for economic and political unity on very much the same lines as the British Cabinet paper of October, although the contentious clause that the Soviet Union should contribute towards the accumulated deficit of the British and American zones was dropped in favour of a vaguer clause demanding 'full understanding on the financial responsibility of each of the Occupying Powers for past and future deficits'. Although this was meant to be a secret agreement, and Bevin made no direct reference to it when he reported back to the Cabinet on the Washington discussions, it was subsequently leaked by Clay as the American Unilateral Statement on German Economic Unity to the Control Council. This drew a horrified response from the Foreign Office, for by doing this Clay had both threatened the presentation of the British position in Moscow, and revealed the extent to which the British were trying secretly to secure joint Anglo–American positions over Germany.[54] They had, however, secured a joint agreement on economic and political pre-conditions for German economic unity formulated closely upon Bevin's three challenges, which was to form the basis of their negotiating position at Moscow the following spring.[55] But the

anticipated difference between the views of HMG and the American Government was, however, found to exist, in that General Clay

[53] Draft Brief for New York CFM, Nov. 1946, FO 945/31.
[54] Report on bizonal negotiations, FO 371/64234. ACC Report, App H III, Section IV, Part 8, FO 371/64558; FO to Berlin, 8 Feb. 1947, FO 371/64509.
[55] Ibid.

expressed the belief that political and economic unity would be worth some additional cost to the occupying powers, whereas the British representatives maintained the view of HMG that no additional cost could be accepted by Britain.[56]

These important discussions in New York, the creation of the bizone, and the constitutional developments proposed for the British zone, all formed the basis for an important document prepared during these months, which was to become the principal diplomatic weapon for the British in Moscow. The 'Bevin Plan' was a very long paper presented to and accepted by the Cabinet on 27 February 1947.[57] This was an ingenious rewrite of the Potsdam Protocol. It claimed to try to maintain the façade of four-power control in Germany, but in reality established stringent conditions for the future economic and political unity of Germany, conditions which it was anticipated that the Soviets would not be able to fulfil, but which would give time to forge strong bizonal arrangements.[58] It would therefore erect barriers against Soviet involvement in western Germany and stall both increasingly determined Soviet propaganda against the bizone and apparently serious Soviet attempts to negotiate over Germany.[59] It was thus a declaration of principles and was privately not considered as a genuine basis for negotiation, or as a supplement to work done by the Control Council or the Deputies.

The Foreign Office emphasized the economic implications of letting the situation drift further, the fear of Soviet intentions in western Europe, and the overriding importance of building upon the American connection in the bizone. 'It seems clear', Bevin was briefed, 'that the Russians intend to put us and the Americans in the dock at Moscow'. Moreover,

[56] Report on bizonal negotiations, T 236/999.
[57] CP(47)68, 'Principles for the Second Control Period', 27 Feb. 1947, CAB 129/17. (See Appendix B.) This was supplemented by papers presented to the ORC, ORC(47)2–12, CAB 134/598. For the Cabinet paper's nickname, see e.g. IY 17070, 28 Mar. 1947, FO 1030/169. It was also known as the New Potsdam, and the Supplementary Principles, Dean minute, 22 Feb. 1947, FO 371/64188.
[58] Interdepartmental working party, 8 Oct. 1946, FO 371/55593.
[59] Indeed, Soviet 'moderation and reasonableness' was reported back to the FO by the Berlin negotiating team, Berlin to FO, 17 Feb. 1947, FO 371/64410.

in Western Germany, particularly the more industrialised parts of the British Zone, the economic difficulties of the last eighteen months have brought about a state of depression and indifference. The Germans are becoming increasingly inclined to lay at the door of the Occupying Powers the blame for their present plight. The absence of any solution . . . is already driving some more politically minded Germans to adopt extreme political views. There can be little doubt that present conditions are favourable to the spread of Communist doctrine and that the Russians are well aware of their opportunities and there are already signs that they are exploiting them.[60]

The original Potsdam Accords were intended to cover the period of direct occupation of Germany, which British officials now considered to have finished: demilitarization and denazification had virtually been completed, and the handover of power back to Germans was beginning. The time was ripe to present the 'logical sequel' to the Accords.[61] So the basic idea of the Foreign Office was:

to revise the Potsdam Agreement with the intention of ensuring that any agreement with the Russians (and the French) about the next stage in the control period for Germany would be based only upon our own terms and would in particular not lead to an increased cost to the British taxpayer, further delay in the rehabilitation of the Western zones, and further and better opportunities for the Russians to penetrate and undermine the economic and political structure of the Western zones, particularly the Ruhr.[62]

But in effect the plan would present the Soviets with an ultimatum with which it would be virtually impossible to comply, unless their influence in Germany was to be neutralized. Germany could then 'play her part in the restoration of a healthy economy in Europe as a whole'.[63] It was, however, clear that 'it is doubtful whether this area can be turned into a going concern without the establishment of central political as well as economic administrations and perhaps without the establishment of a separate currency. This would be tantamount to splitting Germany into two.'[64]

[60] Brief for Moscow, 6 Feb. 1947, FO 944/762.
[61] CP(47)68, 27 Feb. 1947, CAB 129/17. (See Appendix B.)
[62] Brief for Moscow, 6 Feb. 1947, FO 944/762.
[63] CP(47)68, 27 Feb. 1947, CAB 129/17. (See Appendix B.)
[64] Ibid.

In February 1947 'new Potsdam', containing the five British pre-conditions, finally emerged as an appendix to Bevin's lengthy Cabinet Paper prepared before his departure for Dunkirk and Moscow. Bevin explained more fully the reasons for including the two economic pre-conditions which he knew the Soviets could not accept. Even if the Soviets were prepared to accept economic unity without taking further reparations from current production, the condition of the Soviet zone and its need for industrial raw materials would mean a net outflow of goods from west to east. The Soviet Union, moreover, could not be trusted to act in good faith, and would ignore the powers of any central administrative agencies, so that 'the goods from the Western zones could easily be shipped across the Eastern borders of Germany into Poland and Russia. In other words, Russia would continue to take reparation deliveries from current production but in a disguised form.'[65] The only way to combat this was to commit the Soviets to contributing into Germany as a whole until all the zonal deficits had been made good. Distrust thus underlay the Bevin Plan.

The plan also proposed that by 15 August the Control Council should issue a final list of plant and equipment to be removed from Germany, leaving her with capacity to produce 10 million tons of steel per annum (which would also be her permitted output). This was effectively an ultimatum to raise the level of industry to a point that would ensure self-sufficiency and some prosperity for the country. Political questions were inevitably discussed. Bevin explained that British policy was influenced both by the historical experience of a strong, nationalist Germany and by the perceived Soviet threat, or, most alarming, a combination of both. After the First World War Germany was too easily revived, and Europe had had again to learn painful lessons. Now he feared that the Soviets intended to set up a one-party dictatorship, reducing the *Länder* to administrative agents of another highly centralized state. But if this threat were countered with a weak confederal Germany, economic planning and controls would be impossible, and this would reduce the rate at which the German and European economy could be revived. Further, any confederate solution could produce a German backlash,

---

[65] CP(47)68, 27 Feb. 1947, CAB 129/17. (See Appendix B.)

turning 'the Social Democratic Party and many other Germans . . . against us . . . [to] work for a unified Germany even though under Russian auspices'.[66]

Bevin had returned to a theme that had haunted him for nearly a year: the prospect of Germany dominated by the Soviet Union through the manipulation of a centralized German government and administration. For if a German government in Berlin 'fairly reproduced the outlook of the country it would be neither wholly eastward looking nor wholly westward looking. The question would then turn on whether the western democracies or the Soviet Union would exercise the stronger pull.'[67]

What Bevin and his team therefore decided was that a federal system should be established that was decentralized enough to ensure against a revival of German nationalism and to attract American support, and centralized enough to give the Germans some taste of unity to serve as a counter-attraction to a highly centralized Soviet state. The first principle of the federal government would be that all legislative and executive powers would be invested in the *Länder*, except those expressly delegated to the centre. Further, the British plan could be used either for all Germany, or just for the western part, and Bevin talked

of a unified Germany as our aim, and we hope to agree at Moscow on the basic pre-conditions for the breaking down of all zonal barriers. If, as is very possible, we fail to agree, we could proceed without difficulty to implement the conclusions recommended in this memorandum in respect of the British, American, and, if possible, the French zones only.[68]

The priority now was

to keep the iron curtain down (unless we get satisfaction on all our conditions) and build up Western Germany behind it—but only up to an agreed level—so that when a reasonable standard of living and prosperity has been restored there is more chance of drawing Eastern Germany towards the West than vice versa. The moment will then come for unifying Germany, which we hope by that time will, at any rate, so far as the West is concerned, have reached a sufficiently advanced standard of political education and economic rehabilitation to enable the

---

[66] Ibid.   [67] Brief for Moscow, 6 Feb. 1947, FO 944/762.
[68] CM25(47), 27 Feb. 1947, CAB 128/9. (See Appendix B.)

democratic and federalised system which we advocate to have a fair chance of success.[69]

A federal model was conceived as a *via media* between a strong and a confederate state. It would be decentralized enough to satisfy the French, was very closely in line with what the Americans wanted, and was far enough from what the British thought the Soviets wanted to make possible a Western line-up against the Soviet Union, if and when discussions about the pre-conditions for economic unity became difficult. It was central to British strategy for Moscow that there should be a convergence of Western thinking on political questions, although these were of a very long-term nature, and only to be discussed after economic and political pre-conditions had been agreed. A common Western front against the threat of communism, coupled with an attempt to rebuild a genuinely democratic Germany, could bind the Western powers together far more powerfully than national economic interests could. The Bevin Plan also contained political pre-conditions which, alongside the economic pre-conditions, presented a formidable set of principles that required consent before the four powers could co-operate further in shaping the future of Germany.

The effect of the Bevin Plan was clearly to divide Germany— at least temporarily—for the sake of Western interests and lay the blame at Moscow's door. It thus represents a dramatic move forward in the diplomacy of postwar Europe, revealing that the British were ahead of the Americans in their concern to implement a policy to contain Soviet power in Germany and Europe. It was based on an examination of Britain's capacity and willingness to invest more in Germany despite her financial problems, and on a serious assessment of the future security and reconstruction problems of Germany and Western Europe. By building upon those parts of the original Potsdam Agreement—economic unity in particular—which had always most appealed to the British, it combined an ostensible preference for maintaining quadripartite control with what was in fact a radical departure from the existing status quo. With Bevin's determination that the 'principles at stake are too important for compromise', it represented not a negotiating

[69] Objectives for Moscow, undated, FO 371/64244.

brief for the Moscow Council, but a statement of intent, a determination 'to bring matters to a head', and a redefinition of the political agenda for Germany.[70] It was rejected, 'the responsibility for failure . . . should be placed fairly and squarely on the Russians', and Britain and the US could retain and develop their zones alone, which would be preferable to a unified Germany whose economy was dominated by the Soviet Union.[71] Germany was too precious a prize to remain independent.

The Bevin Plan was also intended as an initiative to meet a need within the Labour Party and among public opinion at large, to prove that the Labour Government was not entirely negative and without a European policy. For, as was pointed out in *The Times*, in the sixteen months since Potsdam there had been no authoritative review of Germany as a whole.[72]

Since the Paris Council Bevin had been under pressure from Cabinet and party alike over British expenditure in Germany. Dalton thought that, in effect, the British were paying reparations to the Germans, and that the Germans' endless need for imports 'is one reason why our own people cannot have more food— because we have to spend our scarce resources on feeding Germans'.[73] Bevin was also subjected to a fierce barrage of criticism from members of his own parliamentary party about the general direction of British foreign policy. These attacks came in particular from the Keep Left Group and Labour Party-based journals such as the *New Statesman*. Their assessment of the nature of the Soviet Union and of the kind of socialist response the Labour Government should make was the source of the disagreement. Those on the left of the Labour Party argued that the Soviet Union was motivated by fear and insecurity, for 'the impression made by Russia's conduct of foreign policy is not that of a Machiavellian power pursuing a calculated course of aggrandizement, but rather of a blundering and suspicious giant throwing its weight around and hurting itself and everybody else'.[74] Soviet fear of the atom bomb, which the

---

[70] Ibid.   [71] CP(47)68, 27 Feb. 1947, CAB 129/17.
[72] *The Times*, 10 Dec. 1946.   [73] Dalton, *High Tide and After*, 166.
[74] *New Statesman*, 30 Mar. 1946; Gordon, *Conflict and Consensus*; E. D. Shaw, 'British Socialist Approaches to International Affairs, 1945–1951', (dissertation, Leeds University, 1974).

Foreign Office tended to minimize, the Left still emphasized. They also focused upon the economic weakness of the Soviet economy, arguing that the Soviet Union 'sees everywhere a hostile world organizing military power against her when she is still devastated and enfeebled'.[75] The aggression of the Western powers actually contributed to Soviet defensiveness, for Soviet foreign policy 'makes sense only upon the assumption on which it rests—that world capitalism will overthrow Soviet power if it can'.[76]

Parliamentary pressure came to a head in November 1946 with a motion of censure against Labour's foreign policy backed by fifty-eight Labour MPs. Attlee, although sceptical himself about the direction in which policy was moving, defended his Foreign Secretary by reminding the House that foreign policy was a pragmatic exercise that transcended party politics, for 'we are not acting as representatives of an ideological abstraction, but as the representatives of the people of this country'.[77] This line of argument echoed Bevin's own views on the nature of foreign policy: he himself told a Parliamentary Party meeting that a censure motion would seriously weaken his international standing as well as his bargaining position.

Some Cabinet colleagues were also becoming increasingly critical during the latter months of 1946, although there had been virtually no sustained Cabinet discussion on German policy since the end of the war. The *Daily Worker* alleged that Dalton, Bevan, and Morrison were encouraging the Labour Party rebels behind the scenes during November 1946. Dalton did not deny this. The opposition within the Cabinet turned on the anti-Soviet thrust of British policy and Labour's apparently enthusiastic friendship with the United States, as well as the cost of Britain's overseas policies. Dalton was, as ever, the major critic in the area of expenditure and of Bevin's reluctance to do serious business with the Soviets, asserting that 'if, as we hope, we and the Russians are to march arm in arm into the future, we must get used to the ways of each other . . . we

---

[75] *New Statesman*, 17 Aug. 1946.

[76] Cole, *Intelligent Man's Guide to the Postwar World*, 805.

[77] House of Commons, *Debates*, 18 Nov. 1946, vol. 430; Bullock, *Ernest Bevin: Foreign Secretary*, 327 ff.; Raymond Smith and John Zametica, 'The Cold Warrior: Clement Attlee Reconsidered, 1945–47', *International Affairs*, 61/2 (1985).

shall have to let them do most of what they like in Eastern Europe and Germany'.[78]

Bevan, long a sparring partner of Bevin's, was one of the most critical in Cabinet of constitutional plans for Germany, as he did not believe that Germany could be prevented from attaining the type of constitution which she desired. Morrison was also a long-standing personal and career rival of Bevin's, as well as a critic of Attlee's capacity to control him. The Cabinet was constantly plagued by plots, cabals, and intrigues.[79]

Bevin's tactic within the Cabinet was to ensure the support of Attlee, and to leave him to manage the criticism that foreign policy engendered within the party during the first part of the Labour administration. While he publicly ignored much of the criticism, he was still stung by it, particularly during this period, when he was ill and also absent from the country for long periods. When Attlee cabled him that some colleagues were much disturbed by the state of affairs in Germany, Bevin responded with a general attack upon Soviet policy. 'It is', he retaliated, 'a clash between the expansive policies of the USSR and the resolution of post-war America to stand up to them'. The Soviet Union had 'decided upon an aggressive policy based upon militant Communism and Russian chauvinism . . . and seemed determined to stick at nothing, short of war, to obtain her objectives'. This last comment must be one of the most clear-cut summaries of British perceptions of the nature of the Soviet threat, and Bevin then added that the Soviet Union would even be prepared to use 'Communists and sympathizers in our party in order to work up an agitation to involve the British taxpayer in more liability'.[80] Bevin was clearly more committed to an anti-Soviet stance than many of his colleagues, and to succeed in getting sustained support for his policies he now had to persuade them of the inevitability of standing up to the Soviets after one last public effort to secure

[78] Dalton, *High Tide and After*, 239.
[79] Kenneth Harris, *Attlee* (London: Weidenfeld & Nicolson, 1982), 302 f.; for the most vivid account of Cabinet and Party intrigues, Pimlott, *Hugh Dalton*, chaps. XXV, XXVI. Dalton thought Bevin full of 'bright ideas . . . but dangerously obsessed with Communists!', *High Tide and After*, 157; John Campbell, *Nye Bevan and the Mirage of British Socialism* (London: Weidenfeld & Nicolson, 1987).
[80] Bullock, *Ernest Bevin: Foreign Secretary*, 328 f.; Bevin note, 4 Nov. 1946, FO 800/476; Attlee–Bevin conversation, 28 Dec. 1946, FO 371/64243.

quadripartite agreement over Germany.[81] This hardline approach is very far removed from the conciliatory line that was publicly taken at the time.

But this opposition from within his own party goes a long way towards explaining why Bevin appeared contradictory and hesitant in his public espousal of an anti-Soviet position. The anti-Soviet pressures from the Foreign Office were considerable, but it was only by dressing up the need for a new approach to German policy in the guise of a revision of Potsdam that public and party opinion could be contained at least within the short term. 'Economic unity', minuted Dean perceptively, 'has also become a political catchword. It is the supreme test of our relations with Russia. The economic future of Europe may be said to hang on it. Germany is costing us dollars because the economic unity envisaged by Potsdam has not been achieved: ergo, if economic unity is achieved, we shall save dollars.'[82] Bevin could not yet say publicly that economic unity would not in fact restore prosperity in Europe because it could only operate in an atmosphere of East–West goodwill and he did not trust the Soviets to act in good faith. He could not emphasize that he thought the bizone represented not just the best, but the only way forward for the British because the threat of communism could not be contained for long without American aid. He could not, moreover, explain that any prospects that existed for a Western bloc could not be contemplated as long as the French political system was plagued by communists. Instead, he explained to the House of Commons that he was still seriously seeking an accommodation with the Russians, and simply hinted that the country should not expect too much from the Government at the Moscow Conference. He also emphasized British anti-German feeling, arguing that

[81] Attlee, *As it Happened*, 69; Williams, *A Prime Minister Remembers*, 150; Ivone Kirkpatrick, *The Inner Circle* (London: Macmillan, 1959), 202; see Smith and Zametica, 'The Cold Warrior: Clement Attlee Reconsidered' for a persuasive view that Attlee was more predisposed to trust the Soviets than Bevin was, until he was outflanked by Bevin and the Defence establishment. However, Attlee was also apprehensive about the future, if Britain remained tied to the Potsdam decisions, Attlee to Bevin, 21 Nov. 1946, FO 800/466. Oliver Harvey, *Diary*, 29 Apr. 1946 (British Library, London).

[82] Dean minute, undated, FO 371/64244.

we have to provide for the security of Europe, and I am not yet sure whether even after two wars and two defeats, the Germans really recognise the effects of defeat and the stupidity of war as an object of policy. . . . I am obsessed, above all else, by the possibility of . . . [the] major Powers having differences, which might result in allowing the resurgence of Germany.[83]

At the same time Bevin was able to get the agreement of most of his senior Cabinet colleagues to the Bevin Plan. Dalton's financial arguments in favour of cutting expenditure, which had caused so much friction over Greece, could now be used to good effect by Bevin, who emphasized his desire to prevent the resurgence of a strong centralized Germany as well as the need for upward revision of the level of industry to make her pay her way. The records indicate that the debate on the Plan was fairly muted, and that only Bevan was prepared to take an attacking line.[84]

Another indication of the intense political importance in the international sphere of the German question by mid-1946 was the determined effort by senior members of the Foreign Office— Orme Sargent in particular—to gain control of the decision-making process in Whitehall over German questions.[85] This was a feature of the Attlee Government over Empire and Commonwealth affairs as well, where a line of demarcation has been identified between 'questions of such national importance that they would be determined by the senior ministers as part of their general responsibilities', and 'those that were left, more or less completely, to departmental ministers'.[86]

The postwar division of administrative responsibilities increased interdepartmental antagonism as the question of Germany became more complex and urgent to resolve. The administration of the British zone in areas of constitutional initiatives, civilianization, economic rehabilitation (especially in the Ruhr), and dismantling, came increasingly to depend upon the international environment

---

[83] House of Commons, *Debates*, 27 Feb. 1947, vol. 433.

[84] CM25(47), 27 Feb. 1947, CAB 128/9.

[85] Bevin to Attlee, 14 Aug. 1946, FO 371/55572; Brook note, Sept. 1946, CAB 21/1708.

[86] D. K. Fieldhouse, 'The Labour Government and the Empire–Commonwealth, 1945–51', in Ovendale (ed.), *The Foreign Policy of the British Labour Governments*, 87.

and, in particular, British perceptions of Soviet intentions in Europe. These issues created conflict between the desire for strong action to promote economic recovery and thereby stave off communist infiltration, and the fear of reviving a strong Germany.

After the Paris Council Sargent, with Bevin's support, proposed that the Commander-in-Chief for the British zone should report directly to the Foreign Secretary, not to the Control Office, although Sir Gilmour Jenkins, the Permanent Secretary at the Control Office, retaliated strongly in defence of his department.[87] Throughout the autumn and winter Sargent continued his attacks, criticized the Control Office for inconsistency and hesitation, and tried to exclude it from policy-making, because, as he told Bevin, the whole matter of reassessing policy on Germany was one of power politics which could brook no delay, and it would be hopelessly time-wasting to try to do this through the Control Office. Robertson, a more malleable figure than his American counterpart, was also won over to the Foreign Office line. He changed his mind to the Foreign Office view over the method of socialization in the zone, and by the end of 1946 protested that he did not 'want to remain in Germany unless the organization for the formulation and execution of policy is altered'.[88]

By March 1947 Sargent had succeeded in securing agreement that the Control Office should be merged with the Foreign Office, dealing with less important administrative matters under the Foreign Office's aegis. The unfortunate Hynd was removed from his post and replaced by Frank Pakenham, who was also to have an unhappy tenure of office, and Robertson also became directly answerable to Bevin. The policy-making machine that had existed since the end of the war was no longer compatible with the centrality of the issues involved, and a take-over by the Foreign Office was essential in order that 'the problem of the joint Anglo-American zone can be fitted into the picture of Germany as a whole and the problems of Germany as a whole related to the overall picture of British foreign policy and world

[87] Bevin to Attlee, 14 Aug. 1946, Sargent to Jenkins, 3 Sept. 1946, FO 371/55572.
[88] Sargent to Bevin, 27 Aug. 1946, FO 371/55591; Sargent–Robertson conversation, 13 Dec. 1946, FO 371/55594.

affairs'.[89] It was one more example of the enormous influence that Foreign Office officials could wield, now increasingly secure in the backing of the Foreign Secretary.

The illusion of seeking a quadripartite settlement was also central to relations with Britain's allies. The days of great-power harmony may have ended, destroyed by conflict over the future shape of Germany, by economic crises, and by ideological fears. An alliance born through struggle against a common enemy, it was perhaps inevitable that it could not be sustained in the postwar period. However, Britain was not going to be the first to admit that this was so, as world opinion seemed still to be anxious to see unanimity. To argue publicly that four-power control in Germany was no longer feasible would have brought a further barrage of criticism and propaganda from the Soviet Union, made British relations with the Germans extremely difficult, and strengthened the hand of the Communist Party in France. But, of most importance, it would have thrown the delicate relationship with the Americans into the melting-pot. For the British were all too aware that 'in their simple way, the Americans feel a tremendous urge to get on with the Russians if they can', and Clay had told Bevin in December that Soviet proposals for economic unification and a request for current reparations should be carefully examined. On the other hand, officials were afraid that the Americans might over-react to a crisis and that Britain might then be completely squeezed out of her role as a world power as the unwieldy barge of American power moved into Europe.

So the Bevin Plan was designed very largely with the intention of appealing to the Americans. It set specific dates as targets for progress to counter American fears that the situation was drifting. It emphasized the original Potsdam Accords, and thus the continuity of quadripartite control, to appeal to American legal sensibilities. It concentrated on the constitutional and political issues, areas that would find favour with the Americans, although these were in fact secondary, and would only follow on upon

[89] Brief on future arrangements, 6 Jan. 1947, FO 371/64246. An interesting corollary to these changes occurred six months later when Marshall, no doubt alarmed by the freedom of action Clay had in the War Department, asked to be informed about the take-over of COGA by the FO, Washington to FO, 9 May 1947, FO 371/64422.

agreement on the economic issues. And by widening the field of discussion from economic to political questions

we shall reduce the risk of finding ourselves in a minority of one. . . . The Russians are known to favour a centralised form of German Government. On the other hand, the American views are very similar to our own, while the French, who favour a confederate rather than a federal form, would support us against the Russians if faced with an exclusive choice.[90]

Two high-level meetings were held with senior American officials just before Bevin and his team set out for Moscow, at which the Bevin Plan was presented to the Americans. These meetings reveal a remarkable measure of agreement in Anglo-American views and 'practically identical' attitudes on political and constitutional questions. Both sides wanted, in the long term, the maximum degree of decentralization consistent with security, and there was virtually no disagreement on the division of responsibilities between the *Länder* and any future Central Government.[91] Murphy, however, like Clay, was very anxious to push ahead with political and constitutional reforms within the bizone. But there is no evidence that this was because the Americans wanted to establish a West German government; they were in fact seeking a way out of the constitutional muddle in the American zone, in which so much authority had been given to the *Länder* that their role conflicted with that of the bizonal economic authorities. A division of opinion between Murphy and Freeman Matthews, of the State Department, was also revealed at these meetings. Murphy, like Clay, was far more enthusiastic about granting current reparations to the Soviets in the future than Matthews was. The Foreign Office fervently hoped that the State Department view would prevail: resolving this conflict was to be a major area of British diplomatic activity in Moscow.

The Americans were found to be less well-informed on the revision of the Level of Industry Agreement and had not yet fully decided what they wanted in the area of economic policy, beyond ensuring a reasonable standard of living, the reduction of cartels, and the promotion of private enterprise. On the question of the

[90] CP(47)68, 27 Feb. 1947, CAB 129/17.
[91] Anglo-American meetings, Feb. 1947, FO 371/64244. See also *FRUS 1947* ii, 182 ff.

Ruhr, likewise the Americans were happy to 'go along' with British proposals and accept that four-power control of the Ruhr, with 'Russian troops on the Rhine', was out of the question at the moment.[92] But on the problem of the Polish frontier they were more determined. This issue seemed to be a dead duck for the British because of Poland's geographical position, but the Americans clearly hoped to use it as a negotiating chip with the Soviets over other aspects of the German settlement.

Bevin was in no mood for soft-pedalling to the Americans, but, reminding them of the British war effort, he informed them of the statements he had made to delegates of the Labour Party to the effect that 'we could never again contemplate holding out alone against an enemy for a year or two until others came to help. . . . We must keep very close to the United States.' He also raised tentatively the possible future need to build the German and European economies within a more integrated structure, emphasizing the link between economic disarray and the spread of communism, and mentioning that he knew of the views of John Foster Dulles on the need to plan for Europe's recovery by harnessing the resources of Germany. These profoundly important areas, which were to be discussed in Moscow and were to underpin Marshall's offer four months later, were not, however, the central theme of the talks, which concentrated on the immediate problems of Germany.[93]

But the American response to the Bevin Plan was muted, and must have caused the British some disappointment. Matthews commented disparagingly that

the American idea hitherto had been that the Potsdam Agreement was flexible enough to cover the constitutional and economic arrangements which we wished to see in force for the next period . . . first reaction was that the idea of changing the Potsdam text would cause great difficulties with the Russians and provide them with a useful propaganda weapon.[94]

Before he left for Moscow Bevin told the House of Commons that 'on all questions, our relations with the US are of the most cordial character, and I can assure the Committee that we, for

---

[92] Ibid.   [93] Ibid.; Hogan, *The Marshall Plan*, 17.
[94] Anglo-American meetings, Feb. 1947, FO 371/64244.

our part, shall not allow any wedge to be driven between our two countries and to disturb our friendship'.[95] However, it was clear that, unlike the British, the Americans were still flexible in their attitudes, reluctant to commit themselves to a revision of Potsdam, and ready to do serious business with the Soviet Union to secure a quadripartite solution for Germany, despite the bizone and the agreement over pre-conditions for economic unity. The British plans for Germany were more thoroughly worked out, based on a strong perception of the imminent dangers that communism presented in Germany, Europe, and globally. It was to be their task in Moscow to help to convince the Americans of their perception of the real situation and to act upon these beliefs.

The main thrust of British policy during the second half of 1946 was thus to press ahead with policies that could make the 'Western' option viable, and officials were insistent that there should not be progress over quadripartite policies unless the Soviet Union was prepared to capitulate to Britain's interpretation of the Potsdam Agreement. Indeed any delay in achieving the unification of Germany would be advantageous while conditions and morale in the Western zones were so bad. But '[i]f our reforms are given some time to operate',

German opinion of the Western Powers is likely to change for the better. The French are unlikely to stand out of the arrangements for the unification of the two Zones for long, and a temporary split between Eastern and Western Germany will be complete. The long term result of this temporary split, given some kind of economic recovery, may well be that the Western zones are regarded by the Germans as 'Germany' and the Eastern Zone as the lost provinces. A westward orientation of the Western zones might thus be effected, and a German desire stimulated for a Germany unified on our principles. . . . While a temporary split may even be advantageous to us, we should certainly try not to make the break appear permanent should it occur. We should, if only for the sake of effect upon German opinion, maintain the quadripartite machinery in Berlin.[96]

The first priority was now to secure the British and American zones, not the whole of Germany, for the West.

[95] House of Commons, *Debates*, 27 Feb. 1947, vol. 433.
[96] Brief for New York Council, undated, FO 945/31.

6

THE MOSCOW COUNCIL
March–April 1947

The Critical Meeting

IT was generally anticipated that the Moscow Foreign Ministers meeting would be 'the most momentous session' of the Council and that its failure to bring progress on Germany would bring the 'end of an era'. Contemporary and later writers confirm its importance as a watershed in the postwar period and as vital to the cold-war alignments of the great powers. The collapse of the Council has subsequently been designated as the moment at which it became obvious that wartime unity had finally broken down, ending Rooseveltian aspirations for the co-operative policing of the world. 'I think of it as a very successful failure', wrote Ambassador Bedell Smith, 'this meeting of the Foreign Ministers, in spite of all the frustrations it produced, resulting in clarifying beyond any possibility of misinterpretation the Soviet attitude toward Germany and Austria'. Thus was the iron curtain in Europe rung down. No longer would serious diplomacy be the major instrument of American foreign policy towards the Soviet Union.[1]

The predominant view has been that Soviet intransigence caused the breakdown of the Council. Genuine efforts on the part of the British and the Americans to bring about a settlement were thwarted by the Soviets' implacable public demands and their suspiciously expansionist intentions. 'The Russians themselves could hardly have helped more obligingly to split east from west',

---

[1] *The Times*, 19 Mar. 1947; Georges Bidault, *Resistance: Political Autobiography of Georges Bidault* (London: Weidenfeld & Nicolson, 1967), 144; Edward Mason, 'Reflections on the Moscow Conference', *International Organisation*, 1/1 (1947); Yergin, *Shattered Peace*, 296 ff.; Murphy, *Diplomat Among Warriors*, 376; Kolko, *The Limits of Power*, 349 ff.; Kennan, *Memoirs*, 329 f.; Bedell Smith, *Moscow Mission*, 201, 207; Gimbel, *The American Occupation of Germany*, 120 ff.; Backer, *The Decision to Divide Germany*, calls the Moscow Council the critical conference, chap. 11, heading; Anne Deighton, 'The "frozen front": The Labour Government, the Division of Germany and the Origins of the Cold War, 1945–7', *International Affairs*, 63/3 (1987), 458. For record of the Moscow CFM, FO 371/64206.

one observer commented. Conciliatory gestures were seen as devices to lull the West into a false sense of security, or as in the case of the German economy, to encourage conditions of chaos that would in turn lead to a drift to communism in the West. The Council was the moment at which Kennan's and Roberts's dispatches came to fruition.[2]

The Moscow Council also produced a shift in the direction of French foreign policy, away from its vainglorious and isolated stand on Germany and, eventually, into the arms of the Western powers. Such a shift confirms the most substantial change of direction that both participants and historians have commented on, linking the failure of the Council with the birth of Western Europe under the umbrella of Marshall Aid.[3]

However, the process by which such a fundamental shift took place in Moscow and the role of the British in this change, have barely been examined. Not least because of the future central role of American power and money, analyses have concentrated on the American political, economic, and domestic context of the months leading up to Marshall's offer of aid to Europe. British and American thinking were, it has been assumed, roughly parallel on European questions.[4]

The British documents reveal that this was, in many respects, Britain's conference. The British team played a decisive role in convincing the Americans that German unity was only viable if British conditions were complied with *in toto*, and that the bizonal arrangements were a better solution than any alternative which might give the Soviets scope to encroach into the Western zones and beyond. They isolated Clay and averted serious attempts by the American team to come to an agreement with the Soviets over reparations from current production. They headed off a major

---

[2] Anthony Nutting, *Europe Will Not Wait* (London: Hollis and Carter, 1960), 13; Feis, *From Trust to Terror*; Bullock, *Ernest Bevin: Foreign Secretary*, 393; Frank Roberts, 'Ernest Bevin as Foreign Secretary', in Ovendale (ed.), *The Foreign Policy of the British Labour Governments*.

[3] Young, *Britain, France and the Unity of Europe*, chap. 6; Shlaim, *The United States and the Berlin Blockade*, 28 ff.; F. M. B. Lynch, 'Political and Economic Reconstruction of France, 1944–47, in the International Context' (Ph.D. thesis, University of Manchester, 1981), chap. 4.

[4] Bullock, *Ernest Bevin: Foreign Secretary*, 393 f.; Gimbel, *Origins of the Marshall Plan*, chap. 4; Jones, *The Fifteen Weeks*; Hogan, *The Marshall Plan*. But also see Backer, *The Decision to Divide Germany*, chap. 11.

crisis during the Council over the operation of the bizone, and set in train new arrangements that further committed the United States to the bizone without moving with unseemly public haste away from four-power control. They also played a major part in convincing the Americans that it was no longer possible to wait for the Soviets to co-operate, and that the recovery of Germany, and with it Europe, permitted of no delay. They encouraged the shift of the French towards the West, with promises concerning the Saar and coal allocations. Small wonder that although 'Bevin set out for Moscow depressed and feeling ill . . . [h]e returned in good spirits and much better health, at once impressing his colleagues with the recovery of his old confidence and power of decision'.[5]

The British team that went to Moscow was strong and unified, although 'full of apprehension' about the conference. It included Pierson Dixon, Brian Robertson, and William Strang. Patrick Dean, Oliver Harvey, and Edmund Hall-Patch went to Moscow too, and were able to build upon their acquaintance with senior American officials whom they had met at previous Council meetings. In the British Embassy the Ambassador Sir Maurice Peterson was ably supported by Frank Roberts, and close contact was maintained with Orme Sargent and Gladwyn Jebb, and through Hector McNeil with the PLP. But there were doubts about Bevin's health: he was not allowed to fly and Dalton commented that the Foreign Secretary seemed so unwell that he might possibly not return.[6]

They left the country in the throes of a major economic crisis, which was to lead Dalton to call 1947 the 'annus horrendus'. From 20 January there had been snow and an eight-week freeze-up: coal deliveries to power stations and industry had been affected, power cuts had been necessary from the beginning of February, and the unemployment figures had rocketed up to 2 million. Labour Party economic planning appeared to be in a shambles. To compound these difficulties, government figures published in February showed a disturbing trade deficit of $1.8 billion; the American loan was being used up at an alarming rate, while the daunting prospect of convertibility—promised by the British as a condition

[5] Bullock, *Ernest Bevin: Foreign Secretary*, 393.
[6] Dalton, *High Tide and After*, 211.

of the 1945 American loan—was only four months away. Sargent feared a 'Greek' situation in Britain when the loan ran out, and maybe, even, 'a US administration'. Tremendous pressure was building up to prevent any further expenditure in Germany, where annual costs were estimated at £80 million and rising with the unlimited commitment to the bizone.[7] Economic arguments for restoring the British zone now converged with the security arguments. Dalton and Cripps were strong supporters of Bevin's line that further expenditure simply could not be incurred in pursuit of a four-power settlement.

Despite these domestic worries, the British team went to Moscow with a firm negotiating brief that worked 'strongly against concession'. Four-power co-operation would be taken no further without securing a frame of reference that reflected British and American political and economic interests in Germany. As Hall-Patch tellingly reported, 'we had the advantage of going out to Moscow with our Supplementary Principles in our pocket; and at every point, both before we tabled them and after, we stuck carefully to that framework of policy'.[8] Now that the British had the Bevin Plan (the Supplementary Principles) as a practical way of implementing a new policy of containing the Soviet Union and restoring the Western zones, Dean could sum up the British team's firm new position in the most honest terms, recording that the

truth is that . . . the gulf between us (and I hope and think the Americans) and the Russians is unbridgeable at present. We must be careful therefore not to get into detailed discussions which the public everywhere may expect to lead to a compromise. The sooner the width of the gulf is realised . . . the better. We want to be in the position of pointing out, faintly but unmistakably now, and with ever increasing clarity why we can't agree at this Conference and that Russian intransigence on these matters is the cause . . . unless the Russians come the whole way to meet us, and that they won't do at this Conference. . . . We must not try to paper over the cracks.[9]

[7] Dalton, *High Tide and After*, 187; on Britain's economic difficulties, see Kenneth O. Morgan, *Labour in Power* (Oxford: Clarendon Press, 1984), chap. 8. For Sargent's fears, Jebb letter to Dixon, Dixon Papers, 16 Mar. 1947.
[8] Hall-Patch to Eady, 2 May 1947, T 236/999.
[9] Dean to Dixon, 17 Mar. 1947, FO 1030/3.

The British team also knew that they 'should aim at taking and holding the initiative', keeping difficult questions within the purview of the Ministers themselves. They were 'not prepared to reach agreement or take a decision on any of the individual items . . . until agreement had been reached on general principles' concerning economic unity before reparations or political unity, and, as they thought these principles were unacceptable to the Russians, there was now some chance of securing a Western policy. Thus,

we should avoid any dramatic break and should consent to further discussions, either here or in Berlin, under conditions which do not endanger our basic principles as laid down in the Supplementary Principles. For the rest, if we cannot get our way on the main issues, we should be content to wait till the next session and meanwhile should continue in Western Germany in close collaboration with the Americans and, as far as possible, with the French.[10]

Domestic financial constraints, political objectives, and possession of potentially the richest and most powerful zone now combined to place Britain at the very centre of the negotiating forum in Moscow.

British officials had also assessed the objectives of the other participants at the Council. The Soviets, they thought, wanted

the creation of a unitary Germany with a strong Central Government; the de-industrialisation of Germany to a point where she can no longer be a threat to Russia; participation in an international control to be set up for the Ruhr so as to prevent Western Germany being controlled solely by the Western Powers, and the extraction of reparation deliveries to the amount of $10 billion . . . which could only be attained by large scale deliveries of plant, equipment and manufactures from the Western Zones.[11]

They were also 'having another attempt at gaining German sympathy', of filling up the vacuum between government and people by improving rations, stopping dismantling, and creating a People's Solidarity Scheme for welfare provision. But analysts laid emphasis on the dangers that Soviet policy presented when it softened its line to the Germans, and on its propaganda efforts

[10] Position Paper, 4 Apr. 1947, FO 1030/3.
[11] CP(47)68, 27 Feb. 1947, CAB 129/17.

over the bizone, which they called that 'vast capitalistic ramp aimed at the financial enslavement of Western Germany'.[12] But the Foreign Office was also aware of the Soviet Union's economic problems, including a shortage of consumer goods which had meant taking over 70 per cent of their zone's textile production, despite the fact that the zone was no longer a surplus food area and could 'become a liability rather than an asset if united economically with the Western zones'. Indeed, it was even suggested that, when the Soviet Union had stripped their zone, they might in fact decide to 'throw the remainder into the pool to add to Western embarrassments', if events did not go in their favour.[13]

Bevin explained to Attlee that the Soviet Union aimed 'to cause such confusion in Germany as to reduce the influence of the Western Powers in the Western Zones and eventually to induce the Americans to clear out of Europe'. If the Soviets tried once again to deal directly with the Americans, as had happened in Moscow in December 1945, the consequences would be grave. 'Any attempt at appeasement to Russia', an Imperial Defence College Report warned—and the word 'appeasement' is significant—'is more likely to provoke war. Reasonable firmness, with no sign of fear in our foreign policy, is more likely to sober her.'[14] The Bevin Plan was designed to meet these needs.

American operational policy towards Germany had not yet fully crystallized, and wrangles between State and War Departments continued to plague the administration, and even the wider implications of the 'Truman Doctrine', enunciated on 10 March, were as yet quite undecided.[15] Over Germany 'the Americans wavered all the time', Hall-Patch wrote.

Mr Marshall arrived new to the subject and feeling his way. His advisors were hopelessly divided and he had to make up his own mind without sufficient background. He was very conscious of the danger of Congress

[12] Pink to FO, 16 Jan. 1947, FO 371/64305; Reddaway minute, 26 Mar. 1947, FO 371/64306; *The Economist*, 15, 22, 29 Mar. 1947.
[13] CP(46)461, 17 Dec. 1946, CAB 129/15; Steel to Attlee, 11 Dec. 1946, FO 945/31.
[14] Review of Proceedings of CFM, undated, FO 800/447; COS(47)1, Confidential Annex, 1 Jan. 1947, DEFE 4/1.
[15] Larson, *Origins of Containment*, 312, 320 f.

cutting his appropriations—a danger which imposes on the United States a kind of artificial poverty.[16]

There were also serious specific difficulties over Germany. The bizonal agreement of January 1947 was not operating effectively, for the powers of the Executive Committee for Economics were being continually challenged as undemocratic by the leaders of the *Länder* in the American zone—no legislation intended for both zones had yet been promulgated by them. The fusion agreement was thus partially neutralized, vital industries were being starved of basic supplies, and hopes of a planned recovery were foundering upon the rocks of *laissez-faire* and sectional and state interests. The principal difficulty with American policy in Germany seemed to be the 'tyrant of Frankfurt', General Clay. The United States's 'leave it to Lucius' policy appeared to be having disastrous results, the trouble being that 'Clay has never been quite sure which girl he is married to'. He was caught between the fear that he would run out of funds for administration in Germany and the confusion created now that both the War and the State Departments were taking a strong interest in German affairs. He realized that the fusion agreement reduced the chances of securing four-power agreement in Germany, and interpreted every clause rigidly without an overall vision of rebuilding the German economy, arguing that, if American policy was henceforth to be based on the bizone and not on the Potsdam Protocol and JCS 1067, then this should be done democratically with the political fusion of the two zones.[17] He still thought that 'American objectives in Germany should not preclude serious consideration being given to the utilisation of some current production for reparations in the interest of the European economy and in obtaining economic and political stability for Germany as a whole'.[18] But British officials were reluctant to tackle the Americans yet and were justifiably afraid to reveal their anxieties over the cost of the bizone at the time of the Greek crisis or, most important, to give the

[16] Hall-Patch to Eady, 2 May 1947, T 236/999. In London, Jebb deplored the 'flat-footed, Red Bogey' approach to the Truman Doctrine, Jebb to Dixon, Dixon papers, 13 Mar. 1947; *FRUS 1947* ii, 169 f.
[17] Brownjohn to Robertson, 13 Apr. 1947, FO 1049/868; Makins to Hall-Patch, 9 Apr. 1947, FO 371/65052; Playfair to Turner, 5 Apr. 1947, T 236/1009; *Clay Papers* 1, 333 f.
[18] *Clay Papers* 1, 284.

Americans any impression that Britain was not still trying to make a four-power settlement work. They took comfort in the firm views of Senator Dulles, who was to play an influential role in Moscow, emphasizing Soviet rather than French lack of co-operation at Control Council level, and the overarching need to rebuild the German and western European economies by setting the Ruhr to work in the interests of Europe.[19]

Whilst the German people were unrepresented at the Moscow Council, their influence made itself felt during the proceedings. 'German opinion must considerably affect the stability of the constitutional settlement' because '[w]ith practically no exception, the Germans desire above all things the unity of the country. This is based partly on historical grounds and partly on the erroneous belief that if the resources of the Russian Zone were freely available to the West an immediate improvement in the standard of living would result.'[20] Improvements in the living standards of the Western zones would reduce any chance of German revanchism and there was continual concern about the impact in Germany itself of British policy statements during the Moscow Council.

The four Ministers had before them the Control Council report on Germany and the Deputies' report on a German peace treaty. During the first days of the Council meeting, the agenda consisted of discussion on the four 'ds', as they were known: disarmament, demilitarization, denazification, and democratization, which had formed the core of the ACC progress report and had to be discussed before the Ministers could debate Germany's future. The British delegates felt well prepared for these meetings, thinking that the Soviets intended to concentrate 'on those matters which concern the weakening of Germany and the extinction of elements antagonistic to communism'.[21] Molotov, supported by Bidault, demanded a greater level of industrial disarmament and demilitarization in the Western zones. He accused the British of still keeping military groupings under German officer command, and of failing to destroy war production plants. These accusations worried Bevin, who agreed that military

[19] Dulles, *War or Peace*, 102 f.; Backer, *The Decision to Divide Germany*, 176.
[20] ORC(47)16, 24 Feb. 1947, CAB 134/598.
[21] Brief, undated, FO 371/64560.

formations should be disbanded by the end of 1947.[22] The topics
of denazification and democratization were then largely discussed
together. Bevin felt that the Control Council had, by and large,
done a good job with denazification, and responded tartly to
Molotov's accusations of non-compliance with the decisions of
Potsdam, as well as his accusations about such individuals as
the Nazi industrialist Dinkelbach. Nevertheless, he admitted
that 'we were all in the same boat' on specific instances of
non-compliance.[23]

Democratization produced yet another row between Molotov
and Bevin. In this case the issue was the nature of elections, with
Bevin vigorously opposing Molotov's proposals for proportional
representation in Germany. But these issues were little more
than preliminary skirmishes, noteworthy in that they showed
Molotov and Bevin as the principal protagonists, a fact which
alarmed Marshall, who disliked Bevin's 'caustic' attacks and
counter-attacks, 'well interspersed with propaganda for home
consumption'.[24] Discussion on the four 'ds' formed the background to the meetings on constitutional questions; but the British
team viewed this area of discussion as largely cosmetic, guaranteed
to show that an effort was being made to build a peaceful Western-
style democratic Germany, but not yet lying at the heart of any
great-power solution to the enormous security problem posed by
the future of Germany. The constitutional aspects of the Bevin
Plan would be exploited to try to cement Anglo-American relations
in Germany, and for their potential value if a West German state
was eventually established.

They had not expected that the Russians would be prepared
to talk seriously about constitutional provisions, Foreign Office
analyses of the SED's proposed constitution having shown that
the Soviets, although favouring a strong government, wanted this
area to be left to the Germans to decide in the future. But on 17
March British, American, and Soviet agreement on central
administrations suddenly seemed close, which prompted Bevin,
anxious to slow down any American attempts at bridge-building,
to send a warning shot across the bows of the other Foreign

[22] *FRUS 1947* ii, 240 ff., 315 ff.
[23] Robertson to Douglas, 16 Mar. 1947, FO 371/64560; *FRUS 1947* ii, 307 f.
[24] Ibid. 251.

Ministers, warning that political unity could only follow upon economic unity.[25]

The next day Bevin had his chance to reveal part of the Bevin Plan. Dixon commented with excitement that Bevin 'had the field to himself. This scoop led to extraordinary activity to get publicity at home. . . . [Secretary of State's] feeling was that "we only have leadership to sell" at the moment. But it is partly personal, & though only 9 years in the House of Commons he is as sensitive as any hard-bitten politician to his personal publicity.'[26] Bevin stressed the practical advantages of the constitutional aspects of his plan, and elaborated the steps towards giving the Germans a new future. But Marshall revealed a different emphasis and did not favour the introduction of central administrations, a German advisory body to establish a provisional government, elections, constititional amendements, and finally a new government, as the Bevin Plan proposed. Instead he wanted the immediate establishment of a provisional government consisting of *Länder* Presidents who would organize the central agencies and draft a provisional constitution without first establishing what the powers of the central authority should be.[27] On the following day Molotov and Bidault presented their proposals. Molotov surprised his fellow Ministers by suggesting a constitutional model close to the old Weimar Republic. Bevin reported with some pique that Molotov was 'clearly playing to a gallery of German public opinion' in suggesting that if the Germans voted for federalism the Soviets would not oppose it, but Marshall was anxious to build upon Molotov's suggestion and thought that 'perhaps it was a question of words, for Molotov's proposal had seemed to the American delegation to advocate a federal system, divergences were rather those of degree'. Bidault, isolated by this interchange, was left to plead that provisional governments were as yet premature.[28]

Throughout the debates on constitutional questions Bevin constantly reiterated that 'anything to which the Ministers committed themselves on political principles presupposed that

[25] Moscow to FO, 18 Mar. 1947, FO 371/65052; *FRUS 1947* ii, 255.
[26] Dixon diary, 21 Mar. 1947.
[27] Plenary meeting, 21 Mar. 1947, FO 371/64206.
[28] *FRUS 1947* ii, 276 f.

economic unity was established in Germany'.[29] This effectively reduced this area of discussion to the speculative, but the reported talks about French involvement in central administrations, the composition of any German Advisory Council, the powers of a future central government, and possible voting systems gave a welcome illusion that the Government was seriously trying to negotiate, and that substantial progress had been made in some areas, as Bevin was to report to Attlee.[30]

By mid-April the discussions on central administrations and constitutional arrangements were brought to a close with Molotov accusing the Western powers of walking away from the Potsdam decisions. 'The four ministers were like anglers', *The Times* reflected, 'who had had little luck for many days and by common consent packed up their rods for another season'. The *sine qua non* of economic unity on British terms protected the British negotiators from making more than illusory progress on political principles. How true was de Gaulle's remark that 'constitution making is the last, not the first, step in state building'.[31]

The immediate need was indeed not the framing of a constitution, but the achievement of a viable economy. Within the Potsdam formula this meant resolving the relationship between reparations and economic unity and re-evaluating the Level of Industry Agreement, but for the British it really meant pushing ahead with the recovery of the Western zones as fast as the Americans would follow.

Molotov had stated many times the legal arguments from Yalta and Potsdam in support of the claim that a settlement of reparations should include current reparations and that this should be the first priority of the Allies. The psychological impact of the German invasion of the Soviet Union and the appallingly high number of lives lost was well known in the West, as 'below the Conference table lie the Soviet war dead'. There seem to have been domestic pressures within the Soviet Union to secure some kind of public recognition and acceptance of their position—as

[29] e.g. at plenary meeting, 2 Apr. 1947, FO 371/64206.
[30] Moscow to FO, 18 Mar. 1947, FO 371/65052; plenary meeting, 3 Apr. 1947, FO 371/64206; *The Times*, 3 Apr. 1947; Bevin to Attlee, 16 Apr. 1947, FO 800/272.
[31] CFM(M)(47)121, 11 Apr. 1947, FO 371/64197; *The Times*, 14 Apr. 1947; for de Gaulle's remark, *Observer*, 16 Sept. 1945.

evidenced by Molotov's pleading remarks to Bevin at the end of the Council about the Soviet Union's urgent need for reparations. The American Special Advisor on reparations, the doveish Edwin Pauley, went so far as to argue that, even if the Soviets did not actually receive reparations of $10 billion, a face-saving accounting exercise should be done that would be acceptable to the Soviets. There were also American suggestions that the Soviet Union should be granted substantial loans to enable her to rebuild the country peacefully, which would in turn ease the path of Allied co-operation.[32]

The most difficult task for the British team in Moscow was to stop the American team drifting towards compromise with the Soviets over current reparations. This task became increasingly pressing as the Conference wore on, and reports came in of the failings of the bizone agreement, which threatened the very basis of British policy in Germany.

At the plenaries of 17 and 18 March the Allies again rehearsed their views on economic unity. Molotov 'opened all the stops and pressed all the pedals in describing the damage done to the Soviet Union by Germany during the war. . . . He deplored what he called the "cocksureness" of monopolistic industrialists in the British and American zones', and presented the Soviet Union's own pre-conditions for economic unity, arguing that economic unity could not be contemplated until the bizonal arrangements were annulled, until there was four-power control in the Ruhr, and until there was agreement that current production could be used for reparation purposes.[33] Bevin then read his statement based on the Bevin Plan and once again explained that economic unity was of itself indivisible, that 'we cannot act in some matters as if economic unity had been achieved, while in other important matters the principle is not applied'. The Ruhr would not yet come under quadripartite control and reparations would have to take second place to a balanced German economy.[34] Marshall's

[32] *The Times*, 7 Apr. 1947; Bevin–Molotov meeting, 25 Apr. 1947, FO 371/64206; *FRUS 1947* ii, 395; Mason, 'Reflections on the Moscow Conference'; *The Times*, 24 Mar. 1947.

[33] Dixon diary, 17 Mar. 1947; plenary meetings proceedings, 17 and 18 Mar. 1947, FO 371/64206.

[34] CFM(47)(M)24, 17 Mar. 1947, FO 800/466; *FRUS 1947* ii, 255 ff.; Moscow to FO, 18 Mar. 1947, FO 371/65052.

proposals were very close to those of the British, and emphasized the need for a balanced economy before reparations were taken from current production. He spoke out against the cost of reparations from current production and elaborated upon this by remarking that he did not want to follow Mr Molotov in a retreat from Potsdam to Yalta, and that the Potsdam Protocol superseded the commitments made in Yalta. Molotov, Dixon recalls, 'yelped out that he wanted to speak', and argued most forcefully that Yalta and Potsdam went together. Marshall's legalistic approach surprised Bevin, but the British team decided to give their support as it 'was a triumph for the Americans, & a further showing of their hand'. Bevin wrote to Attlee asking that this should also become British policy.[35]

In the following plenary session Bevin rejected Molotov's pre-conditions out of hand, but then offered to consider payment of reparations from current production when economic unity was achieved and the economy balanced. This apparent compromise was artificial because, to the delight of the British delegation, the Americans were talking in terms of a time limit on the payment of reparations and their suggested time of ten years was far too short a period for the German economy to be set to rights again.[36]

But it was at this moment that the first crisis at Moscow surfaced. The British team had known that the Americans were anxious to reopen talks on the Polish–German borders, and were prepared to support them as it would please the Germans—although they felt that the issue was a lost cause. But when Bevin had a private meeting with Marshall on 22 March, he uncovered something much more serious. Marshall told him that

we had been examining the situation to see if there might not be some procedure such as the operation in Germany of reparations plants for the benefit of the Soviets, they providing the raw materials . . . which would permit a form of reparations from current production without delaying the creation of a self supporting Germany economy.[37]

[35] Dixon diary, 18 Mar. 1947; plenary meeting, 18 Mar. 1947, FO 371/64206; Moscow to FO, 20 Mar. 1947, PREM 8/514; Playfair to Robertson, 1 Apr. 1947, FO 1030/4. The Cabinet had in fact earlier agreed this point, CP(46)292, 23 July 1946, CAB 129/11.
[36] CFM(47)(M)34, 19 Mar. 1947, FO 371/65052.
[37] *FRUS 1947* ii, 273 ff.; Moscow to FO, 23 Mar. 1947, PREM 18/702.

Dixon reported that the Americans are 'ready for a deal which alarms us very much'. They now seemed

ready to pay a price for the unity of Europe . . . [and] seemed to think it would be possible to do a deal with the Russians by agreeing to current reparations in return for a concession regarding the Polish Western frontier. [They] thought the Russians were so anxious to get current reparations that they might be induced, in return for a settlement, to agree to putting the provisional Polish frontier back . . . I suspect at least as far as the Eastern Neisse. Marshall, thinking as a soldier, is obviously deeply impressed by the desirability of pushing the Russian controlled frontier of Europe as far back as possible.[38]

But this idea would enable the Americans to seize the initiative and to continue with four-power co-operation over Germany, thus destroying the basis of the Bevin Plan and driving a wedge between Britain and the United States.

The Americans were told the price that such a settlement would carry, for, as the Soviets had 'pillaged their own zone very extensively, such deliveries will have to be drawn chiefly from the Western zones. . . . [Any] plan for the substantial production and delivery of current reparations from West Germany to the Soviet Union is likely to increase the Soviet influence in the Western zones'. Furthermore, although, as a general, Marshall might like the Polish–German border further to the east, there would be no necessary security benefits, for 'so long as the zones of occupation exist, the Russians will be fully established west of the Elbe'. The Russians would also gain a 'double psychological advantage', showing their sensitivity to Germans in Poland, as well as penetrating the Western zones without yielding up their exclusive hold on their own zone. Bevin wrote a strong letter to Marshall informing him that the British would not accept his scheme because it would impose additional financial liabilities. The situation was serious enough to secure provisional consent from Attlee that the British team would threaten to limit their financial liabilities in the bizone (open-ended under the fusion agreement) if Marshall were to go ahead.[39]

---

[38] Dixon diary, 23 Mar. 1947.
[39] Brief for Bevin, 25 Mar. 1947, FO 1030/4; Moscow to FO, 23 Mar. 1947, FO 800/466; *FRUS 1947* ii, 274.

For several days the British waited. What had long been clear to them was now slowly and agonizingly being grasped by Marshall: the Moscow meeting was the last opportunity to break the clinch-hold of the four powers over their own zones. But the Soviets could not afford to co-operate unless they had guarantees of reparations in the form they so urgently required. Marshall thought that the British might co-operate if the Americans could strike a deal that would at least open the way to constructive negotiation. But he had not bargained for such strong British opposition to a compromise.

While waiting Bevin announced the British proposals 'supplementing and fortifying' the Potsdam Agreement. A 'great day—the launching of "New Potsdam", to which we have been working up for three weeks', wrote Dixon. In a positive and forward-looking speech, written by Dixon and Dean and intended to attract maximum publicity in Britain and Germany, Bevin reiterated his unilateral conditions for progress. The German people, he said, needed at least to be given a sense of direction to enable them eventually to re-enter into 'the society of decent peaceful peoples of the world'. He once again rejected Soviet conditions for unity, but there were no references to the long-term consequences if British conditions were not met. He made no direct threats, no accusations: having taken a stand upon his own interpretation of the Potsdam Protocol, the legal basis of the Council itself, Bevin had created a diplomatic situation in which he could afford to wait for the other powers either to move with him or to appear to break the postwar settlement.[40]

Marshall then rehearsed the principles of economic unity, and the need for the quick completion of reparations. He was not prepared, however, to accept economic unity on the condition that current reparations were paid, as this would, as he put it, be selling the same horse twice. He emphasized that the United States did not want partition as 'a partitioned Germany means a partitioned Europe . . . the United States wants one Germany because it wants a Europe which is not divided against itself. We must not permit our differences to stand in the way of European recovery. The US's responsibilities in Europe will continue. . . .' He pleaded for a spirit of compromise as 'we can never reach real

[40] Dixon diary, 31 Mar. 1947; IY 16034, 24 Mar. 1947, FO 1030/169.

agreement on the basis of ultimatum or immovable positions', proposing that the Foreign Ministers should then meet privately, as real negotiation was impossible under the eye of the world's press.[41] After his speech he telegraphed Truman that 'we are locked in the final discussions regarding economic and political unity':

In the private meeting of 1 April, Marshall offered to see if compensation with current reparations could be made for the loss of any plants already scheduled for reparations, if the four powers agreed to raise the level of industry in Germany further. He added that first, economic unity must be achieved, the Byrnes Treaty should be in place and the scheme should not impose a financial burden on the British. He did not now mention the Polish frontier. Molotov nibbled at the bait but failed to encourage the Americans; Bevin was predictably stony. The granting of current reparations was not intended to be linked in this way with the level of industry and he was, he said, 'unable to follow this form of calculation. . . . The task at this conference was to put Potsdam into operation, to establish a level of industry and to balance Germany's economy. They could then see what sort of country they were dealing with.'[42] Bevin reported on this meeting to Attlee that 'Molotov showed himself eager to accept [Marshall's] proposal, but I realised that a number of coal seams ran under some of the bigger steel works in our zone and that if the value of the concern was assessed above and below ground, there would be no limit to our commitment'.[43] However dismissive and weak Bevin's explanation to Attlee, the British team in fact took the American initiative very seriously, realizing how unsure the Americans were in their views on Germany, and that a major crisis had arisen within their delegation. Clay and Murphy argued that the Germany economy could probably withstand quite substantial demands upon it if it were properly reorganized. But the influence of Bedell Smith and Dulles, Marshall's 'fair-headed boys', was now increasing at the expense of the Berlin experts. After a terrific row with Dulles, Clay, who was depressed about the United States's disorganized and dangerous policy, asked for

---

[41] Plenary meeting, 31 Mar. 1947, FO 371/64206.
[42] Informal meeting, 1 Apr. 1947, FO 371/64197; *FRUS 1947* ii, 303; Clay, *Decision in Germany*, 150.
[43] Review of proceedings of CFM, FO 800/447.

and received permission to return to Berlin. Throughout the conference Dulles had thought that discussions on the minutiae were a waste of time, and that rehabilitation and the restoration of France and Western Europe were what was now required. Marshall was also under strong domestic pressure, both as a result of the Hoover Report of March 1947, which had advocated rebuilding heavy industry in Germany, and from Acheson and State Department officials, who wanted a quick settlement and were afraid of committing further sums of taxpayers' money to Europe.[44]

Truman wrote to Marshall on 1 April. He understood that Marshall's appraisal of the situation had led him to the 'conclusion that the time has come for us to express our willingness to explore the practical limitations and form of a current reparation program', but then poured cold water on the scheme with conditions that included the prohibition of reparations from current production which would diminish the availability of exports. Marshall nevertheless held his own against Truman, reporting that the 'terms which you suggest be made clear, are somewhat too restrictive and may not afford necessary elbow room for negotiation', and would create the impression that the 'offer of current production . . . is wholly illusory'. However, when Marshall presented his offer to the other Foreign Ministers on 3 April, he tacked on Truman's suggestions, contradicting the sense, as a member of the British team remarked, of the whole paper.[45]

Before then British officials had to try to stop discussion on Marshall's alarming deal, and to move the discussion on and away from reparations to other more fruitful areas. In a flurry of activity they rehearsed the British position again for Bevin. Current reparations were simply not on the cards in the short nor probably the long term. Playfair commented that

[w]ith a view to . . . blocking current reparations *de facto* while not objecting to them *de jure*, we have deployed as many claims as we could

---

[44] *Clay Papers* 1, 325 ff.; Murphy, *Diplomat Among Warriors*, 376; Clay, *Decision in Germany*, 149, 152; John H. Backer, *Winds of History: The German Years of Lucius DuBignon Clay* (New York: Van Nostrand Rheinhold, 1983), 176; *FRUS 1947* ii, 161, 306 f.; Gimbel, *Origins of the Marshall Plan*, 179 ff.

[45] *FRUS 1947* ii, 302; CFM(47)(M)97, 3 Apr. 1947, and unsigned comments FO 1030/4.

in advance of them—not only our claims in respect of civil supplies, which we genuinely hope to recover, but also our external occupation costs, which are a pretty hopeless claim . . . we are in a position to attain our end, which is that of stymying current reparations in favour of our prior claims without facing the politically embarrassing necessity of telling our Allies openly that there will never be any.

He deviously suggested that the mention of the ten-year time limit was worth following up, 'as the first charge, if it covers repayment, will operate for more than ten years, in fact there would never be any current reparations if this limit were imposed' because a level of industry of 11 million tons presupposed a balanced economy after only twenty-five years.[46]

'We have come to a point where we have to decide whether or not we are to make some concession in order to reach agreement at this conference', wrote another member of the delegation. The arguments of the Bevin Plan 'work strongly against concession', and any agreement on economic unity that failed to satisfy all the British conditions 'would be more than useless, it would be dangerous'. If Marshall could be privately dissuaded from the plan, 'we are now sufficiently close to the American and French viewpoints on economic matters to make it unlikely that we shall be put in a minority of one as obstructors'. It would be better to bank upon a substantial recovery in the combined Anglo–American zones and to build up Western Germany in close collaboration with the Americans. For, rather 'than subscribe to a bad agreement, it is better for us to prolong the present situation in which the recovery of the Western Zones on the basis of the fusion agreement can continue, unaffected by the economic pauperisation of the Eastern Zone'.[47] It was more realistic now for the British to try to shift the agenda to the level of bizonal industry and the long-term potential of the bizone, and away from reparations.

For by March 1947 the Americans, the Russians, and the British all favoured an upward revision of the level of industry for Germany. The March 1946 agreement had been conditional on a static population level, settlement of the border questions, and

[46] Playfair minute, 1 Apr. 1947, FO 1030/4.
[47] 'Economic Principles', 4 Apr. 1947, FO 371/65052; 'Objectives to be Attained at Moscow', undated, FO 371/64244; Playfair to Turner, 5 Apr. 1947, T 236/1008.

economic unity. However, none of these conditions had been fulfilled and the British proposed a revision to 10 million tons per annum of steel production. These discussions would require great tact, for not only were the Americans undecided about the details, but by 1 April they had seemed to be in a negotiating mood with the Soviet Union.

After the fiasco of the 1 April meeting Bevin had a private open-ended discussion with Marshall on 5 April. He expressed a strong desire to settle matters privately with the Americans and was very reluctant to enter into conference discussions on subjects where there was not a close Anglo–American consensus. The question of the level of industry had now to be tackled, preferably on the basis of the British estimate for the bizone. State Department and delegation pressure, Bevin's intransigence, and his concrete proposals over the level of industry were to have their effect upon Marshall. The British heard that he was planning to see Stalin; as he 'had been holding this in reserve for a showdown' this was good news, but 'we cannot . . . be certain of the American attitude'.[48]

But before Marshall met Stalin, Bevin held yet another meeting with him and now found the American more accommodating. Dixon reported that 'the American Delegation had more or less come round to our figure for steel capacity. They realised that we had thought it out'.[49]

On current reparations Bevin did not want to discourage the Americans unduly, and the American account reports him as appreciating the inefficiency of capital removals as reparations and the difficulties in which Marshall could find himself with Congress if no quick 'solution' to the German problem could be found through a reparations settlement that would enable American forces to be withdrawn promptly from Europe. He therefore proposed suggesting to the Russians a programme including:

(i) economic unity carried out honestly with a proper system of taxation and universal German legislation; (ii) the raising of the level of industry and the establishment of a balanced German economy; (iii) agreement

[48] *FRUS 1947* ii, 309 f. There appears to be no formal British record of 5 Apr. meeting, Moscow to FO, 8 Apr. 1947, FO 371/64508 mistakenly mentions the 5 Apr. meeting, but clearly refers to the 8 Apr. meeting. However, see Hall-Patch to Makins, 5 Apr. 1947, FO 371/65052.
[49] Bevin–Marshall meeting, 8 Apr. 1947, FO 371/64246.

between the four powers as to amounts of their past and present expenditure which would be recoverable.

If agreement could be reached on the above we would be prepared to consider whether, on examination, current reparations could be paid and to what extent. To talk of sending in a bill for 20 billion dollars was just nonsense. The amount of goods which it would be necessary to sell in order to provide that amount would cause another collapse as bad as the Dawes plan.[50]

However positive this might have sounded to Marshall, it was simply a diplomatic window-dressing, a restatement of the economic pre-conditions of the Bevin Plan, and quite meaningless as a strategy to end four-power stalemate.

Bevin then turned to the central question for the British: what should the Americans and British do if the conference broke down? He proposed that policy in the Anglo-American zone should then be based on 'determination of the level of industry, based on an overall allowance of ten million tons of ingot steel. . . . The German people to be told the final score against them. . . . The whole of this programme to fit into the design of the proposals in our "Supplementary Principles".'[51] Under the cover of a Potsdam solution recovery in the West could proceed unhampered by Soviet interference. But Marshall, cautious as ever, would not immediately commit himself to Bevin's plan, which seemed like a last resort that would not relieve American expenditure in Germany, but would rather cement the bizone and with it the division of Germany. At this critical juncture it was the British who were still trying to persuade the Americans about the dangers of Soviet expansionism and the need to contain Soviet power in Europe. Marshall on the other hand was

mortally afraid of agitation in the United States and pressure on the Administration that American commitments in Germany should be reduced on cost grounds. . . . He was therefore prepared to consider seriously whether there could not be some saving of United States expenditure if the Russians would play straight on economic unity. [But if] . . . the Russians would not play, the United States of America would have to face up to the situation.[52]

[50] Bevin–Marshall meeting, 8 Apr. 1947, FO 371/64246.
[51] Ibid.   [52] Ibid.

So Bevin had set the scene for further bilateral action in the Western zones if the conference failed, and for facing constructively the difficulties which were threatening the fledgling bizone, for it was clear, at least within the British camp, that 'economic unity has been dead, is dead and will remain dead for many months to come, and the fusion agreement is the only alternative which exists'.[53]

But Marshall still wavered. On 10 April Bevin reiterated in plenary session his long-held views that German recovery had to be seen in the broader context of Europe's recovery. Europe's reconstruction, moreover, depended upon Germany's health. At the wartime Allied meeting in Tehran there had been agreement that Germany should be dismembered, and dismemberment implied pastoralization. At Potsdam, however, they had opted for economic unity, which implied to him that Germany was now to 'remain a contributor to the well-being of Europe'. Raising the level of industry would help the Ruhr to become 'a European industrial centre which would help to give Europe a new psychology and a new orientation'.[54] He followed this up with a letter to Marshall threatening that if the Soviets did accept the American proposal on current reparations, the British would regard themselves 'as free to take whatever action is appropriate regarding the level of industry' by raising it to 10 million tons of steel production.[55] But Marshall still seemed unconvinced. Clay, now back in Berlin, urged that 'no bilateral agreements be made in Moscow until they have been studied here to determine their full implication': the figure of 10 million tons was, he thought, 'pulled out of a hat', and indeed he wondered whether the fusion agreement should not be annulled and the zones run more independently. Sargent urgently advised Bevin that, in view of 'Clay's attitude, it seems essential to get an agreement approved by Mr Marshall and yourself before the former returns to the United States'.[56]

So once again the British team prepared to exert further diplomatic pressure on the Americans. Robertson drew up a new

[53] Playfair to Turner, 5 Apr. 1947, T 236/1008.
[54] Plenary session, 10 Apr. 1947, FO 371/64206.
[55] FRUS 1947 ii, 474.
[56] Clay Papers 1, 335; Berlin to Moscow, 13 Apr. 1947, FO to Moscow, 15 Apr. 1947, FO 371/65037; FO to Moscow, 15 Apr. 1947, FO 943/498.

Anglo-American memorandum of agreement based upon the Fusion Agreement of December 1946, although some powerful members of the American delegation were sceptical about this, feeling that the British were pushing them too hard and that further, the Bevin Plan should not be the constitutional basis for the bizone.[57]

On 18 April Bevin and Marshall met again. This bilateral meeting was the most significant of the whole Council session, and the one at which the interrelated issues of current reparations, the level of industry, and the problems of the bizone converged. For the 'Western' option to succeed these questions now needed rapid resolution. The meeting was kept completely secret from both the French and the Soviets, and no more than a joint record of decisions taken appears to exist in the records.[58] Bevin proposed a new bizonal 10-million-ton production level, with capital reparations deliveries restarting to the west and to the east. In the record no direct mention was made of current reparations: ending the American capital reparations stop was to be the only sugar for the Soviets on the pill of raising the level of industry bilaterally. The division of powers laid down in the Bevin Plan would be applied to the bizone, so, as Robertson put it, we could 'walk within the framework generally of what had been agreed for the future'. Marshall capitulated, accepting that the bizonal agencies should be concentrated in one centre with the Chairman of the bizonal committees holding executive authority subject to the decisions of a majority of the committee. His sole reservation was over timing and he asked that the decisions should be delayed for six weeks 'to avoid the implication that we had been insincere in our efforts in Moscow to agree on economic unity'.[59]

Marshall's decision to drop serious negotiations with the Russians was also influenced by his unsatisfactory interview with Stalin only three days earlier, for he recounted to Bevin that the 'Soviet Government were just fooling. The US was not going to humiliate herself by remaining in that position . . . he was going to tell the President that he did not believe the Russians

---

[57] Mason, 'Reflections on the Moscow Conference'; *FRUS 1947* ii, 479 ff.

[58] The record is duplicated: *FRUS 1947* ii, 357 ff., and Bevin–Marshall meeting, 18 Apr. 1947, FO 371/64203.

[59] Ibid. See also Dean to Steel, 18 Apr. 1947, FO 371/64508; Moscow to FO, 19 Apr. 1947, FO 1049/743; Review of Proceedings of CFM, undated, FO 800/447.

wanted Four Power Agreement.'[60] So Bevin's proposals had been
perfectly timed.

The agreement at this meeting realized the principal British
short-term economic hopes for Germany. The improvement of
the bizonal arrangements were the only means by which they could
hope to rehabilitate their zone and restore the West German
economy. Their tactics from the beginning of the conference had
been successful, and had helped convince Marshall that the West
could no longer afford to wait, as Germany's and Europe's
economic difficulties were now too acute. The Bevin Plan was
now to provide the blueprint for Anglo-American policy in
Germany.

British interests in Germany could not be secured solely by a
commitment to economic revival in the Western zones. Security
questions had been raised in Paris in the form of the proposed
Four-Power Treaty of Guarantee—the so-called Byrnes Treaty—
and this treaty was discussed once more in Moscow. It was viewed
with some scepticism in Whitehall, but was seen at that juncture
as 'one instrument which may pin down the United States to
maintain forces in Europe for forty years', despite its vagueness.[61]

But Bevin still had far greater hopes for the treaty than his
officials did. He discussed it with Stalin on 24 March and thought
Stalin equally positive. He thought that the Soviets 'want to see
American influence eliminated from Europe. On the other hand,
their deep rooted fear of Germany makes them anxious lest the
Americans should shirk or limit their obligations to assist in
preventing the resurgence of Germany.'[62] His energetic interest
in this treaty during the early days of the Council indicates that,
unlike his senior advisers, he still toyed with hopes that the
Americans could be committed to the defence of Europe without
an open breach with the Soviet Union.

He personally undertook a redrafting of the Byrnes treaty to
include economic measures and a unanimous voting system which
he hoped would make it more palatable to the Soviets. This,

[60] Bevin–Marshall meeting, 18 Apr. 1947, FO 371/64203.
[61] Harvey to Sargent, 3 Feb. 1947, FO 371/64154.
[62] Bevin–Stalin meeting, 24 Mar. 1947, FO 371/64203; Bullock, *Ernest Bevin: Foreign Secretary*, 380.

however, brought a storm of criticism from his own delegation and from Whitehall officials, who suspected that Stalin was simply trying to soften up Bevin.[63] They thought his drafts a *pis-aller*, hard to implement, guaranteed to upset the Americans, and unlikely to satisfy the Soviets. Majority voting on decisions taken within the framework of the treaty were essential in case the Western power ever needed to 'suppress some Communist or crypto-Communist paramilitary organisation' that might spring up in Germany.[64] The Chiefs of Staff were now unsure about sanctioning the treaty until the frontiers and the political character of Germany had been decided. They feared it might let the Soviets into the Ruhr and further argued that it was only to be directed against a resurgence of military power and not against the subversive ideas which they saw as part of the Soviet armoury in Germany.[65] Sargent even went so far as to warn Attlee of the implications of what Bevin was doing, and the Prime Minister felt obliged to write to Bevin, chiding him for his efforts and hoping he would 'bear in mind [American] susceptibilities as the proud authors of the draft treaty and avoid giving the impression that we are unduly critical of their draft'.[66] Only Jebb appears to have supported Bevin's redrafts, and he cogently summarized the implications of failure, although he later realized his prescription came too late. He thought unanimous voting was essential because the treaty presented a genuine possibility of a gesture of goodwill, an act of mutual faith that could slow the remorseless drift to a divided Germany and a divided Europe. For if

we are suspicious of the Soviets, so the Soviets are suspicious of us in that what they no doubt fear is the establishment of some anti-Communist Government in Germany which might make common cause with the West against the Soviet Union . . . if the unanimity rule may involve risks for us, it also involves risks for the Russians. If neither party is prepared to take these risks, then there seems to be only one logical alternative, namely the division of Germany into two parts.[67]

[63] Moscow to FO, 29 Mar. 1947, 30 Mar. 1947, FO 371/64156.
[64] Harvey to Sargent, 30 Mar. 1947, FO 371/64157; Burrows minute, 4 Mar. 1947, FO 371/64156
[65] JP(47)44 Final Redraft, 31 Mar. 1947, FO 371/64156.
[66] Sargent to Attlee, and Attlee to Bevin, 1 Apr. 1947, FO 800/466.
[67] Jebb minute, 16 Apr. 1947, FO 371/64157; Gladwyn, *Memoirs*, 198.

But by the time the Byrnes Treaty was discussed by the Foreign Ministers on 14 April Bevin had been dissuaded from his efforts, the reparations crisis had passed, the British were more confident of continued American commitment to Europe, and, as Dixon commented in his diary, 'the Ams [*sic*] are by now, nearly a year after Byrnes launched it in Paris, rather bored by this badly-drafted treaty'.[68] The wartime spirit that had held the Allies together against Germany had gone, as had Bevin's own hopes for the treaty. In two acrimonious Council sessions all the fundamental areas of disagreement emerged again, although it was now the Soviets and the Americans who were the major protagonists, Bevin being happy to let 'the big boys' fight this one out.

Molotov was clearly afraid that the Four-Power treaty might be recast in a way that favoured the West, and of the possibility of a new and different sort of treaty for Germany that would supplant Potsdam. Over reparations the Western powers had already asserted that the Yalta Agreement had been legally superseded at Potsdam. Molotov now felt the argument would be applied again and therefore wanted any treaty to be 'fully in accordance with the Crimea and Potsdam Conference decisions'. He simply could not afford to emerge at the end of a well-publicized conference on Russian soil with only a treaty that guaranteed an 'illusion of security' but bore no reference to the Potsdam and Yalta formulae.[69]

Bevin, like Jebb, regretted the failure to negotiate the treaty in Moscow. 'I think Russia has made a bad mistake', he told Attlee, 'as bad as she made just before the outbreak of war when she lined up with Hitler'. It was the ever-influential Sargent who then suggested that perhaps the British team could now persuade the Americans and the French to make a tripartite security treaty based on the Byrnes Treaty. With the three powers it would be possible to build in unanimous voting, and the Soviets could even possibly be invited to participate on Western terms, as was the case with the bizone. British delegation members, however, thought the Americans 'wouldn't look at it for a minute'.

But Sargent's idea was a first far-sighted look forward to the Western security achievements of 1948 and 1949.[70]

As well as these discussions there were also to be bilateral talks between the British and the Russians on the revision of the wartime Anglo-Soviet Treaty. The Anglo-Soviet Treaty held attractions of a different nature from the Byrnes draft, for Bevin hoped that talks about revision would improve his stock within the Labour Party and silence those critics who accused him of being anti-Soviet. Its revision might act as an inducement to the Russians to agree to the Byrnes draft, although officials realized that the successful completion of the Byrnes Treaty would make both the Anglo-Soviet Treaty and the Anglo-French Dunkirk Treaty of largely symbolic value, as neither of these latter treaties now answered Britain's perceived security problem, as they did not deal with a possible future threat from the Soviet Union, or the Soviet Union allied with Germany. Keeping down Germany was no longer an adequate means of binding East and West together.[71]

The negotiations on the revision of the Anglo-Soviet Mutual Security Treaty of 1942 took place on the sidelines of the Moscow Council. In January 1947 Montgomery had met Stalin in Moscow, and Stalin had said that he would like the wartime treaty revised in the light of the United Nations Charter. But if senior British officials doubted the value of the Byrnes Treaty, they had even fewer illusions about the value of a revised Anglo-Soviet pact whose main advantage was as a public relations exercise for the Labour Party. They feared the Soviet Union might see the Treaty as a means of driving a wedge between the British and the Americans, who were already very apprehensive of any Anglo-Soviet *rapprochement*, as bilateral treaties could undermine the fragile UN peace-keeping structure. The whole exercise might simply become a political trap to challenge the proposed Anglo-American military standardization agreement.[72] Despite these

[70] Bevin to Attlee, 16 Apr. 1947, FO 800/272; FO to Moscow, 17 Apr. 1947, 26 Apr. 1947, FO 371/64157.
[71] Ibid.
[72] Hankey minute, 10 Feb. 1947, FO 371/66364; Russia Committee, 16 Jan. 1947, FO 371/66362; Warner minute, 2 Feb. 1947, Washington to FO, 3 Feb. 1947, FO 371/66363.

anxieties negotiations began, although Bevin was advised not to worry unduly if they broke down, 'provided we could ensure that the cause of the breakdown could not be shown to be discreditable to us'. The Americans were to be kept in close contact about the progress of the talks and any revisions should include a prior commitment to the Byrnes Treaty.[73] Bevin's own enthusiasm for revising the Anglo-Soviet treaty increased when he got to Moscow, partly because Peterson was very keen to secure its revision and partly because of Stalin's charm when the two met on 24 March. Molotov's Deputy, Vyshinsky, proposed that the treaty should be extended to provide a guarantee of mutual assistance if Germany, or Germany with an ally, should attack Britain or the Soviet Union. Bevin was tempted by the proposal, if it referred to an attack in Europe, but both the Foreign Office and the Chiefs of Staff feared this development because it might mean the Soviets intended to use it to head off Anglo-American co-operation in the Far East. If a non-European power were able to use a European base from which to launch an attack on the Soviet Union, and Germany subsequently joined in that attack, 'should not we be pledged by this formula to support the Soviet Union against that power?'; that is, Britain might actually find herself on the wrong side in any Soviet–American military engagement.[74] Sargent rejected the whole idea of the treaty revision, arguing that the Americans might feel that their presence was not needed in Europe if the British had security pacts with both the Soviets and the French. For 'if you were to come away from Moscow with nothing achieved save an Anglo–Soviet Treaty, would this not make a bad impression in the United States?'[75] Marshall's offer of aid would finally bury any hopes of revising the treaty.

As the Council drew to a close, the Foreign Ministers agreed to meet again in November. The repetitive talks on procedure for a peace conference and the formula for a peace treaty, which had continued alongside the more substantive discussions, only secured a referral back to the Deputies. Indeed, Bevin would have

[73] McNeil to Bevin, 21 Jan. 1947, FO 371/66362.
[74] FO to Moscow, 14 Apr. 1947, FO 371/66365; CM37(47), 17 Apr. 1947, CAB 128/9.
[75] FO to Moscow, 14 Apr. 1947, FO 371/66367.

162 *The Moscow Council*

preferred not to fix another Council meeting at all so that the new fusion and level of industry decisions could begin to produce results.[76] Bevin also had a private meeting with Molotov on 25 April. The flatness and superficial cordiality of this meeting reveals how far apart the two had drifted. Both understood the other's position and appreciated the difficulty of finding a solution that did not interfere with their own national interests. Germany's centrality to the future character of Europe worked against any compromise in specific areas. Molotov argued against hasty action, for 'unless we agreed the main questions of principle, we might be starting on the wrong foot', a point with which Bevin, of course, agreed wholeheartedly.[77]

Bevin's public statements to the press and the House of Commons on his return to Britain echoed this generalized tone. He revealed that nothing concrete had been achieved, but that he was not pessimistic and hoped that the 'Moscow Conference will turn out after all to be one of the best contributions towards the building of a sound peace', an ambiguous phrase to be publicly interpreted as a hope that a four-power settlement could yet be achieved.[78] Privately, Bevin was pleased that the Council had convinced the Americans that policy could no longer be allowed to drift, and that he had successfully outmanœuvred the Soviets.[79]

The Moscow Council was the most positive proof for Whitehall that the Americans would follow a policy in line with that enunciated by Byrnes in September 1946 and did not intend to withdraw from Germany at the earliest opportunity, or do a deal with the Soviet Union. In a lengthy paper reflecting on the Moscow Council Hall-Patch later thought that Marshall had had three options open to him in March 1947:

(a) a firm policy *vis-à-vis* Russia, which involved backing Western Europe (on the lines of Greece and Turkey) at what might prove to be considerable expense;

Plenary session, 24 Apr. 1947, FO 371/64206; Embassy meeting, 20 Apr. 1947, FO 371/64201.
[77] Bevin–Molotov meeting, 25 Apr. 1947, FO 371/64203.
[78] House of Commons, *Debates*, 15 May 1947, vol. 473; Bevin press statement, 25 Apr. 1947, FO 371/64600.
[79] Summary of Decisions of CFM, 24 Apr. 1947, BEVN/II/5/8.AHQ/9236 (Churchill College, Cambridge).

(*b*) doing a deal with the Russians and staying in Europe on terms, which would involve more expense in Germany (e.g. on current reparations) but might make it unnecessary to give such full financial support to Western Europe; and
(*c*) pulling right out of Europe.
I do not think Mr Marshall ever contemplated (*c*), but he wavered very much between (*a*) and (*b*). He came down finally on a rather over-aggressive version of (*a*).[80]

Six weeks in close contact with British perceptions of German and European problems at the same time as having a taste of Soviet negotiating tactics had made a decisive impact upon Marshall. By agreeing to raise the level of industry and to restructure the organization in the bizone the Americans had shown a commitment to the recovery of Western Germany, and with it Europe, that went far beyond their previous generalized concern over European recovery. In Moscow the Americans cut their 'cold war' teeth over Germany. Britain's contribution to this shift is incontrovertible. Bevin and his officials knew that the Americans needed British leadership in Germany and Europe; they had witnessed the divisions and uncertainties in the American camp and were able to act as a major protagonist in Moscow. Despite tensions over China, Japan, and Greece, and the dilemma of the increasingly alarming dollar gap, there was now a closer understanding between the British and the Americans than at any time since the end of the war.

France's place in the diplomatic ring was now also becoming clearer. The British attitude had been that as long as France remained hidebound by her insistence on a prior settlement for the Ruhr, the Saar, and the Rhineland little could be done with the French zone. The Anglo-French Treaty of Dunkirk was a symbol of goodwill to encourage the French rather than a relevant security pact. This Treaty, and a small loan also made to France in March 1947, were the limits to which the British would go while the Communist Party played such a powerful part in French politics. As Bevin reportedly told Bidault, 'we can't carry on a conversation between two Great Powers, with a third Great Power in the cupboard with a listening apparatus'. France's position at Moscow had been very ambiguous. Domestic pressures tied Bidault's hands,

[80] Hall-Patch to Eady, 2 May 1947, T 236/999.

although the Soviets had rejected France's own territorial claims in July 1946. Dixon had long thought it clear that the French were 'playing a blackmailing game and would do anything with anybody in order to get more coal from Germany'.[81] Further, to complicate Britain's relations with France, the Americans were split over their French policy, with powerful sections of the State Department favouring a rehabilitation of liberated Europe at the expense of Germany. However, Dulles had talked to Bidault in Moscow about France joining the bizone and Bidault hoped that a political situation might soon develop which would 'permit that decision being made'. Other Americans, such as Clay and Murphy, felt that the French were the root cause of the breakdown of quadripartite control in Germany.[82]

But France could not sit on the fence indefinitely. Both Britain and the United States were prepared to make concessions over the Saar. Molotov was also trying hard to bargain Soviet agreement to a transfer of the Saar against four-power control in the Ruhr. When this failed and the Soviets then refused to commit themselves to any change on the Saar, the French position shifted noticeably towards the Western camp.[83] Bevin had met Bidault on 14 April as the secret preparations were being completed for the new Anglo-American agreement, to talk about a Western deal which would bring more coal to France. An agreement with France would help her to accept a bizonal decision which placed the recovery of Western Germany as Europe's first priority.[84] Bevin assured Bidault that he would like more coal to go to France from the Western zones. After brief trilateral discussions, a sliding scale was agreed for increasing coal exports to France as production rose in the Ruhr. Publicly Bidault hoped for more and there were serious doubts about the relationship between the bizonal level of industry and the sliding scale. *The Economist* feared that 'the Ruhr miner bears on his shoulders one of the main planks of Anglo-French and American–French

    [81] Dixon diary, 15 Mar. 1947; Young, *Britain, France and the Unity of Europe*, 50 ff.; on Dunkirk Treaty see Zeeman, 'Britain and the Cold War'.
    [82] *FRUS 1947* ii, 162; Gimbel, *Origins of the Marshall Plan*, chaps. 4, 14.
    [83] Plenary session, 10 Apr. 1947, FO 371/64206; Bedell Smith, *Moscow Mission*, 208 f.
    [84] Anglo-French conversation, 14 Apr. 1947, FO 371/64203; Vincent Auriol, *Journal du Septennat, 1947–1954*, i. *1947* (Paris: Armand Colin, 1974).

understanding'. Sooner or later, Bevin hoped, 'Communist parties, particularly those in France, might be led to assume policies tending towards the best interests of their countries rather than purely Communist policies', but for now, the Moscow Council had exposed the contradictions of the French position.[85]

One of the dilemmas for the student of the Moscow Council is why the Soviets failed to present their case clearly, to negotiate on economic issues either in plenaries or even bilaterally, although they were prepared to make concessions on constitutional questions. It is clear that they initially sought to do business in Moscow, and perhaps hoped to form some kind of wider understanding between themselves and the Americans. But not only did they fail to pick up Marshall's offer at the private meeting of 1 April, which could have led to further talks on current reparations, but they also let their tenuous rapport with the French slip away during those six weeks. Furthermore, they completely failed to drive home the fact that the bizone was an ultimatum representing a breach in the spirit, if not the letter, of the Potsdam Accords.

From British and American records it is possible to conclude that Molotov was diplomatically hamstrung at Moscow and was given virtually no negotiating leeway, although there also emerges a strong sense that they felt that 'we have our principles too'. There was a real difficulty for the Russian negotiators in that the Potsdam and Yalta Accords were settled at head-of-government level, whereas the Moscow talks were only taking place at foreign minister level: 'the CFM could only adhere to the agreements reached by the three powers since they were subordinate to their Governments', Stalin told Marshall.[86] This attitude was most clearly seen in the Soviet reaction to the American claim that the Potsdam Accords superseded those made at Yalta, and explains their alarm that the Byrnes draft might in its turn supersede the Potsdam Accords. Although the Truman Doctrine was barely mentioned there can be no doubt that it sent a tremor of alarm through the Kremlin, as the propaganda outpourings show, and probably resulted in a very close re-examination by the Russians

---

[85] Lynch, 'Political and Economic Reconstruction of France', chap. 4; Gimbel, *Origins of the Marshall Plan*, 197; *The Economist*, 26 Apr. 1947.
[86] *FRUS 1947* ii, 341 f.

of their own and of Western foreign-policy objectives for the short and for the long term.

Although Stalin was conciliatory to Bevin and Marshall, the Council must have represented a grave disappointment to the Soviet leadership. By the end of the Council the British and the Soviets were left in a position of dreadful symmetry, each country holding on to what it valued in Germany, their mutual hostility far too strong to break that deadlock. Soviet fear of the United States was now greater than their fear of an immediate resurgence of German power, they had failed to drive any kind of wedge between the English-speaking powers, they had failed to secure an agreement on reparations, much needed for both economic and psychological reasons, and were just left hoping that there might be a rapid change in the political leadership in Britain and the United States. But the skilful publicity efforts of Bevin in Germany and in Britain had helped to ensure that an anti-communist consensus was far closer than it had been at the beginning of the year, even within the left of the Labour Party.[87]

Francis Williams has argued that Attlee and Bevin were

throughout the whole of the post-war period to play for time. They had to fight a holding operation. It was one which Britain's limited resources and pressing economic and defence problems made it virtually impossible for her to win without American help, only obtainable if the United States could be brought to realise that her own interests, no less than those of Britain and Europe, required her to oppose the expansion of Soviet power in Europe.[88]

The Bevin Plan had a crucial role in playing for time, enabling Britain to take a leading place in Moscow as befitted one of the great powers, while coaxing the Americans into further commitments in the Western zones. It created a quasi-legal and viable basis for strengthening the operation of the bizone and with it an American commitment not to a unified Germany but to the rehabilitation of Western Germany. Its construction even allowed for a four-power settlement in Germany if the Soviets, isolated, dispirited, and overwhelmed by the economic efforts of the war

---

[87] Windsor, *German Reunification*, 17; Jonathan Scheer, *Labour's Conscience: The Labour Left, 1945–51* (London: Unwin Hyman, 1988), 63 ff.

[88] Williams, *A Prime Minister Remembers*, 160.

and Western refusals to pursue an effective reparations policy, simply backed down.

Over the next two months the pattern of Anglo-American relations was again to alter dramatically. Marshall's speech of 5 June 1947 was to reveal that the Americans were now prepared to pick up the gauntlet of aiding European economic recovery, a challenge to which only they could rise. Bevin's response would be to confirm the underlying trend of British policy, reinforcing the division of East and West and rehabilitating the economies of the Western zones and of Western Europe.

PART III
From Moscow to London
April–December 1947

7

TAKING OFF THE GLOVES

ON 5 June George Marshall delivered the best-remembered speech of his career, offering American aid to any European government willing to assist in the task of European recovery, and adding that 'any Government which manages to block the recovery of other countries cannot expect help from us'. The United States would be willing to bridge the gap between what the European countries needed and what they could afford to buy, so that the balance could be tipped against economic collapse in Europe. But any assistance was to be in the form of a cure, not a palliative. The countries of Europe had to come to some agreement as to the requirements of their continent. This was an offer which had fundamental political as well as economic implications, as its purpose was 'the revival of a working economy in the world so as to permit the emergence of political and social conditions in which free institutions can exist'.[1]

The genesis of and motives behind this speech have been exhaustively analysed on both sides of the Atlantic.[2] Much of the debate about American intentions derives from the fact that there were many strands of opinion within the United States about the economies of Britain, France, and Germany, the threat of communism, as well as the willingness of Congress to pay large sums of aid to Europe. The divisions between the State and War Departments have already been touched upon. Within the State Department itself Acheson had argued that the Greek and Turkish

---

[1] Marshall speech, 5 June 1947, CAB 21/1759.
[2] The literature on this subject is enormous. See e.g. Kennan, *Memoirs*; Jones, *The Fifteen Weeks*; H. B. Price, *The Marshall Plan and its Meaning* (Ithaca: Cornell University Press, 1955); Bullock, *Ernest Bevin: Foreign Secretary*, chap. 10; Gimbel, *Origins of the Marshall Plan*; Alan S. Milward, *Reconstruction of Western Europe, 1945–51* (London: Methuen, 1984); Max Beloff, *The United States and the Unity of Europe* (Westport: Greenwood Press, 1976); Lipgens, *A History of European Integration*, i; Michael J. Hogan, *The Marshall Plan: America, Britain and the Reconstruction of Western Europe, 1947–1952* (Cambridge: Cambridge University Press, 1987); Robert A. Pollard, *Economic Security and the Origins of the Cold War* (New York: Columbia University Press, 1985); William C. Cromwell, 'The Marshall Plan, Britain and the Cold War', *Review of International Studies*, 8/4 (1982).

171

problem was 'only part of a much larger problem growing out of the change in Great Britain's strength and other circumstances not directly related to this development'.[3] He agreed with Marshall that a State Department planning section should look at European problems as a whole and had himself in May delivered a major but largely unnoticed address in Mississippi on the same lines as Marshall's later speech. Some State Department officials were working on the assumption that a genuine all-Europe plan was envisaged,[4] while a further group, including William Clayton, Under Secretary of State for Economic Affairs, envisaged large American grants for three years to stem the deteriorating balance of payments situation in Europe, as one 'political crisis [in Europe] after another merely denotes the existence of grave economic distress. . . . *The United States must run this show*.'[5] There was already a fear that the Soviet Union might benefit politically from Europe's economic problems, but State Department officials did not think that these problems had been deliberately provoked by the Soviet Union; Europe's own failure to recover from the effects of the war had brought about the situation.

George Kennan, whose Policy Planning Staff were working on the European problem, thought that aid should be offered as 'a proposal for general European (not just western European) co-operation', probably through the Economic Commission for Europe. This would be done

in such a form that the Russian satellite countries would either exclude themselves by unwillingness to accept the proposed conditions or agree to abandon the exclusive orientation of their economies. . . . If the Russians prove able to block any such scheme in the Economic Commission for Europe, it may be necessary for the key countries of western Europe to find means of conferring together without the presence of the Russians.[6]

'Our principal contributions consisted', he later reflected, 'in the insistence that the offer should be made to all of Europe—

[3] *FRUS 1947* iii, 197.
[4] For example, W. W. Rostow, *Division of Europe after World War II: 1946* (Texas: University of Texas, 1982), 75 n. 50.
[5] *FRUS 1947* iii, 230 ff. (Emphasis in original.)
[6] Ibid. 228.

and that if anyone was to divide the European continent, it should be the Russians, with their response, not we with our offer.'[7] That the onus for any division of Germany and Europe had to be borne by the Soviet Union was a philosophy that Bevin and his Foreign Office officials had held since 1946, but one that was not yet shared by all Kennan's colleagues.

The Labour Government was not taken completely by surprise by Marshall's speech. Even before Acheson's tip-off to British journalists it was known in government circles that the Americans were planning a major new initiative after their failure to secure four-power agreement in Moscow and the decision to raise the bizonal level of industry.[8] The loans to Britain, the World Bank, and the International Monetary Fund had all proved inadequate to the task of restoring Europe's economy. Inverchapel informed Bevin on 26 May that the Administration hoped that 'it will prove possible to formulate a long range policy . . . a large-scale programme of foreign aid is indispensable not merely for the political stability of the world, but also for the domestic prosperity of the United States'.[9]

In an important report Inverchapel then considered proposals for a United States of Europe, a popular concept in the United States. It was certain

that the desirability of some steps in the direction of unification, or rather the integration, of the economics of Western European countries is much in the minds of high State Department officials. . . . Britain and France would find it mutually beneficial to give the lead in the negotiation of arrangements such as Belgium and Luxembourg had concluded.[10]

But Clayton and Acheson had had to 'eat practically every word that they had uttered before Congressional Committees during the past three years', and were now primarily concerned with what was politically possible, not with what was economically necessary. The countries of Europe needed to display willingness and to put forward their respective problems as a common one with some

---

[7] Kennan, *Memoirs*, 343.
[8] Leonard Miall, 'How the Marshall Plan Started', *Listener*, 4 May 1961.
[9] Washington to FO, 26 May 1947, FO 371/62386.
[10] Ibid.

common plan to convince the American Congress: a new slogan had to be found.[11]

This view was echoed in a leader in *The Economist*, which argued that more grants would not be forthcoming to Europe and any aid would have to be represented not merely as assistance to the improvident but as the foundation of some good constructive purpose. And if 'the difficulties in the way are simply the unreasonable recalcitrance of the Europeans, let the US use its great power to knock their heads together to impose agreement'.[12]

The time for knocking European heads together was yet to come. Bevin and his officials were already constructing an approach to the Americans for aid for western Europe. But unlike the Americans, the Foreign Office wanted to separate the economic problems of Britain and of continental Europe. The link between the two was Germany, and in particular the drain the bizone was making upon Britain's dollar supplies. A note to the American Ambassador (for his 'private eye' only) explained that British expenditure had made a contribution to underpin the American zone as well as Britain's own. Precious dollars were being drained into Germany, and Britain would be in no position to budget for foreign exchange expenditure in Germany beyond the end of 1947.[13]

On 4 June, the day before Marshall's speech, Bevin produced a paper for an interdepartmental discussion on the position in continental Europe, assessing the possibilities open to American policy there. For, as the Committee for European Economic Co-operation report was later to reveal, western European countries faced an acute financial crisis in mid-1947; a dollar shortage and the possibility of economic collapse could result from the harsh winter of 1946–7, if more American aid was not forthcoming. Bevin's short analysis had a political emphasis focusing on the current trends of Soviet policy in western Europe. He argued that the Soviets were hoping to exploit food shortages, particularly

[11] Washington to FO, 30 May 1947, T 236/782; Washington to FO, 30 May 1947, FO 371/62386.
[12] *The Economist*, 31 May 1947. Barbara Ward, on the staff, had also reported to the FO that a new lend-lease programme was going to be suggested, Warner note, 3 May 1947, FO 371/62386.
[13] Undated note to American Ambassador, T 236/782.

in France, where he thought that they hoped eventually to induce civil war. The Soviets themselves hoped for a good harvest after which they would be able to build up their zone and increase the calorie ration to 2,000, while in the bizone the ration would be 1,500 at most. This would clearly have an enormous impact on British policy in Germany, and could lead to further disillusionment and a possible shifting of any magnet of economic recovery to the East, with grave political consequences.[14]

In Whitehall perceptions of Britain's problem in Europe were political, and centred on the need for short-term aid. The delicate fabric of political as well as economic recovery seemed under threat from a planned communist onslaught. Bevin argued that the whole of western Europe needed food within a fortnight on a lend-lease basis, with no conditions attached. In particular, he attached great importance to making the French government strong enough to withstand the attacks by the communists. At the Treasury and the Board of Trade officials warned that short-term aid would not be popular with the Americans, who felt 'that Europe must do all it can to help itself before looking to the United States for further aid, which they are reluctant to give piecemeal and without any European over-all plan'.[15]

Thus, when Bevin first heard of Marshall's Harvard speech he had already been turning over in his mind future avenues of policy towards Germany and Europe. He also realized that the speech had implications not only for Europe's recovery, but also for Britain's future relationship with the United States. As Oliver Franks was later to reveal:

first came the realization that his [Bevin's] chief fear had been banished for good. The Americans were not going to do as they had done after the first world war and retreat into their hemisphere. They had enlarged their horizon and their understanding of the intention of the United States to take in the Atlantic and the several hundred million of Europeans who lived beyond it. The keystone of Bevin's foreign policy had swung into place.[16]

Marshall's speech, however, was a declaration of high policy and left important practical questions unanswered. Was the

---

[14] Bevin note, 4 June 1947, meeting of 9 June 1947, T 236/782.
[15] Notes from Treasury, Board of Trade, FO, 5 June 1947, T 236/782.
[16] *Listener*, 14 June 1956; Jones, *The Fifteen Weeks*, 255 f.

scheme to include the Soviets? At a hastily convened meeting with Bevin, officials concluded that they had to find out from Clayton (expected in London shortly) whether the scheme was to be an all-European one. Hankey in the Foreign Office argued that the Soviets would co-operate but not sincerely, only seeking political advantage. Waley thought Marshall's speech explicitly anti-Soviet. But one thing was certain: France would have a major role to play. Telegrams were dispatched to both Washington and Paris indicating that a speedy and serious British response could be expected.[17]

Another question was how any scheme would be executed, as there existed no machinery for implementing such an initiative. The UN's Economic Commission for Europe (ECE), replacing the Emergency Economic Committee for Europe, had only met once, in Geneva in May, and was the only obvious candidate. But it was run by the apparently unpopular Gunnar Myrdal, had no established machinery, and, worst of all, the Soviets were able to command six out of seventeen votes on the Commission, which would give the Soviet Union every chance to sabotage any scheme from within. But this organization had been founded on American initiative, and therefore American advice would again be needed.[18]

Specifically, Britain's response was to be firmly within the context of the 'Western' option, rather than that of a highly integrated, and possibly unified, European economy. American help should be concentrated on 'a three pronged drive to increase production, first in this country, secondly in conjunction with France and the Western Allies, and thirdly in Germany. For this drive to be successful food and coal supplies in all three areas must be sufficient.' Aid had to be part of the drive to 'revive the economy of the British and American zones in Germany and to settle a level of industry'.[19] Berlin was asked for immediate advice

[17] FO meeting, 5 June 1947, FO 371/62548; Waley note, undated, T 236/782; FO to Washington, FO to Paris, 9 June 1947, CAB 21/1759. (Many files in the FO 371 series on Marshall Plan are retained by the FO; therefore this account is largely drawn from other files in the FO 371 series, Cabinet, Treasury papers, and *FRUS*.)

[18] 'Economic Commission for Europe', FO 371/62773; Bevin paper, 9 June 1947, T 236/782.

[19] Bevin paper for 7 June meeting, T 236/782; GEN 179/5, 6 June 1947, CAB 130/19.

and was warned that the Foreign Secretary did 'not want generalizations or lengthy lists'.[20]

Bevin also emphasized the importance of associating the French government fully with the enterprise, despite French hostility to German recovery and the political difficulties that the threat of communism suggested there. He was determined to press ahead with German rehabilitation, dragging the French along with him if necessary, and encouraging them with the information that he was taking into account the definite idea of bringing the Ruhr up to its maximum production as quickly as possible, and assisting France to get its maximum production.

On 13 June Bevin responded publicly to Marshall's speech at a Foreign Press Association lunch. By then Marshall had announced that aid should be offered to all Europe and that he would make no further statement on the matter of any diplomatic approach to European nations until they themselves had responded to his proposal for aid to Europe. Privately Bevin was disappointed, feeling that Marshall had confused the long-term and the short-term issues, the European and the world situation. But publicly he quickly picked up Marshall's cue, telling his audience that

the speech which Mr Marshall delivered at Harvard may well rank as one of the greatest in the world's history . . . when the United States throws a bridge to link east and west it is disastrous for ideological or any other reasons to frustrate the United States in that great endeavour. . . . We are glad to know that any possible source of misunderstanding has been eliminated by including Russia in the American proposal and therefore removing any idea that there is anything ideological in this proposal.[21]

Only when Clayton visited London could Whitehall try to discover what the Americans really intended and also be able to discuss the separate problem of the British dollar shortage. For, despite his publicly expressed relief that Marshall's offer was intended for all of Europe, Bevin certainly did not want the Soviets included, as this would strengthen their position in the Ruhr, in the Western zones, and across Europe and would give them the

[20] FO to Berlin, 11 June 1947, FO 371/65359.
[21] FO to Washington, 13 June 1947, T 236/782.

chance to undermine the scheme from the inside. The briefing papers for Clayton's visit give an excellent insight into Britain's continuing preoccupation with her role as a European and world power and her reluctance to decline into a position in which, she feared, she might have a relationship with the United States comparable to that of the Yugoslavs with the Soviet Union. Britain also hoped that the American initiative might even enable the West to draw at least some of the satellite countries out of the Soviet orbit—possibly Czechoslovakia (hopes for Yugoslavia seemed to have been dropped) and Poland—for 'Russia cannot hold its satellites against the attraction of fundamental help'.[22] This was in contrast to Whitehall's traditionally pessimistic approach to Eastern Europe and, it was hoped, might encourage the Americans even if it ultimately proved to be unsuccessful.

British officials hoped to set up a small task force of experts drawn from a representative group of European countries, for example Britain, France, Poland, Czechoslovakia, Belgium or the Netherlands, Denmark—but not the Soviet Union—to examine Marshall's offer. The affairs of Germany could be covered by the British, French, and American representatives—no mention was made of the Soviet zone. They anticipated that Jean Monnet would lead the French team and Oliver Franks the British. By September the small group would prepare a plan which would 'fire the imagination of the American people and the Congress'. It would have to be 'simple, striking and concrete . . . in the long run its form may be more important than its substance', and it should emphasize the efforts which Europe was making to achieve her own reconstruction despite the handicaps. The ECE would not be completely bypassed as this would be a blow to the prestige of the United Nations, would probably be unacceptable to the Americans, and might also lead the Soviets themselves to raise the issue there. The task force should instead present an agreed resolution to the ECE when they met in Geneva on 5 July. Bevin expected that the showdown with the Soviets would come at this point, as the resolution 'would doubtless give rise to controversy. It is hoped, however, that a majority of Governments will be prepared to endorse the action taken and to co-operate.'[23]

[22] *FRUS 1947* iii, 268; 'European Reconstruction', 17 June 1947, T 236/782.
[23] Ibid.

It was decided not to bring up the question of Germany at the Paris talks as the French would want to see plans for the future of Germany adjusted so as to facilitate the execution of the Monnet Plan, but if the matter was raised, we

should take the line that it is clear that the plan will have to be drawn up on certain assumptions regarding the future level of German industry and German exports and that we regard a prosperous Germany as an essential feature of a healthy European economy; but that we are not prepared to discuss these points at this stage and that so far as the Anglo-American Zones are concerned, we shall need to work out an agreed Anglo-American policy. If the French feel that it will be to their advantage to come into the Fusion Agreement so much the better.[24]

Bevin was clearly not prepared to let French policy towards Germany muddy the waters at this early planning stage. Neither were Soviet sensibilities to impede progress, and he told the Cabinet before he left for Paris that he would press on urgently with the preparation of a plan, whether or not the Soviet Government were prepared to co-operate on British terms. The 'Western' option was rapidly becoming a reality, and Bevin could now begin to discard the cloak of a dual policy.

Paris, 17–19 June 1947

Bevin's neatly mapped out scheme was to receive a setback during the Anglo-French talks in Paris. These largely centred on the question of inviting the Soviet Union to the European talks, which was not part of the British plan at all. The British and the French agreed that it was essential to avoid the impression of bypassing the United Nations, that a steering committee and *ad hoc* committees would be needed, but discussions beyond this floundered. There was no agreement on whether the steering committee should be set up by invitation, as the British wanted, or through a procedural conference. Moreover, the French insisted on Paris, not London, as the place for discussions, as they correctly thought that London had an 'anti-Soviet flavour'.[25] (The British later rationalized this setback by arguing that not using London

[24] CM54(47), 17 June 1947, CAB 128/10.
[25] Report of Secretary of State's visit to Paris, CAB 21/1759.

would prevent Britain's being too closely associated with failure if Marshall Aid came to nothing.) The French did accept that Germany would have to be represented on the Technical Committees, and that German production must be taken into account, but there was no agreement over the volume or nature of production, over socialization, or over coal questions. Indeed, Bidault stated baldly that

the main concern of the French Government was to disarm domestic criticism to the effect that Russia had not been given in good faith a full and cordial opportunity to join in discussions at the 'start. . . . We must avoid the impression of putting a pistol to M Molotov's head either by mention of a date for a further meeting or by not offering M Molotov some place of meeting other than London or Paris . . . [or] any suggestion that the meeting would be held anyhow whether the Russians accepted or not.[26]

Bevin was furious at this and retorted that he was 'not prepared to go to Moscow merely to court a rebuff'. Petulantly, he added that if 'there was any desire to collaborate on the part of the Soviet authorities they would surely be able to authorize M Molotov to come to Paris or London for this important purpose'.[27]

On 18 June the talks hit another difficulty. The French Ministry of Information leaked the fact that the British and the French intended to act bilaterally to set up a European Economic Committee to consider the plan. Although this was quickly denied by the Quai d'Orsay, there was now considerable pressure to send Moscow an invitation to talks and an agenda was prepared in case the invitation was accepted. This agenda was to be proposed by one of the Western powers 'without giving any indication [to the Russians] that it had been agreed in advance'.[28]

The Paris talks were a partial disappointment to Bevin and his team, as they were now faced with the possibility that the Soviets would participate in the planning of a European response, rather than have it presented to them as a *fait accompli* at the ECE. However, they knew that privately Bidault did not in fact want the Soviets to be involved any more than the British did, which was very much in line with the ambivalent attitude to the Soviet

[26] Report of Secretary of State's visit to Paris, CAB 21/1759.
[27] Paris to Moscow, 18 June 1947, T 236/782.
[28] Report of Secretary of State's visit to Paris, CAB 21/1759.

Union that he had exhibited over the past year. During the talks he told American Ambassador Caffery that the French Government hoped the Soviets would refuse to co-operate and that, in any event, the French would be prepared to go full steam ahead even if the Soviets refused to do so. Bevin told Caffery much the same thing.[29]

Bevin was still in an impatient and threatening mood on his return from Paris, and he warned the Commons that 'the guiding principle that I shall follow in all talks will be speed. . . . I shall not be a party to holding up the economic recovery of Europe by the finesse of procedure, or terms of reference, or all the paraphernalia which may go with it. There is too much involved.'[30] Then on 22 June the Russians accepted the Anglo-French invitation to come to talks in Paris on Marshall's offer.

London, 24–26 June

But before Bevin returned to Paris he was to meet Clayton in London. On leaving the United States Clayton told a press conference that his visit was not connected with Marshall's speech, that he would probably do a great deal of listening, but that it was very unlikely that he would offer advice to the Europeans. In fact he took with him a memorandum from Marshall, drafted by Acheson, Lovett, and Kennan, about the aid programme, which stated that

it is generally recognized in the United States that a stable and self-supporting Europe is a matter of immediate interest to the American people. . . . But they are naturally concerned that future aid should be productive of more effective results. . . . And unless the American Congress can receive some convincing reassurances on this point, we doubt that its members would feel justified in making further appropriations.[31]

[29] *FRUS 1947* iii, 260; Waley to Bridges, 19 June 1947, T 273/240; CP(47)188, 23 June 1947, CAB 129/19.
[30] House of Commons, *Debates*, 20 June 1947, vol. 438.
[31] *FRUS 1947* iii, 247 ff.; Cromwell, 'The Marshall Plan, Great Britain and the Cold War'.

No mention was made of the Soviet Union, and the tone of the memorandum clearly shows that at this critical juncture the Americans still wished at least the appearance of leadership to rest with the Europeans.

The four Anglo-American meetings held in London covered both immediate and long-term questions concerning aid as well as Britain's role in Europe. The first meeting was attended by Attlee, Bevin, Cripps, and Dalton, and Ambassador Douglas as well as Clayton. Bevin was the principal British spokesman. This was the first occasion in the postwar years when senior British and Americans aired together their differing views about Britain's European and world role. Bevin told the American team that what was required was immediate short-term aid for Europe. This was an economic and political priority as the 'first European need is food. We need a better pipeline and security of rations.' The bizonal ration had to be increased to 1,800 calories by the end of the year: 'Give me 5 million tons of grain and I will break the production problem in Germany', which would in turn help to ease Britain's own economic difficulties, he promised.[32] Behind this rather simplistic remark lay the theme that controlled German recovery, not European integration, was central to Britain's own political and security interests.

The American team, however, was less than impressed. They preferred a continental, not a piecemeal, approach. They wished to know 'why in 1947—two years after the end of the war—they [the Europeans] still find themselves in such serious economic and financial difficulties' and insisted upon statements of European needs and production capacities. For long-term reconstruction they wanted 'some proposals regarding a closer integration of European economy . . . a firm plan for Europe including European integration was necessary to convince Congress'.[33]

Bevin then turned to his conception of Britain's world role. She could not just be likened to the other European powers for she was a major actor in German and European politics at a time when Europe was threatened by both economic collapse and militant communism. She wanted to work with the United States,

---

[32] The meetings were held on 24–26 June, *FRUS 1947* iii, 268 ff., and GEN 179/12, CAB 130/19.
[33] *FRUS 1947*, iii, 272 f.

and knew that the Americans needed her leadership in Europe, but now what Britain needed was 'some temporary interim solution' to relieve her own economic difficulties.

The chronic troubles of Europe are interwoven with politics and our dollar problem really comes from Europe. Europe can contribute materially to the solution but Britain with an Empire is on a different basis . . . if the US took the line that the UK was the same as any other European country this would be unfortunate because the UK could contribute to economic revival. . . . [But] if the UK was considered just another European country this would fit in with Russia's strategy, namely, that the US would encounter a slump and would withdraw from Europe, the UK would be helpless and out of dollars and, as merely another European country, the Russians, in command of the Continent, could deal with Britain in due course.[34]

Dixon made much the same point in his diary a few days later. The Soviets, he thought,

want to keep Europe, and GB, in a state of economic disorder for the next few years, with the double object of disrupting the British Empire, communising Europe, and getting their own economy on Communist methods into shape—the final objective being a Europe run politically and economically on Communist methods.[35]

The British had been honest about their financial difficulties but they did not want to go into an American programme and not contribute to European recovery, as this would sacrifice the 'little bit of dignity we have left'. They would not, however, contemplate going into an immediate customs union with other European countries, as Europe's problems were so urgent that a 'full blueprint for Europe would take too long for the present emergency'. But more American aid to Britain would enable her to play her part for Europe and would also help Bevin, and 'stop a back-biting of . . . foreign affairs moves by people at home who were pinched by the British financial position'.[36]

Bevin then turned to the political implications of Marshall's offer. 'I went ahead on the Marshall Plan without asking questions', he reminded Clayton, 'and I feel that it is the quickest

[34] Ibid. 292, 271.
[35] Dixon diary, 2 July 1947.
[36] *FRUS 1947* iii, 277, 279, 270.

way to break down the iron curtain' and lure the Soviet satellites, in particular the Poles and the Yugoslavs, away from the Soviet Union with fundamental help toward economic revival. The Americans did welcome Britain's leadership and accepted her role as 'chief occupying power' in Germany, although they criticized the administration in her zone. But Clayton and Douglas now preferred to concentrate on the economic questions, were intolerant of special pleading on the part of one country, and in general seemed to have been reluctant to discuss the strategic implications of what was being offered.[37]

The most important topic was, however, the participation of the Soviet Union. Here, Clayton said that he now realized that

there would have to be a radical change in the Russian position regarding European recovery and other related matters before the American people would approve the extension of financial assistance to Russia. . . . Russia did not need food, fuel and fiber and would thus have little basis for participating in the short term phase.[38]

But Bevin still sought clarification, for 'if Russia did not get in on the short term scheme they [*sic*] would not play in the Marshall Program'. Would the Americans then still support Britain? The answer was affirmative. In their joint *aide-mémoire* it was made clear that 'while it is hoped the scheme will cover Europe as a whole, the US Administration would be satisfied if it could be started with the Western countries of Europe as a nucleus, on the understanding that the scheme would be open to other countries if they so desired'.[39]

Bevin had confirmation of this important decision in a telegram of 24 June, when Balfour reported from Washington that Kennan thought that

should it prove impossible to secure Soviet or satellite participation on reasonable terms, the United States would look for the elaboration of the western European project as a pis-aller. . . . [Indeed], the state of Soviet Russia's own economy was such that she was in any case ill-placed to make a substantial contribution to a constructive project.[40]

---

[37] *FRUS 1947* iii, 268, 270, 284 f.   [38] Ibid. 291.
[39] *Aide-mémoire* , 25 June 1947, GEN 179/13, CAB 130/19.
[40] Washington to FO, 25 June 1947, CAB 21/1759.

As with the bizone, the West would proceed independently, but would still publicly offer the Soviet Union participation, throwing the onus of refusal onto her. Thus both Kennan and Clayton came to the same conclusions about Soviet participation, though through different analyses of the Soviet position.

The theme of these discussions laid down the parameters of an Anglo-American debate about Britain's relation to continental Europe that was to last over twenty years. Bevin certainly 'stood up to the Americans' in June 1947 as befitted a great power, but he had to modify his instinctive reaction to the Marshall proposal, which had been to ask for more short-term aid to Britain to enable her to play the kind of leadership role she wanted to carry in Europe. After the Anglo-American talks Bevin had a much clearer picture of the direction he and Bidault could take in Paris. Of greatest importance, he and his officials knew that despite the ambiguities of Marshall's original offer, it was not to be contingent upon Soviet participation. If the Russian satellites could be drawn in on Western terms, so much the better, but the involvement of the Soviet Union was not the *sine qua non* of the plan, and this prized information was to give the British an enormous diplomatic advantage over the Russians in Paris. The task was now to ensure that the Soviets did not participate, and to achieve this in a manner that would enable the blame for the dividing of Europe to be cast at the feet of the Soviet Union.[41]

Paris, 27 June–3 July

Tripartite talks on Marshall's offer opened in Paris the day after Clayton's meetings with the British ended. Bevin was now well prepared, confident, and in 'fighting form'.[42] He knew that the principle of self-help and mutual aid had to underpin a European response which would allow of no special pleading by individual countries. Bevin and his officials had also decided that their request for aid should not be too timid: they would leave the Americans to

[41] Bullock, *Ernest Bevin: Foreign Secretary*, 416; Edmonds, *Setting the Mould*, 167 f.; Kennan, *Memoirs*, 326; Memorandum for Dominions, 2 July 1947, T 273/240.
[42] Dixon diary, 27 June 1947.

do any scaling down of requests. The Americans had now accepted that the ECE did not have to be the initial vehicle for aid, and that the Anglo-French plan for a small steering group supported by technical committees was also acceptable. The Anglo-American *aide-mémoire* thus gave the team a thorough brief, despite Bevin's deceptive protestations to Molotov that there was nothing more to know about the American offer than that which Marshall had publicly stated. Despite his earlier failure to construct an Anglo-French-led task force, the Paris talks could still ensure that the Soviets would eventually exclude themselves from the aid programme. It was not yet clear what role Britain herself would play in this programme, but American aid would bring a breakthrough towards the recovery of the Western zones of Germany, thus helping to contain the westward drift of communism and fulfil the real thrust of British policy. Germany's role in any aid programme would inevitably be raised in Paris, but this issue could not now be avoided and Bevin would deal with it by arguing that

it is probably inevitable that a certain measure of priority should be recognized in the case of devastated members of the United Nations, but every effort should be made by the United Kingdom representative to ensure that the Plan provides an adequate economy to Germany with particular reference to the part she can play in European reconstruction.[43]

Germany, the key to European reconstruction, would now have a role to play.

Although Soviet aims were unknown, there was great Soviet curiosity about the offer, and public scorn about its intentions. A *Pravda* columnist thundered that it

is easy to see that Marshall proposes or rather demands quick formation of notorious western bloc but under unconditional and absolute leadership of American imperialism. Spiral of Truman Doctrine begins unroll. From retail purchase of several European countries Washington has conceived design of wholesale purchase of whole European continent.[44]

Ironically, it was Truman himself who was later to call the Truman Doctrine and Marshall Plan two halves of the same walnut.

---

[43] Preparations for tripartite talks, CAB 21/1759.
[44] *FRUS 1947* iii, 295.

Molotov arrived in Paris with a delegation of nearly one hundred, a sign either of his seriousness or possibly of Soviet intentions to put pressure on the French Communists to destabilize the French Government or block French participation. The story of the following five days of discussions marks, as Bevin whispered to Dixon during one of the sessions, 'the birth of the Western bloc'.[45]

The combative atmosphere of the talks was set at the first meeting on 27 June. Bidault presented a slightly modified draft of the secret Anglo-French agenda. Molotov asked what exactly the Americans had in mind and how receptive Congress would be. These meetings, he said, showed the willingness of the three powers, but they were working on very little information. What had gone on in previous talks with the Americans? Should not the three powers ask for more information before deciding their response? Bevin, feigning innocence, replied that there was nothing more to know. As an old lending power, Britain herself would say no to any erstwhile borrowers until she knew what their scheme was. Conditions cannot be imposed by borrowers on lenders, Bidault added. Molotov pressed on, arguing that it would be impracticable to make decisions on incomplete information. Bidault then suggested that Marshall's offer of 'friendly aid in the drafting of a European programme' should be further explored, but Bevin was totally opposed to this until there was a plan.[46]

The following day Molotov decided to try another tactic. He was irritated by Bidault's robust stand, yet clearly did not want to give the British and the French any pretext for a diplomatic break because of Soviet intransigence. He therefore suggested that it would be improper to discuss the position of Germany except within the context of the Council of Foreign Ministers. Bevin and Bidault both stood firm and asserted that Germany had a major role to play and could be represented by the Allied occupation powers. Molotov then tackled the question of national sovereignty and aid. He feared that an inquiry into the resources of the participating countries amounted to violation of their sovereignty. Bevin and Bidault replied that to avoid this would mean that a

---

[45] Dixon diary, 2 July 1947.
[46] Accounts of the meetings can be found in 'European Reconstruction', 27 June 1947, CAB 21/1759, *FRUS 1947* iii, 297 ff., and Dixon diary.

European plan could not be drafted and that this would not guarantee the best use of Europe's resources as a whole. This unsatisfactory and inconclusive meeting drew to a close in a raging thunderstorm, with the prospect of a day's rest for the Foreign Ministers to consider each other's proposals.[47]

The conflicting issues of national sovereignty and an all-European approach were already of irreconcilable difference. It was plain that Molotov had reason to complain about the infringement of sovereignty: as Dixon noted, American aid 'really would have the effect of interference with the economies of states. The United States obviously would not give dollars, for example to Rumania, without exacting improvements in the Bank of Rumania', but Molotov's 'hungry satellites are smacking their lips in expectation of aid'.[48]

Bevin decided to try a new initiative that would give the appearance of seeking compromise. With Bidault's blessing he rewrote the draft response to Marshall, but he received short shrift from Molotov, who said quite correctly that it represented no change on the important issues. Molotov himself then proposed a scheme that looked superficially like the new Anglo-French one, but which would be based on a composite programme of national requirements. Bevin remarked that this looked like a request for a blank cheque, wondering what Moscow's reaction would have been to such a suggestion from another country.[49]

While these unproductive talks continued, Dixon suggested that Duff Cooper return to London to get final clearance from Attlee that the British and the French could proceed alone if and when the Soviets pulled out. Dixon exerted considerable pressure on Bevin not to refer back to the Cabinet for further instructions, which would have delayed the meeting and might have created the appearance that there was a chance of compromise. He wanted to avoid the 'dangerous ambiguity if the Conference ended on this note, and suggested to the S of S [*sic*] that he should add that it must be clearly understood that we are going on alone'.[50]

---

[47] 'European Reconstruction', 28 June 1947, CAB 21/1759; Dixon diary, 28 June 1947.

[48] Ibid.; *FRUS 1947* iii, 301.

[49] 'European Reconstruction', 1 July 1947, CAB 21/1759; *FRUS 1947* iii, 302.

[50] Dixon diary, 2 July 1947; Rothwell, *Britain and The Cold War*, 282–4.

Bevin was again more hesitant and reluctant than his senior advisers to force a showdown against the Soviet Union.

The final meeting, which represented the first open break between East and West, reportedly had all the characteristics of an elaborate farce, as Molotov now seemed to have recognized that East–West agreement was impossible. So he reverted to the familiar theme of Council discussions: reparations and German recovery. The Western powers were now planning to allocate the resources of Germany before reparations had been completed: they appeared to be getting their own way. He then issued a last challenge to Bidault, asking if this was also what France wanted. Did she now also favour the raising of the level of industry? He challenged both Britain and France to deny that the new organization would be able to interfere with European countries. This meeting ended with an open Soviet threat that these Anglo-French efforts could lead to a very different result than the reconstruction of Europe. Molotov and his team then departed.[51]

As the Russians left Paris, Bevin again met with Bidault. They decided to send invitations to all European countries (except Spain and the Soviet Union) in the hope that some of the Eastern European countries might still be tempted to look west for economic aid; and also to the Allied representatives in Germany. The idea of a small steering committee was now dropped in favour of the French proposal to hold a conference first. Bevin and Bidault now also had a frank exchange of views about Germany, for Bevin knew that when the excitement of the Soviet departure had died down, the way in which the German question was handled might well determine the success or failure of the project. 'It is vital', he told senior officials the following day, 'to keep France informed of German policy to keep them with us over Marshall Aid'.[52]

Bevin's aim in Paris had been to secure Soviet exclusion from Marshall's offer if their diplomats would not agree to Western conditions, and to do this without actually ejecting the Soviets from the discussions. This was entirely consistent with the Whitehall strategy for dealing with the Soviet Union at the Council

[51] *FRUS 1947* iii, 305 f.; Bidault, *Resistance*, 150 ff.; Auriol, *Journal*, 296.
[52] 'European Reconstruction', 3 July 1947, CAB 21/1759; meeting with Secretary of State, 4 July 1947, FO 371/65069.

of Foreign Ministers. Negotiation was never seriously considered. If aid were granted to all Europe, it should be in a manner that would introduce Western methods and ideas across Europe and thus undermine Soviet influence or even the Soviet system itself. Indeed, the all-Europe solution could threaten the Soviet position in Europe generally and lead 'the rulers of the Kremlin [to] fear for their own position and the regime if Europe under American water cans handled by British gardeners blossoms into a happy Western Garden of Eden'.[53] But it was more likely that the terms presented would lead the Soviet Union to exclude herself, which would enable the Western zones and the countries of Western Europe to be put back on their feet with American financial support.

Given American conditions and French support, it is hard to see how the conference could have been concluded differently unless the French Government had collapsed or the Soviets had capitulated to Western conditions. It was ironic that Bevin himself was later to object to many of the features of Marshall's offer to which the Soviets also objected. These battles over European recovery were yet to be fought with the Americans, and during the 1950s Britain's reluctance to participate in schemes that would decrease her power of independent decision-making became a feature of West European politics.

On 8 July Bevin reported back to the Cabinet. Describing the events in Paris, he argued that 'from a practical point of view it is far better to have them [the Soviets] definitely out than half-heartedly in', obstructing from the inside. This had been achieved by confronting the issues of principle from the start. 'Any other tactics might have enabled the Soviet to play the Trojan horse and wreck Europe's prospects of availing themselves of American assistance . . . at least the gloves are off, and we know where we stand with them.'[54]

On his return to London Bevin also saw American Ambassador Douglas and reminded him that German recovery and in particular the question of coal production had to remain at the forefront of negotiations. The level of industry and the issue of socialization could not now simply be subsumed into the politics

[53] Dixon diary, 2 July 1947.
[54] CP(47)197, 5 July 1947, CAB 129/19; CM60(47), 8 July 1947, CAB 128/10.

of American aid. The British cold warrior also sent a strong and
alarmist message back to Marshall. Bidault had shown 'great
firmness' in dealing with Soviet coercion and with attempts to bring
down the French Government. But the breakdown of the Paris
talks would lead to great East–West tension and he interpreted
Molotov's warning of 2 July to mean that the Soviet Union would
use every 'subversive device to prevent other European nations
from joining in the formation of a program and would employ
every method to create internal trouble'. Speed was essential,
and temporary financial assistance imperative. Bevin was now
primarily concerned that, if communism was not to take hold
in France, she would need help before the autumn. It was this
threat of communism, so persuasively articulated by Bevin, which
was later to help to sell the aid programme to Congress.

Britain had thus seized the opportunity to institutionalize a
divided Europe in the same way that creating the bizone had
institutionalized a divided Germany. The Marshall Plan represents
a willingness by Britain to exploit American economic largess as
an instrument of cold-war politics. Western Germany might now
be harnessed to European recovery through an aid programme;
maybe this would eventually act as a magnet to the Eastern zone
and to some Soviet satellite countries. But the priority was now
to build upon this breakthrough. Attlee later called the Soviets'
actions in Paris 'a declaration of the Cold War': the same comment
could also be made of British policy at this critical moment.[55]

Towards a Western Bloc

The next five months were to be among the most complex in early
postwar British history. Ministers and officials from the Foreign
Office, the Treasury, and the Board of Trade became embroiled
in immensely complicated sets of negotiations in Berlin, Paris,
London, and Washington on closely interrelated subjects, and
the stakes were never higher. The recovery of Germany and the
success of Marshall Aid were essential to Britain.[56] The summer

[55] *FRUS 1947* iii, 310 ff.; Attlee, *As it Happened*, 170.
[56] Yergin, *Shattered Peace*, 320. For a detailed account of the diplomacy of these
months, see Bullock, *Ernest Bevin: Foreign Secretary*, chap. 11.

convertibility crisis added an acute sense of urgency to an already difficult situation, and in October planning also began for the London Council of Foreign Ministers. Despite shifts to accommodate the changing international and economic situation, Bevin and his officials retained a number of specific objectives with regard to Germany that ran like threads through the various sets of negotiations.

First, it was axiomatic that the recovery of the Western zones should not be delayed. The initiative seized in Moscow to reorganize the bizone and raise the level of industry there must not be lost. A healthy democratic Western Germany that was economically self-sufficient was essential to retain the balance of power in Europe. The exclusion of the Soviets from Marshall's offer meant that, at least in the short term, the division of Europe might soon be an accepted fact. The alternative to recovery still seemed to be a communist Germany, and maybe with it, a communist Europe.

Second, although it seemed that Marshall's offer at last gave the promise that Europe would not be abandoned by the United States, giving the Americans the right sort of leadership to maintain the balance between sustaining their commitment and possible over-zealousness was still a major priority. This was not easy, for, in the last resort, British officials knew that their leverage was minimal if their own position was ever seriously challenged. They could never forget that the quantity and conditions of aid were not secure. The surge of Western European political confidence and the economic recovery to which Marshall Aid contributed has tended to overshadow how dangerous and unclear the postwar world looked in the first half of 1947, and it would be unhistorical to ignore these uncertainties for British decision-makers.[57]

Third, the appearance of France at the centre of international diplomacy made the resolution of Germany's problems increasingly urgent. Until mid-1947 Bevin had been content to leave France somewhat in the wings. However, now that Bidault had accepted that Marshall Aid would mean that German recovery had to take precedence over reparations, France seemed to be moving tentatively into the Western camp. French participation was

[57] Interview with Lord Franks, Feb. 1985.

essential to the success of any aid programme, but the margin of safety in France, from both an economic and a political viewpoint, was extremely thin. So British diplomats had to move within the constraints of French policy, charting a course between ensuring Germany a major part in the aid programme for European recovery and not provoking the French into denouncing aid as a device to restore Germany at the expense of herself and other West European countries. So during these months Bevin and his officials had to follow a difficult line between the gradual realization of American power in Europe, French sensibilities, and Britain's own quest for a continued leadership role, despite her economic difficulties.

The linchpin for the successful recovery of Western Germany was acceptance of a new level of industry agreement. Any new Western agreement 'engaged in a breach of Potsdam', but would represent a definite commitment by the Americans to the economic recovery of the Western zones and a means of settling the lingering sore—for both East and West—of reparations.[58]

After the Moscow Council confidential Anglo-American talks had opened in Berlin. A new bizonal level of industry of 10.7 million tons of steel production (excluding the Saar, and 11.5 million tons if the other zones co-operated too) was agreed in July. Bevin wanted this to be a final decision, so that reparations could then be 'implemented resolutely and firmly, and that such a plan would be presented to the German people in the best way . . . in the light of connexions with the Marshall Plan'. But Clay thought that it should serve only as a means to force the Soviets back to the negotiating table to agree a revised quadripartite plan, and that reparations deliveries were not to be restarted to the Soviet Union until economic unity was achieved.[59]

Bidault's reaction to the plan was vehement. He accused the British and Americans of giving priority to Germany while aid was still uncertain: the level of industry was 'within the competence of the CFM . . . nothing can be done now either legally or in

[58] *FRUS 1947* ii, 1043.

[59] ORC(47)6, 7 July 1947, CAB 134/599; Berlin to FO, 20 June 1947, FO to Berlin, 10 July 1947, FO meeting, 15 July 1947, all FO 371/65190.

194 Taking off the Gloves

fact to prejudice the decision'. The continuation of his government was at stake as 'we have 180 Communists [in the Assembly] who say: "the Marshall Plan means Germany first". If something permits them to say this again . . . I tell you the government will not survive.' He was not mollified by a promise that the Council of Foreign Ministers would still make the final decisions about Germany.[60]

This outburst was particularly awkward, coming as it did just as the Committee for European Economic Cooperation (CEEC) was about to start work in Paris, so Bevin reluctantly decided that the new plan would have to be put into cold storage whilst further talks were held with the French, despite some American disagreement.[61] By postponing the announcement of a new level of industry, Bevin hoped that the greater prize of aid would not be jeopardized by the French before talks even got going. It was more important now to emphasize publicly what Germany could contribute to European recovery than to discuss the permissible extent of her own recovery. So he wanted the CEEC negotiators to examine 'the principal items which Germany will have available for export and her requirements necessary to make such exports available. In this way it might be hoped that discussions on the level of industry could be avoided'.[62] But it was clear that such a postponement could only be temporary, as 'Germany is an integral part of the European economy and . . . we ourselves are initially interested in obtaining for the western zones fair and equitable treatment and . . . it is entirely contradictory to our interests that the western zones should be regarded as a milch cow'.[63] The Cabinet were also reminded that it was not yet at all clear what exact role the Americans had in mind for Germany, and that their advice was being urgently sought.

The same problem emerged again at the beginning of August, when it became certain that the anticipated production figures for the three Western zones would exceed the agreed March 1946 levels. Bidault now threatened to resign if the new 10 million tons steel production figure was taken as a basis for calculation and

[60] Paris to FO, 17 July 1947, FO 371/65192; *FRUS 1947* ii, 997 ff.
[61] Paris to FO, 19 July 1947, FO 371/65191.
[62] CP(47)209, 22 July 1947, CAB 129/20.
[63] FO to Washington, 21 July 1947, FO 371/65191.

it seemed for a while as though the July crisis would be repeated.[64] The work of the CEEC was temporarily suspended while delicate negotiations took place. The French compromised on a 'possible' production figure of 10 million tons of steel, with an obscure rider that the actual level of steel production would depend on decisions taken elsewhere (presumably the Council of Foreign Ministers). It still had to be seen publicly that 'the place laid for Germany at the Marshall table is quite clearly below the salt'.[65]

The Americans then took an independent initiative to try to placate French sensibilities about Germany. In talks with Clayton and Douglas, but behind the backs of the British, Bidault and Monnet managed to secure a provisional agreement from the Americans for international control of the Ruhr. Whitehall responded furiously to this attempt by the Americans privately to bargain away Britain's major negotiating asset, and it reawakened old anxieties about the French as partners in Europe and in particular about Monnet's role. Such an agreement, Makins felt,

appeared to give the French much of what they had been striving for since the war in the Ruhr in return for their agreement to the level of industry proposals and without any obligation in regard to the terms on which they would be prepared to come into the Fusion Agreement. This struck me as an outrageous price to pay for French concurrence. One always expected to pay a little blackmail to the French, but not on this scale.[66]

Bevin told Douglas that the British would pay no price whatsoever for French co-operation beyond indicating a future sympathetic consideration of the question. To Bidault's chagrin, the Americans then backed down, and also agreed to tripartite talks on the level of industry.[67] These talks took place between 22 and 27 August in London and revealed that Bevin and his officials were not prepared to concede without a fight either to American initiatives or to French pressure, and forced the French to accept the new

[64] Paris to FO, 10 Aug. 1947, FO 371/65194.
[65] Haviland to Franks, 18 July 1947, FO 371/65192.
[66] Report on Douglas–Makins conversation, 17 Aug. 1947, FO 371/64513; *FRUS 1947* ii, 1029 ff., 1038 n. 91.
[67] Ibid. 1041 f.

level of industry. By way of compensation they were allowed an extension to the sliding scale of coal and coke deliveries to France from Germany as steel production rose. French aims, as always, focused on wishing the Ruhr to produce more coal but less steel, a conundrum that was to persist until the formation of the Coal and Steel Community.[68]

The relationship between Marshall Aid and the German problem remained an uneasy one, in part exacerbated by the role which Britain herself wanted to play in the programme. At the end of June Bevin had emphasized and re-emphasized that Britain could not be considered simply as another continental European country, but that her sterling position, and her Empire and Dominions, entitled her to play a role as the United States's partner in European recovery. He then even had the audacity to suggest to Douglas on 25 July that the British should be given relief 'to the tune of a billion dollars which . . . will be sufficient to carry . . . [us] over the hump by the middle of next year, and which . . . will place Britain in a position where she can provide assistance to France and play her role in Germany'.[69] Britain continued to separate the revival of Germany and Europe from her own particular problems.

This was made particularly clear when the Americans at last stepped into the CEEC negotiations, after Bevin had refused to persuade the Committee to transform 'sixteen shopping lists' into a coherent response to the Americans. The resulting report of the CEEC reflects the ambiguous role that Germany had been given and the delicate path that Bevin had trodden during these months.[70] The Eastern zone was deemed to have excluded itself by not returning the questionnaire that had been sent to all invited countries, and indeed the German question was relegated to one-and-a-half pages of the report because, it said, the Western zones had created special difficulties, Germany's future and the extent of reparations were not yet decided, and the CEEC was not the body to do that job. The report concluded that 'the

[68] FO to Paris, 24 Aug. 1947, FO 371/65196; Anglo-French meeting, 27 Aug. 1947, FO 371/65201; FO to Washington, 1 Sept. 1947, FO 371/65197.
[69] Quoted in Milward, *The Reconstruction of Western Europe*, 63.
[70] *FRUS 1947* iii, 372.

German economy must not be allowed to develop to the detriment of other European countries, as it has done in the past'. But it also said that

if European co-operation is to be effective, the German economy must be fitted into the European economy. . . . In particular the output of the Ruhr coalfield . . . must contribute to the rehabilitation and economic stability of the whole of Europe. . . . Other Western European countries cannot be prosperous as long as the economy of the Western Zone is paralysed, and a substantial increase of output there will be required if Europe is to become independent of outside support. . . . Western Germany, like the participating countries, will require help.[71]

This ambiguity reflects a major triumph for British diplomacy. Britain had correctly assessed the ebb and flow of European and French opinion. If France had withdrawn from the CEEC, Marshall's offer would have collapsed. But Bevin had no intention of letting French national interests and, in particular, the coal requirements of France's own recovery programme, override the fundamental relationship between aid and the recovery of the Western zones. On the other side, Britain had to pay lip-service to American concepts about European integration without sacrificing her own world role. In the middle of the convertibility crisis this balancing act was exceedingly difficult to maintain and British diplomacy had to be doubly resourceful and ingenious to compensate for the weakness of the British economy.[72]

Bevin may have retained the place he wanted for Germany in the CEEC Report, but on the question of the socialization of German industry in the bizone he had to accept a loss of authority over the future structure of the major heavy industrial complexes in the British zone. American suspicions had been growing that the British were not making a good job of industrial management in their zone because of their desire for 'experimenting in the Ruhr', and Clayton warned in June that the Americans regarded British management of the coal-mines as 'pathetic'. The Americans wanted a five-year trusteeship over the mines, with ownership

---

[71] *General Report, Committee of European Economic Co-operation* (London: HMSO, 1947), Appendix B.
[72] Milward, *The Reconstruction of Western Europe*, 129 f.; Meeting with Secretary of State, 25 July 1947, FO 371/64246.

vested in the *Land* of North-Rhine-Westphalia until eventually the Germans could be allowed to decide how their own industries should be managed.[73]

Part of Bevin's difficulty was that the socialization plans were very close to his heart, and he felt that to give them up would damage his relations with the trade unions as well as his stock with his party in the House of Commons. But he was pressurized to put his plans on ice and to agree to the trusteeship plan as advocated by the Americans after extensive talks in Washington. This compromise still met with French dismay as they feared that too much power would be given to Germans, despite the measure of international control which would remain. The end of Bevin's socialization ideas marks an important step forward in a more active American policy and the inevitable tilt towards the Americans' predominance in European affairs that accompanied their greater financial involvement in Europe's economic recovery.[74]

Although embroiled in the Marshall Aid talks, tripartite discussions on the level of industry, and the difficulties of the socialization programme, officials did not forget that another CFM was to be held in November. The organizational and financial arrangements for the bizone had to be as secure as possible by then, to withstand further anticipated attacks on it by the Russians.

At Moscow Bevin had persuaded Marshall that the bizone's organization had to be improved, and discussions on this subject then took place between British and American officials. British officials were striving to create a 'Bizonal super agency', as 'in a world of abundance only a few central fiscal controls are needed to direct the general economy, but in times of scarcity, as in Germany today, when nearly all materials have to be rationed, very strong central powers are needed to make any plan work'. But Bevin rejected political fusion as premature.[75]

---

[73] *FRUS 1947* ii, 929 ff.; Gimbel, *Origins of the Marshall Plan*, 211 ff.

[74] *FRUS 1947* ii, 959 ff., 973 ff. For a fuller account of British policy towards the revival of Germany, Ian Turner (ed.), *Reconstruction in Post-War Germany: British Occupation Policy in the Western Zones, 1945–55* (Oxford: Berg, 1989).

[75] CCG *Aide-mémoire*, 13 Apr. 1947, FO 1032/1652; Pakenham–Robertson meeting, 18 Apr. 1947, FO 1032/1653.

The situation was further complicated as Clay did favour political fusion, though not to strengthen the powers of the centre, but rather to increase the powers of the *Länder* at the expense of the central government; and indeed also suggested that he was interested in getting a return on American investment, and not in the rebuilding of Germany. He thought that perhaps, while not formally disbanding the fusion agreement, the British and the Americans should run their zones in a more independent fashion.[76] Serious disagreements over this issue mark the months following the Moscow Council, and even as the Council ended Robertson warned that 'the Fusion Agreement is in suspended animation'. If no agreement was reached, Bevin warned the Cabinet, he feared the issue would have to be referred back to Marshall.[77] But after intense discussions the common interests of both the Americans and the British in Germany enabled them to agree to establish an Economic Council of fifty-two German representatives from the *Länder*, who controlled the activities of the five German Executive directors. These directors were appointed by an Executive Committee of eight Germans, one from each *Land*, and all their decisions were subject to allied Anglo-American approval. This agreement took the political arrangements for the bizone even further than was anticipated at Moscow.[78]

The financing of the reorganized bizone was threatened by Britain's financial crisis which loomed like a shadow over the diplomatic exchanges of summer 1947, culminating in the suspension of convertibility on 15 August. When the coal talks finished in Washington on 12 September, Strang began very private talks on the refinancing of the Fusion Agreement. They ran from 8 October to 17 December, continuing even while the London Council was in progress. Britain's financial situation was parlous and the bizone had cost £81 million by 1947, but Strang did an impressive job in convincing the Americans that, as Clay put it, 'while Great Britain needs America's help, America needs Great Britain's in Germany'. Britain succeeded in achieving a

---

[76] Appendix A, Annex 1 of report on meeting of 28 Apr. 1947, FO 1030/169.

[77] DMG to Clay, 25 Apr. 1947, DMG to Bevin, 28 Apr. 1947, FO 1032/1653; CP(47)143, 30 Apr. 1947, CAB 129/18.

[78] *Clay Papers* 1, 344; Penson to Makins, 2 May 1947, FO 371/65068; Brief for CFM, 3 Nov. 1947, FO 371/64629.

maximum dollar liability of £28 million for 1948, and no payments for November and December 1947. Their sterling contribution in the bizone was reduced from 50 per cent to 25 per cent, which pleased the Treasury.[79]

The reorganization of the bizone, and the prospect of less crippling financial responsibilities for Britain there, was to form the basis of a stronger Anglo-American front at the next Council meeting. By the summer of 1947 a temporarily divided Germany was, even in Germany, seen as inevitable, if not desirable, and it was reported to the Foreign Office that both Kurt Schumacher and Konrad Adenauer 'had expressed their conviction that the foundation of a West German state was an essential preliminary to the re-absorption of the East'.[80] This is why planning for the Council was focusing so strongly on presenting to the Soviets a united Western front that permitted of no compromise or Soviet dilution of Western conditions.

The diplomacy of late 1947 was made easier for Britain during these months by the Soviet Union's reaction to the abortive Paris talks. The United States was now singled out for particular criticism, and *Pravda* reported—with some accuracy—that 'the belated inclusion of the Soviet Union in the offer . . . was simply a ruse to put the USSR and the countries of Eastern Europe in the invidious position of rejecting the plan when in fact Mr Marshall had never intended it to apply to more than Western Europe'.[81] An all-European programme would inevitably have meant Western influence in the East, while rejecting aid would prepare the ground for the formation of a Western bloc; but this latter option was the lesser of two evils for the Soviet Union, who then also put pressure on the Czechs and the Poles not to participate in the CEEC deliberations.

Ferocious public attacks upon the Marshall Aid talks were combined with persistent Soviet challenges about the legitimacy of the other German talks. The August tripartite level of industry talks in London were signalled out for particular criticism,

[79] Berlin to FO, 29 Sept. 1947, FO 371/64514; Dalton note, 1 Sept. 1947, FO 371/65072; CM96(47), 18 Dec. 1947, CAB 128/10.

[80] Berlin to FO, 23 Aug. 1947, FO 1032/2197.

[81] Berlin to FO, 12 July 1947 and 2 Aug. 1947, FO 1049/712.

drawing a private admission from Bevin that the spirit of Potsdam was clearly being breached by the British and the Americans.[82] But the overall effect of these attacks was now to harden public and Labour Party opinion behind Bevin as he reaped the benefit of his diplomatic triumph in Paris.

It was therefore hardly surprising that by the end of July the Anglo-Soviet trade talks and the talks to renegotiate the Anglo-Soviet pact broke down. The Soviets began to tighten their grip on the East: peasant parties in Bulgaria and Poland were threatened when their leaders were arrested. In September 1947 the Cominform was formed amidst vitriolic attacks upon Western socialist leaders' attempts to 'cover up the rapacious essence of imperialist policy under a mask of democracy'.[83] Both Roberts's and Kennan's assessment was that the Soviet Union was reacting to a deep fear of Western intentions, but the inevitable conclusion seemed to be that the Soviet Union was set to conduct a battle for the hearts and minds of West Europeans.[84] Strikes in Italy, industrial unrest in France which was to bring down Ramadier in November, and attacks upon social democracy all pointed the way to an assault upon Western-style democracy, and whatever the Soviet Union intended, the effect of her actions was to bring the Western powers more closely together and to persuade American public opinion of the need for financial aid from the United States.[85] In Britain the trade union movement swung round behind Bevin after its annual Conference. The Keep Left group had published *Keep Left*, criticizing the direction of the Labour government's foreign policy, in May, only weeks before Marshall's offer to Europe, but Bevin was firmly defended by Dennis Healey's pamphlet, *Cards on the Table*, which was written after Bevin suggested that the Foreign Office should co-operate with the Labour Party in drawing up a reply to *Keep Left*. It described the public and visible side of Labour's foreign policy since the war, concentrating upon Soviet attacks on Britain and Soviet attempts to expand into areas of British interest. Britain

---

[82] Washington to FO, 20 Aug. 1947, FO 371/65195; *The Economist*, 26 July 1947.

[83] Cominform declaration, quoted in Bullock, *Ernest Bevin: Foreign Secretary*, 485 f; Barker, *The British Between the Superpowers*, 92 ff.

[84] Moscow to FO, 7 Oct. 1947, FO 371/62672; Kennan, *Memoirs*, 357 ff.

[85] Washington to FO, 8 Oct. 1947, FO 371/62672.

had sought to counter this with a pragmatic and non-ideological Anglo-American response. This book, which was widely discussed on its publication, acted as the major platform for a defence of Labour policy. Its publication happily coincided with the withdrawal of the Soviets from the Marshall talks in Paris, an act which was presented as further evidence of Soviet unwillingness to co-operate.[86]

With increasing international polarization, and with firmer domestic support, what then were British aims and hopes for the London Council, ostensibly called to prepare the way for a peace treaty and a four-power settlement of the German problem? One thing was certain; Bevin did not intend to waste time over the meetings, and 'had no intention of uttering an unnecessary word' now that the foundations for the 'Western' option were being laid. Soon the duality that had marked British policy to Germany from the end of the war could be ended, as it became clearer that it was not possible to deal sensibly with the Soviet Union. So Bevin would 'bring matters to an end quickly and find the best ground on which to break'.[87] Senior Ministers now argued with him that 'a continuation of the status quo or even an accentuation of the present split between the West and the East . . . would suit us better than the establishment of a spurious "economic unity"'.[88] This would get public support too, for the changed international climate meant that 'it should not be too difficult to put our case in a convincing light'. Britain, Dean explained,

did not rule out a temporary split, but. . . . the objective, in the event of a split, would be so to reconstruct Western Germany that it acted as a magnet to the Eastern Zone. There were two factors involved. In the first place the Germans wanted to be united and all the forces would operate in this direction. Secondly if we acted quickly and did not let ourselves be held back by technicalities, the Western Zones, being the richer half, had a good chance of speedier recovery.[89]

[86] Ian Mikardo *et al.*, *Keep Left* (London, 1947); Denis Healey *Cards on the Table* (London: Labour Party, 1947).
[87] Note to Strang, 3 Nov. 1947, FO 371/64629.
[88] ORC(47)50, 22 Nov. 1947, CAB 134/599; ORC(47)8, 24 Nov. 1947, CAB 134/597.
[89] FO to Washington, 13 Nov. 1947, FO 371/64633.

Bevin explained to Bidault that 'at Moscow he had not been entirely certain of public opinion at home. Since then the party meeting at Margate and the TUC conference had shown that the country were squarely behind him. People in this country realized what the Russian game was and expected the CFM to break down.'[90] The British therefore intended the Council discussions to be kept at a very general level, focusing only on Western conditions for progress. Indeed, Strang wanted to add to the conditions for economic unity by insisting that Soviet ownership of basic industries should be ended, as he feared the Soviets might still try to secure a compromise which would jeopardize the success of the bizonal financial talks.[91] There was not to be another report from the Control Council, as the last one had led to so much discussion of technicalities in Moscow; indeed the Deputies' meeting in London from 6 to 22 November could not even agree upon an agenda for the CFM. Control Commission officials briefly proposed that one last effort should be made to try to secure Soviet co-operation before the Western powers turned their attention more vigorously to bizonal political fusion, but in Whitehall officials decided that the ostensible objectives of Britain remained those catalogued in the Bevin Plan, which would be tabled once again. Even ideas for a fresh Cabinet paper on the subject were rejected until the outcome of the Council was known.[92]

During October and November preliminary talks were held with both France and the United States to try to establish for the first time a common Western negotiating line at a Council meeting. All three powers now confirmed that quadripartite unity was only acceptable within the context of the Bevin Plan, but they knew that even this was no longer really on the political agenda because of the prospect of Marshall Aid.

The French were particularly preoccupied with the security implications of the new Europe that was now taking shape. Bevin met Ramadier on 22 September and the two talked generally of Anglo-French economic co-operation and the political power of the two if their strengths—and colonial interests—were linked.

---

[90] Bevin–Bidault conversation, 25 Nov. 1947, FO 800/465.
[91] Washington to FO, 28 Oct. 1947, FO 371/64629.
[92] Control Commission paper, 4 Nov. 1947, FO 1030/34; Robertson to FO, 3 Nov. 1947, FO 371/64629; FO to Washington, 19 Oct. 1947, FO 371/64207; Dean minute, 26 Nov. 1947, FO 371/64631.

Bevin returned, albeit briefly, to the ideas he had entertained since 1946 of harnessing Anglo-French interests into a Third World Force, and Ramadier suggested enthusiastically that, in such a front, the two could act as peacemakers between the Soviet Union and the United States. Whitehall officials were much more sceptical and by early October these grandiose schemes had been put into cold storage again.[93] The British still remained unmoved by French attempts to increase coal production and deliveries from the Ruhr to France while at the same time keeping steel production down, but on 7 October Hector McNeil dined in New York with Bidault, who told him that 'he had burnt his boats as regards the Russians. He said he had tried to follow a middle path for two years . . . Russian moves had shown that they were determined to have two worlds rather than one.' He wished for tripartite conversations in real secrecy before the Council to evolve a common policy. But he was apprehensive of Marshall, whom he found to be rather vague in conversation.[94]

So the French were invited to talks in London between 19 and 22 October to consider merging the French zone with the bizone to form a trizone. They were anxious about the policing of what would be a new eastern border for Germany and favoured bilateral military talks, and British officials now found that they had to restrain French enthusiasm for Western co-operation, but agreed to investigate the possibility of a security system responding to the needs of the two countries possibly through the application of the Byrnes Treaty on a three-power basis, to keep the Americans in Europe.[95]

As these talks were progressing in London, in Washington Strang had private talks with Hickerson, the American Director of European Affairs about the next Council meeting. He reiterated that the British were 'doubtful about the desirability of immediate German unification since this might extend the scope of the Marshall Plan to all of Germany under conditions whereby the Soviets nevertheless would be able to syphon out Marshall Plan

[93] Young, *Britain, France and the Unity of Europe*, chap. 8, Duff Cooper to Bevin, 16 Oct. 1947, FO 371/67674.

[94] New York to FO, 7 Oct. 1947, FO 371/64207.

[95] Anglo–French meetings, 20–22 Oct. 1947, FO 371/64629.

assistance through reparations claims and in the earmarking of current production'.[96] However, the Americans—with elections imminent—once again appeared reluctant to accept the consequences of what was happening in Europe. They did not welcome French plans for tripartite talks before the Council, or want to discuss future joint action, if and when the Council broke down. Hickerson told Strang that there should be a clean break between quadripartite negotiations and any subsequent discussions for a re-enforcement of Western zonal fusion, and that social occasions, not official discussions, could be used in London for the Western powers to get their ideas into line.[97]

Despite this setback, new Anglo-French talks opened to discuss more detailed questions relating to Germany. But these talks turned into an exercise in reassuring the French, who were themselves now in the throes of a profound political crisis and terrified because there was no Anglo-American contingency plan if there was a final breakdown with the Soviets. Hall-Patch reassured the French that the Americans and British would stand firm and not accept half-way measures that could leave Germany subject to Russian economic or political exploitation; but that they could not immediately offer improved security arrangements in return for France's joining the bizone. The security issue was becoming increasingly important, for Bevin was under Treasury pressure to run down troop levels in Germany and there were fears that the Russians might make a spectacular offer to withdraw many of their troops from the European theatre if the Western powers would do the same. (Bevin had no intention of withdrawing troops as it would be much easier for the Soviets to return their troops to Europe if the occasion arose, but such a Soviet offer would have made excellent propaganda.)[98]

Massigli then expressed equally grave doubts about what would happen if the Soviets did capitulate to Western demands. Once again Hall-Patch assured him that there was absolutely no prospect of letting discussions develop to a point where specific questions

[96] Washington to FO, 28 Oct. 1947, FO 371/64629; *FRUS 1947* ii, 676, 688.
[97] FO to Washington, 3 Nov. 1947, FO 371/64633; *FRUS 1947* ii, 694.
[98] Duff Cooper to Bevin, 16 Oct. 1947, FO 371/67674; Bevin to Attlee, 24 Oct. 1947, FO 800/366; Moscow to FO, 29 Oct. 1947, FO 371/64629.

would be raised, with any leeway for compromise. Soviet capitulation to Western demands was not even an option to be hoped for.[99]

On the day before the Council opened Bevin gave a warning to the Cabinet that he was not optimistic about its outcome. But this would be the last chance to get agreement, and if it failed 'he would have to ask the Cabinet to consider a fresh approach to the main problems of our foreign policy': the dual policy would be ended.[100] He now knew that he had secured a general measure of Western agreement that a break with the Soviet Union was probably inevitable, he had the backing of the Cabinet, Commons, and public opinion, and he had also secured a bizonal reorganization, a tripartite agreement on a new level of industry, and the prospect of Marshall Aid upon which to build. The international agenda was moving towards the creation of a German trizone in a divided Europe. After the Council, Britain, the United States, and France would be openly contending with the Russians for Germany.[101]

It was with considerable skill that Bevin played his meagre hand in these months, in particular in his building up of a united Western front and the mobilization of public opinion for the forthcoming meeting with the Soviet Union. He had thought out his strategy well, he had clear long-term aims and a good sense of timing, all of which enabled him to play cold-war politics on a large scale and with what were to be impressive results.

[99]   FO to Washington, 6 and 10 Nov. 1947, FO 371/64633.
[100] CM90(47), 25 Nov. 1947, CAB 128/10.
[101] Hall-Patch to Bevin, 21 Nov. 1947, FO 371/64632.

8

THE LONDON COUNCIL NOVEMBER–DECEMBER 1947

The Dismal Council

THE fifth Council of Foreign Ministers, and the last that was to be held for eighteen months, has generally been recognized as a failure. Both traditionalists and revisionists have described it as a futile meeting and a mere reworking of old arguments that could lead nowhere.[1]

The changed international climate that Marshall's offer brought about meant that by the summer of 1947 there was no serious expectation in any official quarter that the Council could now bring profitable four-power discussions on Germany.[2] The Moscow Council had exposed the ideological gap between East and West, and to bridge that gap would require either much goodwill and a readiness to compromise on all sides, or a dramatic reversal of policy by one of the Allied powers. There was no evidence that either of these options was realistic. Soviet reaction to the CEEC had been vehement, and strikes in France and Italy were seen as a communist-backed attempt—with an eye on the forthcoming Council—to destabilize these countries so that perhaps the United States would not think them worth saving.[3] Whitehall thought the Soviet Union would now act quickly to extend its political and economic systems into the Western zones with the object of winning Germany over to communism, and thus undermine one of the principal pillars of the Marshall Plan. The Russians might make superficially attractive proposals and compromises which would bind 'the other three powers to a joint policy in Germany as a whole, which would in practice have allowed them a free hand to operate directly and through German

---

[1] Gladwyn, *Memoirs*, 206; Murphy, *Diplomat Among Warriors*, 382; Bullock, *Ernest Bevin: Foreign Secretary*, 493.
[2] Tel. 1240, 23 Aug. 1947, FO 1030/169.
[3] *FRUS 1947* i, 813; Moscow to FO, 26 Nov. 1947, FO 371/67683.

Communist stooges in the Western Zones, while at the same time they prevented, on grounds of military security, any penetration either political or economic of the Eastern Zone by the Western Powers', but which would nevertheless keep the Council process going. Alternatively, they could try 'wrecking activity' in the Council sessions to drive a wedge between the Western Powers, and then set up a German government when the conference failed.[4]

Britain's strategy still rested upon the Bevin Plan. But Hall-Patch now warned Bevin that

the only way of making substantial progress in time to check, or, if possible, to forestall Russian action will be if the three Western Powers can agree on the broad principles of their combined action before the Conference disperses. To wait until after and then attempt to reassemble representatives of the three Governments from their own countries and from Berlin would be dangerous.

The form of a provisional German government had to be agreed with the Americans in London, and arrangements made to bring the French into the bizone.[5] This, rather than negotiations with the Soviets, should be the real British agenda for the Council.

Bevin saw the other Foreign Ministers before the Council formally opened. He assured Bidault of his intention not to let matters drift or to raise matters that might endanger Anglo-French relations, such as Germany's economic recovery, or central administrations, or the Ruhr.[6] His meeting with Molotov, however, was far more acrimonious. He warned the Russian that Britain had been at war for one day in three over the past thirty years, and now wanted peace, but that this was the wartime Allies' last chance for quadripartite agreement. When Molotov complained that he was being threatened, Bevin replied that 'he had seen no threats; that he had gained exactly the opposite impression'.[7] But Harold Nicolson's account of this meeting, given to him by Bevin at the end of a long reception at Buckingham

---

[4] Fraser minute, 10 Nov. 1947, FO 371/64499; Russia Committee, 11 Sept. 1947, FO 371/66372; Hall-Patch to Bevin, 21 Nov. 1947, FO 371/64632.
[5] Ibid.; undated brief for CFM, FO 1032/2196.
[6] Bevin–Bidault meeting, 29 Nov. 1947, FO 800/465; Auriol, *Journal*, 629.
[7] Bevin–Molotov meeting, 24 Nov. 1947, FO 800/447; *FRUS 1947* ii, 731; Bevin to Bidault, 25 Nov. 1947, FO 371/67683.

Palace, is far more colourful. He recounted that Bevin and Molotov had had a real heart-to-heart talk in Bevin's flat. 'Mr Molotov', Bevin demanded:

'what is it that you want? What are you after? Do you want to get Austria behind your iron curtain? You can't do that. Do you want Turkey and the Straits? You can't have them. Do you want Korea? You can't have that. You are putting your neck out too far, and one day you will have it chopped off. . . . You are playing a very dangerous game . . . if war comes between you and America in the West, then we shall be on America's side. Make no mistake about that. That would be the end of Russia and of your Revolution. . . . What do you want?'

'I want a unified Germany,' said Molotov.

'Why do you want that? Do you really believe that a unified Germany would go communist? They might pretend to. They would say all the right things and repeat all the correct formulas. But in their hearts they would be longing for the day when they could revenge their defeat at Stalingrad. You know that as well as I do.'

'Yes,' said Molotov, 'I know that. But I want a unified Germany.'[8]

However much this account may be embroidered, Bevin's hostile and intimidating line can hardly have been conducive to setting a positive atmosphere for the negotiations of the following weeks.

Bevin also met Marshall before the Council opened. Bevin recounted to him his meeting with Molotov, then concentrated on the fusion talks, not the Council meeting agenda. The British knew that the American team was still not an entirely cohesive one. Marshall, moreover, was anxious about Congress, and wary that precipitate trilateral action might appease 'over-heated' American public opinion now, but would then be regretted later. His caution worried both the British and the French teams. However, when Marshall met Bidault and the Frenchman repeated that France wished to join the bizone after the Council, Marshall was pleased and urged Bidault to avoid discussing the Ruhr or the level of industry at the Council, as this might disrupt common Western positions.[9]

[8] Harold Nicolson, *Diaries and Letters, 1945–62* (London: Fontana, 1971), 107 f.; Bevin and Molotov also met socially on 26 Nov. 1947, FO 800/447.

[9] Bevin–Marshall meeting, 24 Nov. 1947, FO 800/447; *FRUS 1947* ii, 730 ff.

During the early days of the Council Ministers concentrated on an agenda, a possible peace treaty, and Austria. Bevin tabled the Bevin Plan again and warned that Germany presented an overtly ideological challenge to East and West. Dropping completely the circumspection of earlier Council meetings, he demanded to know if the Ministers wanted 'a central German Government which is so designed and so organized that it makes one particular ideology more capable of being adopted, or do we want a free country?' A politically united Germany could only be acceptable if it was created 'on a basis of democracy as we know it'. He referred back to the Paris Council and reminded his colleagues of the fears he had expressed then that Europe could be dominated by one power.[10]

But in general the plenary sessions do not reveal more than entrenched positions and uncompromising speeches. The private Western meetings are far more revealing about British intentions. One of the first of these was held on 2 December, when Bevin and his senior officials had lunch at the American Embassy. Bevin said he thought Molotov was wasting time and he was going to have another talk with him so that he could show the world that if the Council did break down, Britain had at least made an effort to reach a settlement. He fully understood that Marshall's offer of aid had placed the Soviets in the dilemma of either risking losing their satellites or facing a Western bloc, but he was more anxious now in case the Soviets disrupted the still fragile Western understanding. He pressed for interim aid for France, to help her retain her 'key position' in Europe. But in a characteristically intransigent mood he discouraged Marshall's suggestion that the Council should meet in private session.[11]

On 4 December the two met again for another discussion on tactics. He now found Marshall more belligerent, and anxious to demonstrate to the American people that, if the Council broke down, it had done so on matters of principle. He proposed presenting an ultimatum to the Russians, listing six or seven main points of principle. American public opinion was baying for blood: Marshall knew he could 'break off and tell the Russians to go

[10] CFM(47)(L)7, 26 Nov. 1947, FO 800/466.
[11] Bevin–Marshall meeting, 2 Dec. 1947, FO 800/447.

to the devil', but he too wanted to give domestic public opinion good reasons for any break.[12]

Bevin thought this too dramatic. He felt 'the country was behind him in expecting us to take our own measures to adjust German economy if the discussions here failed', but favoured a subtle approach, sticking to the Bevin Plan and waiting for the right moment to break with Potsdam, after France had a promise of interim aid. He repeated that such a promise would give the Western powers 'greatly increased momentum at this conference'. Roberts, who had now taken over as Bevin's Private Secretary, reported that Marshall had been persuaded by the British team, supported by the Soviet experts in the American team, to adopt the strategy that the Western powers could continue with their own arrangements 'without any blowing of trumpets'.[13] This advice was to prevail.

On 5 December the major question of economic principles was reached in the formal discussions. The Bevin Plan was immediately accepted by Marshall, who attacked Molotov's accusations that the United States meant to set up a government in western Germany and then challenged him to explain how Germany was meant to pay $10 billion in reparations. The harsh realities of the existing situation in Germany, a division which had retarded its rehabilitation and that of Europe, could not permit a pretence, a façade of a central Government. He would accept 'an "all German" Government just as soon as there is an "all Germany" to be governed and "all German" work to be done'. Bidault, albeit somewhat reluctantly, also accepted the Bevin Plan as a basis for discussion.[14]

Sargent, who played a central role throughout the Council and had continually urged closer Anglo-American co-operation, still felt that the Americans 'have no clear idea of what to do after the Conference if it ends in a deadlock, and have not yet got accustomed to the idea of having immediate discussions with us and the French'.[15] But Bevin himself at last felt confident in the support of his own parliamentary party, as MPs had 'indicated

[12] Bevin–Marshall meeting, 4 Dec. 1947, FO 800/466; *FRUS 1947* ii, 750 ff.
[13] Roberts to Bevin, 6 Dec. 1947, FO 371/64249.
[14] CFM(47)L/19, 5 Dec. 1947, FO 371/64249; for Bevin Plan, CFM(47) (L)7, 7 Nov. 1947, FO 371/64249.
[15] Sargent to Bevin, 8 Dec. 1947, FO 371/64250.

their disgust at the spectacle of the futile and somewhat undignified proceedings of the past two weeks'.[16] But although the three held a secret meeting on 7 December, he still found it impossible 'to get real conversations with the French or USA'. The French were particularly anxious to push ahead with tripartite talks because of the serious political crisis at home, hoping that, even if de Gaulle returned to power in the next several months, he would not be able to undo agreements which had already been concluded. But Marshall again suggested a final effort to negotiate properly with the Soviets in private session to find grounds for a compromise, and seemed reluctant to accept that the Council process served no further purpose for the Western powers.[17]

After discussion with Robertson Sargent came up with three practical papers on tactics and future political and security policy for Germany. It was vital that there should be no delay over political questions: he had long been convinced that the Soviets intended taking a lead in Germany and that the Western powers therefore had to act to contain the threat to their interests there. If and when no four-power solution emerged at the Council, a modified version of the Bevin Plan—leaving out the early consultative stages—could be implemented quickly, if the Americans and the French agreed. The Germans would be reassured by this, although it would mean a 'trial of strength' between West and East and French agreement would not be easy to secure.[18]

On 20 December Sargent produced a Cabinet Paper entitled 'Possibility of a Three-Power Treaty on German disarmament', to meet possible French sensitivities over his proposed constitutional provision. In it he again suggested (as he had done during the Moscow Council) reworking the Byrnes quadripartite treaty on a three-power basis. By

using the present draft four-Power treaty as a basis, and by drafting it in such a form that it would be open at any time for the Soviet Union to adhere, we should avoid the appearance of a three-Power treaty directed solely against the Russians, which would have a very bad effect

[16] *FRUS 1947* ii, 754.
[17] Bevin comment on Sargent minute, 8 Dec. 1947, FO 371/64250; *FRUS 1947* ii, 756.
[18] Sargent to Bevin, 8 Dec. 1947, FO 371/64250.

on public opinion and would dangerously exacerbate a relationship already seriously strained.[19]

Sargent wanted to apply the principle of the creation of the bizone—which was still technically open to the Soviets and the French to join—to resolve Western Europe's security problems. Although the more moderate Attlee was not enthusiastic about this proposal, as such discussions 'would bring home to the world the new alignment between East and West', this extremely important paper was to play a major part in the post-Council period.[20]

Even as the British were evolving their post-Council strategy, Molotov was making a last attempt to compromise and keep the Council alive. His alarm at the way the tide was flowing was deepened by his knowledge of the supposedly private trilateral meeting of 7 December.[21] At the next plenary he delivered a long and vitriolic speech attacking the Western Powers. The bizone had not only divided Germany but had failed in its public aim of reviving the economy of the Western zones. So the West had turned to the United States, which was offering them a form of political usury quite outside the normal framework of international credit. He also set forth once again the Soviet position on economic and political principles, which, like the Bevin Plan, had not changed since Moscow. Molotov again demanded four-power control of the Ruhr, the abolition of the bizone, and reparations of $10 billion, including current reparations, before the Russians could agree to a level of industry of 10–12 million tons. He also argued that the Bevin Plan, like the proposed Byrnes treaty, was really intended to supersede the Potsdam Agreement, although he reminded his colleagues that the Potsdam Protocol had been agreed at head of government, not just Foreign Minister, level.[22]

Molotov then rained a shower of concessions upon the heads of the other Foreign Ministers. These included an agreement to discuss economic principles using the Bevin Plan as a working paper and to consider reparations from current production not as a prerequisite to economic unity, but in parallel to it. He also

[19] CP(47)326, 10 Dec. 1947, CAB 129/22.
[20] Minute on CP(47)326, 12 Dec. 1947, PREM 8/512.
[21] Moscow to FO, 10 Dec. 1947, FO 371/64631.
[22] *FRUS 1947* ii, 757.

agreed to a common import–export programme and the next day agreed that sums advanced by controlling powers to pay for imports by Germans should be a first charge on Germany's foreign exchange resources. On 11 December Molotov then accepted the British text on decartelization, a level of industry of 11.5 million tons of steel, and a proposal to give more authority to the Control Council over the allocation of coal and steel.[23]

Bevin and Marshall were by now both highly sceptical about these concessions. Possible compromise had not really been hoped for at the Council, and Marshall assessed that Molotov was not only 'playing for time but is consistently, almost desperately, endeavouring to reach agreement which really would be an embarrassment to us in the next four to six months'.[24] He also feared that Bevin might now waver. But the British team were quite unmoved as they had been expecting just such tactics to try to sabotage Western unity and still held that further negotiations would restrict the capacity of the Western powers to put their zones in order, 'Germany would remain in chaos and we should have gained nothing'.[25]

On 15 December Molotov suggested that the German People's Congress attend the Council, no doubt to show that the Soviets were prepared to deal more directly with the Germans. This suggestion was smartly turned down by Bevin who criticized Molotov's attempts to establish a 'bogus democracy' in Germany, and now voiced doubts as to whether 'the CFM is a body which can ever reach settlement of the German and the European problem'.[26] Before Molotov could respond to this, Marshall suggested—to the surprise of both Bevin and Bidault—that the Council be suspended. Molotov accused the Americans of simply wanting a free hand in Germany, and on that sour note the Council adjourned.[27]

So by 16 December the end of a negotiating phase had been reached, although the Council was adjourned rather than irrevocably abandoned. On 18 December Bevin also explained

---

[23] *FRUS 1947* ii, 757, 760, 762, 765.   [24] Ibid. 765.

[25] Sargent to Bevin, 12 Dec. 1947, FO 371/64631; Clay, *Decision in Germany*, 345.

[26] Plenary session, 15 Dec. 1947, FO 371/64646; *FRUS 1947* ii, 770 ff.

[27] For Bevin and Bidault's surprise, Bevin–Bidault meeting, 17 Dec. 1947, FO 371/67674.

to the Cabinet and the House of Commons his perceptions of what had happened at the Council. It is clear that not all ministers were happy with the course of events in London, and Brook reminded Attlee that, whilst no doubt he and Bevin wanted to avoid general discussion on the future at the moment, the Economic Policy Committee meeting of 16 December had revealed that some ministers needed reassurance about the future direction of British foreign policy.[28] Bevin first explained to the Cabinet that he intended to make a statement to the House of Commons that afternoon, telling them that reparations had been the occasion, rather than the cause, of the Council's breakdown. He promised another Cabinet meeting soon after the American and French delegations had left London, and then he would present a comprehensive memorandum considering future European policy. He reassured them that agreement had been reached on a new financial arrangement for the bizone, which would relieve Britain of a substantial part of her obligations there. Although some dollar liability for the zone remained, the arrangements secured could be considered as 'constituting assistance to the United Kingdom comparable to the interim aid which Congress was affording to France and Italy'.[29]

That afternoon Bevin addressed the Commons and painted a grim picture of Soviet policy, thus laying the ground for the diplomatic realignments of the new year. The Soviets had ordered their immediate neighbours not to participate in Marshall's offer, had attacked the Western powers in the United Nations and Control Council, and were waging a propaganda war. The CFM should have been a businesslike instrument for the drafting of the peace treaties, which built on the wartime experience of meetings between the Alliance powers so that 'the responsible Ministers of four Great Powers would be able to get to know each other and express their views freely to one another, and thereby promote a spirit of friendship and understanding'. Although the Foreign Ministers had secured treaties for the satellite powers and Italy, the Council had subsequently 'alternated between carrying out its original function and being used for

---

[28] Brook to Attlee, 17 Dec. 1947, PREM 8/512. (The records of the Economic Policy Committee do not reveal the extent of these anxieties.)
[29] CM96(47), 18 Dec. 1947, CAB 128/10.

entirely different purposes', for the Soviets had been determined to create an 'unrepresentative and bogus' central government for Germany and had therefore caused the Council to fail.[30] In May 1946 Bevin had said that if there was to be breakdown with the Soviet Union over Germany, the Soviets must appear responsible for it: in December 1947 he conveyed just that impression. Skilfully, he left it to the former Conservative Foreign Secretary Anthony Eden to spell out the implications of his statement. This Eden did in resounding tones, declaring that

> there is no choice open to us but to do everything in our power to promote recovery in that part of Europe where we are still free to act— that is to say, Western Europe. . . . The Marshall Plan is there as a framework and within that framework we can work successfully and, I trust, speedily and finally. It is evident that Germany will have to play her full part in that. . . . In the interests of the world we should take account of [the] realities of this breakdown and go ahead with those who will work with us as speedily as we can.[31]

It was to immediate problems and private diplomacy that the three powers returned after the adjournment of the Council. During the following three days intensive talks took place between the Western powers. There were three questions relating to Germany that now had to be tackled and resolved: how to increase industrial output in the Western zones, what constitutional arrangements were needed to set up a provisional government, and how best to bring the French into the bizone. Bevin again stressed the need for a 'superior economy' for the Western zones and was told that, with Marshall Aid, a balanced economy could be secured in five years.[32] On the same day that the new financial arrangements were agreed, Bevin and Marshall also decided to try to secure four-power currency reform. Marshall was very enthusiastic about this approach and 'emphasized that in making a quadripartite approach we should make it clear that we really wanted Russian agreement and were not merely making a gesture'. Robertson and Bevin, however, were privately sceptical as to any success that might be achieved between the four powers.[33] Robertson and Clay also met to decide how to proceed towards

[30] House of Commons, *Debates*, 18 Dec. 1947, vol. 445.   [31] Ibid.
[32] Bevin meeting with officials, 16 Dec. 1947, FO 371/64250.
[33] *FRUS 1947* ii, 1138 ff.; Robertson–Clay meeting, 18 Dec. 1947, FO 371/64250.

a provisional government for the Western zones. They concluded that the Economic Council's activities should be expanded, and that it should be renamed the Council. They hoped that the zones would have an elected Chamber by the summer of 1948 as well as a constitution based upon the Bevin Plan.[34]

The French now hoped to get a favourable settlement with international control in the Ruhr, as well as agreed security arrangements before joining the bizone. Both Bevin and Marshall knew that the French would fight hard for such acceptable guarantees and Robertson feared the consequences of delay. For, as Auriol noted in his diary, 'nous ne parlerons d'envisager la fusion des zones occidentales qu'après un accord préalable sur le Rhin. En effet s'il y a un trizone contrôlant la Ruhr, comment sera garantie la sécurité de la Rhénanie?'[35] But Bevin did not intend to compromise to France's economic interests in the Ruhr, although he had sympathy for their security concerns. The French, he thought,

visualise a possible clash in Western Europe arising from the present tension between the great Powers and they consider that they would be the principal sufferers. They cannot withdraw from Europe as is open to the Americans, and to a lesser degree ourselves. . . . The French are really concerned about the possibility that France may be faced with the danger of attack by the Red army. If we are to carry the French with us in the reconstruction of Western Europe and in our German policy, we must try to satisfy them on this score.[36]

Bevin promised Bidault guarantees of security as and when France joined the bizone. But it was essential to move very carefully to avoid 'giving the Russians a slogan or a plan with which to come out against the Western Powers and embarrass all three'. The security issue, masked while the economic recovery of Europe was at the front of the stage, was to be the major issue of the next year.[37]

The collapse of the Council had thrown the Americans into considerable disarray, and indeed Marshall even toyed with

---

[34] Ibid.   [35] Auriol, *Journal*, 629.
[36] CP(48)5, 5 Jan. 1948, CAB 129/23.
[37] Bevin–Bidault meeting, 17 Dec. 1947, FO 371/67674; G. Elgey, *La République des Illusions, 1945–51* (Paris: Fayard, 1965), 381 f.; John Baylis, 'Britain, the Brussels Pact and the Continental Commitment', *International Affairs*, 60/4 (1984); Nicholas Henderson, *The Birth of NATO* (London: Weidenfeld & Nicolson, 1982), 1.

the idea of reconvening the Council in Geneva.[38] Bidault also
reported that, in his meeting with Marshall, the American had
only considered the prospects of a trizone, and that he 'had been
unable to get anything very precise out of Mr Marshall, either
as regards procedure for co-ordinating the ideas of the three
Western Allies or as regards fundamental points of policy. . . .
Although the situation which had been clearly foreseen, had
now been brought about, the Americans seemed to be rather
overwhelmed by the results of their own action.'[39] Having failed
to persuade the Americans to be prepared for failure before the
Council opened, British officials now had the task of moving
Western diplomacy forward. Bevin told the Cabinet that these
days were like 'introducing a friendly but sometimes difficult new
partner into a firm where our present partner is at times liable
to take an independent line'.[40] He knew well the vagaries of the
American foreign policy machine and had already warned Dulles
that 'the Russians could walk around the Americans as long as
the Americans allowed themselves to be entangled in their lengthy
Congressional procedures'.[41]

During these discussions Bevin took and held the leading role
with his allies, showing both skill and determination to construct
the viable Western policy which he had worked towards over the
previous eighteen months. He was confident and ready to take
the initiative. He told Bidault and Marshall that the *Daily Herald*
and the trade unions were backing him, and he intended to make
decisive but quiet progress, anxious not to lay himself open to
the charge of appearing too aggressive towards the Soviet Union
'until we had our plans ready'.[42]

He then set forth to Bidault the real context of Britain's overseas
interests in most revealing remarks:

Europe, as he saw it, was now divided from Greece to the Baltic and
from the Oder to Trieste. It would be difficult, if not impossible, to
penetrate the countries east of these lines. Our task was to save Western
civilisation. He himself felt that we should have to come to some sort of

[38] Report of conversation between Roberts and Bedell Smith, 17 Dec. 1947,
FO 371/64250.
[39] Bevin–Bidault meeting, 17 Dec. 1947, FO 371/67674; Marshall–Bidault
conversations, 17 Dec. 1947, FO 371/64250.
[40] CP(48)5, 5 Jan. 1948, CAB 129/23.
[41] Bevin–Bidault meeting, 17 Dec. 1947, FO 371/67674.   [42] Ibid.

federation in Western Europe whether of a formal or informal character. . . . As an Englishman, he hoped it would not be necessary to have formal constitutions. Everything should be flexible, but we should act quickly.[43]

Britain and France had a clear role as leaders in this new enterprise and had to tell the Americans that they must face up to the situation: 'If we and the French played our part it would not be good enough for the Americans to expect us to take action while they themselves were not ready to take any risk until a much later stage. They had to be persuaded that we were all in this together as Allies.'[44] A certain amount of guile was essential, as although they might be 'prepared to take the right steps in Europe, it would still be necessary for the French and ourselves to advise them, while letting the Americans say and think that it was they who were acting'. This conversation reveals most starkly and unequivocally Bevin's perceptions of Britain's unique role as leader in Germany and Europe, a role he had first elaborated to Clayton in June. Then, his exposition had focused upon Britain's world role despite her economic difficulties. Now he focused upon her role spearheading an ideological struggle against communism, which explains why he had emphasized the ideological aspects of East–West differences at the Council. The real issue was where power should rest in Germany and in Europe, and, to maintain a favourable balance of power and to prevent Soviet power from seeping westwards, Western Europe had to be as powerful as Eastern Europe. He therefore advocated confidential Anglo-French military talks to give a lead to the Americans.[45]

And France, from her ambivalent position in 1945, was now in a position to begin to play a major part in the consolidation of Western Europe. This shift had been a long and tortuous process, in which Bevin had given encouragement to France but had been unable to act very positively towards her while the threat of communism within France remained. This brake upon co-operation was more important than France's attitude to Germany, which, although an irritant for British officials on the ground, also conveniently served to hold up progress in the Control Council. Indeed, Bidault concluded the meeting on a note

[43] Ibid.   [44] Ibid.   [45] Ibid.

of self-congratulation for the new diplomatic picture, remarking that it was French obstinacy over central administrations which had stopped the advance of communism into Germany.[46]

On the evening of 17 December and on the morning of the 18th Bevin and Marshall met again to discuss issues of a new German currency, Berlin, and security questions. Bevin now elaborated upon his concept of a 'spiritual consolidation of Western civilisation. . . . an understanding backed by power, money and resolute action', with Americans and Dominions supporting a Western European group. By Western civilization he clearly meant an anti-Soviet bloc, for he added that 'if such a powerful consolidation of the west could be achieved it would then be clear to the Soviet Union that having gone so far they could not advance any further'.[47] He linked this analysis to an appreciation of France's security needs, along the lines either of a three-power treaty on the Byrnes model, or of a Western European treaty that would involve the Benelux countries and Italy, and he told Marshall he wished to set up an Anglo-French committee to work on these problems. Marshall, it seems, did not quite grasp the broad sweep of Bevin's thinking but said he had 'no criticism of the general idea' though he favoured reaching an understanding on immediate objectives. But Marshall added that he continued to be 'most anxious in regard to the general international situation to avoid a "frozen front", which was tragic to contemplate'.[48] These interchanges are the clearest indications that Bevin and his officials were far more acutely aware of the future shape that international politics should now take, even to the extent of wanting to take a lead over a possible West European–American security grouping.

In two subsequent Cabinet Papers Bevin was to develop the broader issues raised by the establishment of the reconstructed Western zones in the family of Western European nations.[49] He made quite explicit the economic and political components of his

[46] Bevin–Bidault meeting, 17 Dec. 1947, FO 371/67674.

[47] Bevin–Marshall meetings, 17, 18 Dec. 1947, FO 371/64250 (non expurgated version).

[48] Ibid.

[49] CP(48)5, 5 Jan. 1948, CAB 129/23. Gladwyn Jebb, then Chairman of the influential Russia Committee, prepared much of this paper: interview with Lord Gladwyn, Oct. 1985; CP(48)6, 4 Jan. 1948, CAB 129/23.

policy to combat a Soviet strategy that was inherently aggressive and expansionist. Britain would be 'hard put to it to stem the further encroachment of the Soviet tide. It is not enough to reinforce the physical barriers which still guard our Western civilisation. We must also organise and consolidate the ethical and spiritual forces inherent in this Western civilisation of which we are the chief protagonists.'[50] In any future democratic system in Western Europe American and Dominion backing was essential, as was the eventual inclusion of both Spain and Germany, without which no Western system would be complete. All these countries sense 'the imminence of the Communist peril and are seeking some assurance of salvation'. For if 'we are to preserve peace and our own safety at the same time, we can only do so by the mobilisation of such a moral and material force as will create confidence and energy on the one side and inspire respect and caution on the other'. Soviet accusations of an offensive Western alliance were now anachronistic, for the only alternative for the West would now be 'to acquiesce in continued Russian infiltration and helplessly to witness the piecemeal collapse of one Western bastion after another'.[51] Bevin's Cabinet Papers are a leading statement of a cold-war mentality and of the core assumptions that subsequently came to dominate British and American policy towards the Soviet Union. They contrasted Western civilization with Soviet ideology, which was by implication not even Western in origin. Bevin painted a picture of a struggle that was not merely military, a struggle in which major countries could fall like dominoes in the face of communist subversion. Bevin and his officials had long argued that Western democracy required economic health, and this thinking had underpinned Britain's emphasis on the recovery of her zone since 1946. But civil liberties, human rights, and what Clay called 'ideas and ideals' were now openly to the forefront.[52]

Bevin explicitly charged Britain with the duty to spearhead this incipient ideological battle. She had the moral and political resources to do so. As the chief protagonist she had the obligation to act resolutely and give 'strong leadership in order to secure its

[50] CP(48)6, 4 Jan. 1948, CAB 129/23.
[51] Ibid.
[52] Clay, *Decision in Germany*, 348.

[Western Union's] acceptance in Europe on the one hand and in the Dominions and the Americas on the other'.[53] Churchill's well-rehearsed aphorism about Britain lying at the centre of three interlocking circles is given a radically different meaning within such a cold-war context, a meaning that is closest to that advocated in his Fulton speech. However, Bevin further cast Britain as the leader of Western Europe, the United States, and the Dominions in the struggle against communism.

Thus, by 1948 Bevin was in crusading spirit. He now had growing confidence in American and French support and his battles with sections of his own party and public opinion in Britain were largely won. As many of his officials had long foreseen, it had become obvious that a divided Germany, at least in the short term, was an essential ingredient to contain communist infiltration and Soviet power, and to restore a balance of power in Europe and the world that would be favourable to the West. But it was to be nearly two more tense years before a West German state and a network of European and Atlantic alliances gave the framework to ensure to Western satisfaction that the balance of power in Europe did, after all, appear to rest in their favour.

[53] CP(48)5, 5 Jan. 1948, CAB 129/23.

CONCLUSIONS

By December 1947 the Council of Foreign Ministers, which had been established at Potsdam, had clearly failed to fulfil part of its avowed purpose, that of preparing a peace treaty to decide the future of the defeated Reich. The failure of the fifth Council meeting also brought the collapse of the whole Potsdam process, including, in 1948, the 'noble experiment' of the Control Council in Germany.[1] Effective decision-making had now openly returned to the capital cities, which, it can be argued, it had never really left. By January 1948 Bevin could finally bring into the open his fears about Soviet intentions and his determination to build a Western Europe that could withstand the onslaught of communism. It was clear that a provisional government for the Western zones of Germany could not be far away—and Bevin knew that he had much support from within Western Germany itself. The ideological battle for the heart and soul of the German people was now in full swing, combating 'fear to dull the hearts and distorted information to capture the minds of peoples powerless to resist'.[2] Marshall Aid would, it hoped, serve as the basis for the economic recovery of Western Germany and Europe, and interim aid consolidated France's position in the Western camp, although the latter's economic competitiveness with Germany and her preoccupation with the possibility of a German revival were to colour Anglo-French and Franco-German relations in Europe for many years to come.[3]

So, less than three weeks after the collapse of the Council, Bevin elaborated to the Cabinet his policy on Germany and on a Western Union. Released from the shackles of Potsdam, Germany's future could now be seen within its ideological framework, revealing the need to create a democratic, Westward-looking Germany, not a police state with 'the revival of the Gestapo under another name'.[4] The Western powers would have to secure Western Germany and Western Europe with American backing, and

[1] Clay, *Decision in Germany*, 348.   [2] Ibid.
[3] The best short introduction to this subject is Young, *Britain, France and the Unity of Europe*, but there is as yet no definitive study of France's part in the diplomacy of these years. For reference to France's own 'duality' of policy, *FRUS 1946* i, 566 f.
[4] CP(48)5, 5 Jan. 1948, CAB 129/23.

Britain's role, indeed her duty, was publicly to lead this new crusade to restore a healthy balance of power in Europe. Molotov's departure from London thus marked a milestone in British policy on Germany and with it the cold war, and was the moment at which the dual policy of the British government came to an end, revealing the true dimensions of cold-war politics.[5] It was the end of a phase of politics that can be dated from the beginning of 1946.

For by early 1946 there had emerged in the highest echelons of the Foreign Office what we would now identify as an operational code, a cold-war mentality towards the Soviet Union. Suspicion of Soviet policies in the Mediterranean region, Iran, Southern and Eastern Europe, and Germany quickly overtook fears of resurgent German nationalism. Moscow's actions came to be seen as a blend of Soviet communism and Russian imperialism: coherent, well co-ordinated, denying co-existence with the West, and aiming ultimately at world domination. The Soviet Union was perceived as posing the overriding threat to British interests, although the worst scenario still remained that of Soviet communism fuelled by German economic might. It became clear to policy-makers in Britain earlier than it did to those in the United States what the implications of Soviet expansionism were for Europe, and that, if all Germany could not be secured for the West to sustain a favourable balance of power, then at least the western part of Germany had to be made safe for liberal democracy and a free economy. In Washington Kennan's Long Telegram caused a sensation, but in Whitehall Roberts's précis of the Long Telegram and his many other reports served to confirm already existing fears and suspicions of the Soviet Union. Britain, however, could not act alone, and France was still too weak and unreliable. It was axiomatic that the Americans had to be apprised of the political and security consequences of 'drift' in Germany and shown how their influence should be brought into Europe to balance the might of the Soviet Union.

So in one sense Britain's postwar European policy simply reflected her long-standing preoccupation with the European balance of power. Traditionally, Britain had acted to preserve the balance of power in continental Europe, sitting in splendid

[5] And was accepted as such, ibid.

isolation and ready to restore the balance when necessary. From 1945 onwards, officials had pragmatically assessed Britain's interests and then worked to redress a balance of power that increasingly appeared to favour the Soviet Union. The extent and nature of this new threat required a new kind of response which was active and global and admitted of no appeasement or concession in areas of vital interest. It was to lead to the division of the principal central European power into two separate countries and, uniquely, the long-term military presence of both British and American troops on continental European soil.

The first clear evidence of Whitehall's move to counter the new dangers to the balance of power was the Cabinet Paper of 3 May 1946.[6] This first presentation of a 'Western' option involved ending the Potsdam formula for governing Germany as a single economic unit through four-power co-operation. Based on considerations of security, it regretfully posed the possibility that Germany might have to be divided permanently to stop the spread of communism westwards. It was no hastily compiled summary of tactics on the eve of an international conference, but the culmination of a far-reaching, pragmatic, and pessimistic analysis of the dangers that lay ahead, and of Britain's options for dealing with them. That analysis reflected the ideology, assumptions, and world-view of the Foreign Office, supported by the Chiefs of Staff. But Bevin and his officials rejected any idea of publicly breaching the Potsdam agreement yet, and preferred a 'go slow' approach until sure of their support. Yet the seeds of Britain's containment policy lie in this Cabinet Paper.

This 'Western' option was to be clearly revealed in the creation of the bizone. It was Bevin's threat in Paris to 'organize' the British zone, perhaps the most logical consequence of the military zonal division, that provoked Byrnes's offer to merge the zones economically, a response which provided Foreign Office officials with a unique way out of the four-power quagmire in Germany. They, and later Bevin, then fought tenaciously against American vacillation and intransigence to secure the best agreement they could with the United States, although the bizone was outside the spirit, if not the letter, of Potsdam. It represented the first and most important building-block in an incremental process that

[6] CP(46)186, 3 May 1946, CAB 129/9.

was to lead to a divided Germany. It further implied the need for some kind of joint financial and political arrangements in the future, although Bevin preferred initially to settle for only such constitutional changes as would bring the British zone as close to the American zone as practical realities and British constitutional preferences would allow.

The so-called Bevin Plan of February 1947 was the next major landmark in the development of British policy.[7] Designed to meet a diplomatic need at the Moscow Council, it was a partial interpretation of the Potsdam Protocol which stressed the precedence of economic unity over currrent reparations or political unity. Its dense legalistic phraseology obscured the fact that it made four-power control in Germany impossible except on British terms. American acceptance of the Bevin Plan at the Moscow Council represented a further commitment to a Westward-looking bizone and to Anglo-American co-operation in checking Soviet influence in Germany, although the rapidly changing climate of opinion within the United States itself was not yet directly reflected in any American willingness to take a lead in European affairs.

It was Marshall's offer of 5 June 1947 that gave Bevin and his officials the first real opportunity to speed up the economic recovery of the Western zones and to institutionalize the United States' role in Europe. The energy with which Bevin and his officials sought to realize this was further evidence of their strong commitment to the Western zones' economic recovery, rather than to German unity. Bevin's determination to organize Western Europe against the Soviet Union was made public after the London Council in his Western Union speech of January 1948, when for the first time Britain's operational policy converged with her declaratory policy.

Given the climate of public opinion in Britain, the true direction of Britain's interests in Europe could not be disclosed publicly at home until memories of wartime Soviet heroism had begun to fade and fear of postwar Soviet ambitions spread. What also emerges is that the 'Western' policy had its roots in the Foreign Office, although by mid-1946 Bevin saw the strategic dilemma in which Britain was placed, and realized that the 'Western' option, despite its dangers, best represented British interests. Bevin himself

[7] CP(47)68, 27 Feb. 1947, CAB 129/17.

did have the broad but not uncritical support of Attlee, but the enormous legislative pressures and the difficulties of keeping abreast of the complex domestic and international issues that faced the Labour Government meant that other ministers and the Cabinet did not take a consistent and informed interest in German policy until the stark conditions in the British zone and an increased awareness of the difficulties in the great-power alliance became all too apparent. Bevin, however, was always sensitive to criticisms of his policies from within his own party, whether expressed privately or in the House of Commons, feeling that such criticisms were disloyal and made his task harder in the many rounds of international diplomatic encounters that he faced. The summer and autumn of 1946 were particularly difficult for him, and this was a period when even Attlee began to doubt the assumptions behind British policy towards the Soviet Union. But by the end of 1947 there seemed to be no ears to listen to the voices of opposition in the Labour Party or to the hopes of the Keep Left group. The Conservative Party had shown little opposition to Bevin's policies; the Cabinet were in general support in so far as they were fully informed of the implications of what was happening. Little notice was taken of the prescient questioning of the future Conservative Prime Minister Harold Macmillan, who thought MPs should ask themselves whether it may 'not be that the apparent chauvinism of Soviet policy is a form of insurance, not of expansion, that security, not imperialism is their instinctive goal'.[8] By the end of 1947 party and trade-union criticisms had become muted, as Bevin's determination to reveal the difficulties of dealing with the Soviet Union began to pay dividends.

The formulation of policy, however, depended in large measure upon the perceptions and persistence of senior Foreign Office officials, supported by the Chiefs of Staff, although Bevin's trade-union experience and his personal dislike of Molotov always contributed to his own anti-communism. A determination by leading figures in the Foreign Office never again to fall prey to the folly of appeasing a totalitarian government underpinned many British officials' distrust of the Soviet Union. This distrust was indeed consistent with the anti-communist sentiment which had fuelled appeasement in the 1930s. It was further reinforced by

---

[8] House of Commons, *Debates*, 26 Feb. 1946, vol. 419.

overseas reports of Soviet activity, analyses of Soviet intentions and the nature of marxism–leninism (particularly those from Moscow), and diagnoses of Britain's future strategic requirements made by the influential military establishment. Once convinced of the Soviet threat, Foreign Office officials remained consistent in their determination to restore a favourable balance of power in Europe.

Political and strategic considerations also had a priority in the Foreign Office that overrode the economic constraints of postwar Britain herself, although there were strong economic arguments for revising the Potsdam formula, as Britain's desperate need for more dollars for Germany placed her in an increasingly vulnerable position with each month that passed. The prospect of a reparations settlement that would both constrict the economic recovery of the British zone and present a continual drain of resources eastwards, coupled with the daily cost of running the zone, enabled a strong, if somewhat uncomfortable, alliance to be forged by the Foreign Office with the Treasury (although their respective masters, Bevin and Dalton, remained firmly antagonistic to each other). This alliance helped the creation of the bizone to be in part presented as a means of saving British money, although until the end of 1947 there was no limit to the extent of Britain's financial commitments to this expensive option.

Moreover, by 1947, as the centrality of the German question became increasingly obvious, the Foreign Office secured a very firm grip on the policy-making machine within Whitehall. They ensured that the Control Office was marginalized in the decision-making process and won Brian Robertson, the one official with real authority on the ground, round to the Foreign Office point of view, although he was to remain an uneasy ally. It has also been argued that, because of his own insecurity, Bevin quickly adapted to the attitudes of his peers in the Foreign Office.[9] This may well have been so, but his own constant ill-health, his preference for broad generalizations rather than details, his enormous workload, and his own suspicions about Soviet

[9] This was a view widely held by Bevin's contemporary critics; for a more recent assessment, see Michael Blackwell, *Attitudes Concerning Britain's World Role Held by Policymakers in the Aftermath of the Second World War (1945–47)*, (Ph.D. thesis, University of East Anglia, 1981).

diplomacy are more convincing reasons for the power that the established and competent bureaucracy was able to exercise. The German question was only one area of policy-making at a time when, as Bevin himself put it, 'all the world is in trouble'. The pressure of work affected Minister and officials alike, and clearly contributed to the considerable degree of official freedom during these years when the outline of British policy was laid down.

The Labour Government was in the vanguard of the policy of containment of the Soviet Union in Europe, and the main European contributor to what has been called the postwar American 'Empire by invitation' in Europe.[10] Britain's policy was predicated upon traditional perceptions of the need to maintain a favourable balance of power in Europe, and her self-perception of her role as a major world and European actor. These were deeply ingrained beliefs, 'the habit and furniture of our minds', as Lord Franks has written, not assumptions arrived at by a conscious decision.[11] It is quite untrue to argue that in the immediate postwar era Britain's own crippling weakness drove her into a flight from her global responsibilities. Her weakness rather compelled her to intensify and build upon her 'special' relationship with the United States, her Imperial and, particularly, Dominion links, and even her relationship with France. She still felt she had a role to play at the top diplomatic table, and the policy to contain Soviet power in Europe and elsewhere was clearly not the nostalgic pipedream of officials seduced by Britain's prewar power. It was based both upon an ideological fear of the tenets of marxism–leninism and upon an assessment of the realities of power politics in Europe, learning from what seemed to be the disastrous errors of appeasement and realizing the kind of support that Britain herself would need to retain her status and play her part as a great power.

---

[10] Geir Lundestad, 'Empire by Invitation? The United States and Western Europe, 1945–1952', *Newsletter 15/3* (Society for Historians of American Foreign Relations, September 1984). For the most coherent view of American containment, see John Lewis Gaddis, *Strategies of Containment* (Oxford: Oxford University Press, 1982); and for Kennan's criticisms about the US's misinterpretation of what he meant by containment, Thomas H. Etzold and John Lewis Gaddis, *Containment: Documents on American Policy and Strategy* (New York: Columbia University Press, 1978), 384.

[11] Franks, *Britain and the Tide of World Affairs*, 3 ff. Lord Franks has argued that this way of thinking lasted until the fiasco of the Suez crisis. Suez was the 'lightning in a dark night', which revealed that the 'normalcy' of Britain's great-power status would not return; comments made during a seminar, All Souls College, Oxford, 25 Jan. 1985.

The point at which Soviet power in Europe had to be contained was the border between the Soviet and Western zones of Germany. Control of the British zone gave Britain a chance to build a model of containment that extended far beyond a simple military barrier. For, as both Kennan and Roberts saw, the essence of controlling Soviet expansion lay in rebuilding sound economies and political structures. This prospect of recovery could offset any appeal of communist doctrine, and further serve as a basis for Western-style democracy which had so patently failed to flourish in Germany when confronted with economic depression before the war.

Confirming the zonal division of Germany agreed during the war also dealt, at least in the short term, with the continuing and very real fear of German power felt by the wartime Allies. For, although the creation of a West German state was to fly in the face of national self-determination, it was also an effective response to the threat of an immediate revival of German nationalism, and was in essence a double containment, controlling both German and Soviet power. It also emphasized what the British had realized very soon after the war, that it was simply not worth making too great an issue of Eastern Europe, as the presence of the Red Army in the region meant that confrontation would only drive the Soviets from the negotiating table over an issue of the greatest consequence to them—the security of their own western borders. The agreed zonal division of Germany thus came to reflect an acceptance of a military status quo in Europe, and to serve for the West as the basis for reining in both German and Soviet ambitions.

It was also perceived in Britain that containment of the Soviet Union at the border between the Western and Soviet zones could serve as a basis for a future realistic and pragmatic conduct of diplomacy with the Russians in Europe. The 3 May 1946 Cabinet Paper referred to the permanent division of Germany, and in October of that year a senior Foreign Office official asked whether it was not possible that

in the end we may have smoother relations with the Russians in Germany if we accept the division and cease to quarrel so much about what they do in their zone and what we do in ours, than if we indulge in an internecine warfare for the body of a unitary Germany, the results of which . . . will inevitably be regarded by the losing side as fatal to its own security? The stakes are so high that it is bound to be a very bitter struggle.

But officials later doubted whether such a bizarre solution could last, or whether it would and should not serve as the basis for the eventual reunification of Germany within a Western bloc. For the Germans' own desire for unity would

> prove too strong for this [permanent division]. It is probably the strongest force in Germany today. An irridentist movement is certain to arise sooner or later. The problem for us is to bring this unity about as soon as possible, but in such a way as to ensure that the forces of attraction operate from the West upon the East and not vice versa as the Soviet Union intend with their aim of dominating the whole of Europe. We want to see established in the Western Zones in Germany a political and economic system to join which the Germans in the Eastern Zone will exert all their energy, and which will in the end prevail . . . true unity . . . can only be achieved under the auspices of ourselves and the other Western powers and not of German nationalism or Soviet Communism.[12]

Whatever the intended consequences were, with its heartland divided in such an unnatural way, the effect of the division of Germany was that Europe remained at the top of the international political agenda, and with it remained Britain, still capable of influencing events, manipulating the image of her continuing power, and preserving her own interests in what nevertheless became an increasingly bipolar world.

The crucial relationship that underpinned British policy was, however, that with the Americans. It is in this area that access to British official sources has revealed perhaps some of the most interesting new insights. For, at least over Germany, American policy appears in this period as neither simply leading a response to Soviet expansionism, as the traditionalists would have us believe, nor thrusting greedily towards new markets, as in the revisionist view. Indeed, it was the United States' uncertainty about how to act as a great power, how to manage her enormous economic and military prowess, and how best to carry her own public and Congressional opinion with her that continually preoccupied British officials. This was reflected in the ambiguities about German policy that the perpetual conflict between the American War and State Departments created on the one hand, and the

---

[12] Hankey minute, 25 Oct. 1946, FO 371/55592; CP(48)5, 5 Jan. 1948, CAB 129/23.

shrill tone of the declaratory policy encapsulated in the Truman
Doctrine on the other.[13] In an operational sense, this uncertainty
about the Americans drove British officials to fight through the
autumn of 1946, and then again in the spring of 1947, to ensure
that Byrnes's Paris offer matured into a workable 'Western'
solution for Germany, and also to lead the response to Marshall's
generous but ambiguous offer of financial aid for European
recovery. The Anglo-American relationship was the most
important axis of international politics in the immediate postwar
years, and was critical to the future shape of Europe, yet it is
easy now to underestimate the depth of uncertainty that existed
in London about the United States's intentions before the relief
brought by Marshall Aid removed some of the memories of
1919.[14]

It remains to be asked whether there existed a genuine
alternative for the Labour Government to the policy that it
followed during these crucial years, or whether it was inevitable
that each particular incremental, but ultimately divisive,
step would be taken. This is an important question, first because
the division of Germany between East and West was a major
cause of the cold war, and as Britain was clearly not a junior
partner in the years 1945–7 before the superpower mould
became set, she must carry some responsibility for the cold war,
along with the United States and the Soviet Union. Second,
we are now experiencing the effects of the disintegration of
cold war structures built in the immediate post·war years.
The events of 1989 throughout Eastern Europe exposed the
fragile and provisional nature of the post·war settlement. The
balance of power in Europe, Germany's borders, and her
relations with her eastern and western neighbours are once
again key issues in European and global power politics. Any
judgement is directly coloured by the world around us.

Until 1947 many on the Labour Left tried in vain to construct
an alternative foreign policy for Britain, attracting some of the
brightest MPs towards their course. This is well known. It is

---

[13] Indeed, as Larson points out, even within the Truman Administration, the
apparent scope of the Truman Doctrine did not immediately imply the practical
implementation of a global, or even a European, containment policy, *Origins of
Containment*, 325.
[14] A point made most emphatically by Lord Franks, interview, Feb. 1985.

equally interesting that Clement Attlee himself was sceptical about the tone and assumptions of policy, challenging in 1946 Bevin's vision of Britain's global role and her perceived strategic requirements. Whether or not Attlee would have been able to stand up to the combined strength of Bevin, his officials, and the Chiefs of Staff, we shall never know, as he was not prepared to take up this challenge. What the disagreement does make clear is that the Foreign Office view of what was needed to protect Britain's interests was not a unanimous and foregone conclusion, and that the criticisms and fears voiced were both serious and substantial.

This book makes clear that failure to resolve the German problem through a Council of Foreign Ministers became the immediate cause of the diplomatic breakdown between East and West over the future of Germany, and with it the cold war. It is apparent that the Council system was entirely the wrong way to approach the delicate but crucial problems confronting the Allies, and that private diplomacy could perhaps have contributed to a less antagonistic international atmosphere. The semi-public Council negotiating process condemned it to failure when the stakes were as high as they were over Germany, for the temptation to use the Council for national propaganda was too great to resist, and no side ever forgot the interest of its own domestic constituencies in Council business. Council sessions never provided an atmosphere in which the participants could collectively come to understand the problems of postwar recovery and reconstruction which they were—with the exception of the United States—all experiencing, nor did they give participants a chance to alter or compromise their positions without considerable risk. Any conciliatory move by one power came to be interpreted by the others as being disingenuous or as having a sinister ulterior motive.

But the record shows that the behaviour of the British teams at these meetings was not even seriously directed at prolonging four-power harmony. Publicly Britain posed as the impoverished defender of four-power unity,[15] but the principal thrust of her

---

[15] German historians, in particular R. Steininger and J. Foschepoth (eds.), *Die Britische Deutschland und Besatzungspolitik, 1945–1949* (London: German Historical Institute, 1984) have been less convinced by this posture than some British scholars.

policy was not to give way to any issue of principle, and to build up an anti-Soviet bloc while creating the impression of continued loyalty to her wartime allies. It is clear that at the Council meetings both the Soviet Union and the Western powers were evolving their responses to what each perceived as a complex threat to its interests, a threat which was not simply military, but also economic, ideological, and psychological in character; and in these years diplomacy was not yet a gladiatorial combat between the two superpowers. Council meetings both reflected and reinforced the divisions between the Allied powers and became a form of diplomatic trench-warfare. Sterile arguments were rehearsed and rehearsed again in an increasingly suspicious and antagonistic atmosphere. For the historian, the Council meetings reflect the failures of policy-makers at Potsdam, and serve to chart the downward spiral of great-power relations.

Whether there existed a genuine alternative for the British government during these years is a question that is also bedevilled by lack of access to Soviet primary sources—or even to British intelligence reports—and it is still an open question what the Russians really had in mind after the War. We might be better able to tell whether genuine policy alternatives existed for Britain in the 1945–7 period if it were possible to know more accurately what Russian policy towards Germany really was, and whether uncertainty or fear of a strong Germany even within the Soviet camp dominated Soviet thinking.[16] It has, however, been shown that there was a clear ideological inclination within the Foreign Office to perceive the Soviet Union as both untrustworthy and expansionist, and this contributed in large measure to a reluctance to work seriously with them in Germany, a task which would have required appreciating the constraints upon the Soviets' diplomatic activity, their economic and political difficulties, and their fear of the bizone and of the possible nature of Marshall's offer of aid. But once British officials were predisposed to consider that any Soviet initiative or compromise had the ulterior motive of driving a wedge between the Western powers, or catching them off their guard, it was inevitable that compromises could not be achieved in the confused atmosphere of the early postwar world.

[16] Dean minute, 22 Oct. 1946, FO 371/55592.

The documentary record makes it clear that in Britain officials genuinely feared the Soviet Union and that this fear grew with the passage of time, whether or not it was in fact a misperception about Soviet intentions. But it has also to be said that it was assumed that Britain had herself to maintain a place as a world power, and that her own strategic interests, whether in Europe or in the Mediterranean or Middle East, might not be less-well served by a Soviet–American *rapprochement*, for such a collaboration could have left Britain herself an impoverished second-rank power, without a world or European role. Anglo-American solidarity was needed both to confront Soviet power and as an affirmation and bulwark to Britain's own great-power status. But, despite her success in persuading the United States to redress the balance of power in Europe on British terms, Britain was to find herself playing an increasingly junior role anyway, as American self-confidence and assertiveness increasingly dominated Western policy in Europe and South-East Asia, and the confrontational and military interpretation of containment so feared by Kennan, and avoided by Britain, came to dominate the international politics of subsequent decades.

APPENDIX A
Extracts from Protocol of the Proceedings of the Berlin Conference, 2 August 1945*

Top secret   BERLIN, *2 August 1945*

The Berlin Conference of the Three Heads of Government of the U.S.S.R., United States and United Kingdom which took place from the 17th July to the 2nd August, 1945, came to the following conclusions:–

I.—*Establishment of a Council of Foreign Ministers*

A. The Conference reached the following agreement for the establishment of a Council of Foreign Ministers to do the necessary preparatory work for the peace settlements:–

'(1) There shall be established a Council composed of the Foreign Ministers of the United Kingdom, the Union of Soviet Socialist Republics, China, France and the United States.

(2) (i) The Council shall normally meet in London, which shall be the permanent seat of the joint Secretariat which the Council will form. Each of the Foreign Ministers will be accompanied by a high-ranking Deputy, duly authorised to carry on the work of the Council in the absence of his Foreign Minister, and by a small staff of technical advisers.

(ii) The first meeting of the Council shall be held in London not later than the 1st September, 1945. Meetings may be held by common agreement in other capitals as may be agreed from time to time.

(3) (i) As its immediate important task, the Council shall be authorised to draw up, with a view to their submission to the United Nations, treaties of peace with Italy, Roumania, Bulgaria, Hungary and Finland, and to propose settlements of territorial questions outstanding on the termination of the war in Europe. The Council shall be utilised for the preparation of a peace settlement for Germany to be accepted by the Government of Germany when a Government adequate for the purpose is established.

---

* FO 93/1/238, 2 August 1945, Butler, Rohan, and Pelly, M. E. (eds.), *Documents on British Policy Overseas Series I*, Volume i, 1945. (HMSO, 1984), 1262 ff. Reproduced by permission of the Controller of Her Majesty's Stationery Office.

(ii) For the discharge of each of these tasks the Council will be composed of the Members representing those States which were signatory to the terms of surrender imposed upon the enemy State concerned. For the purposes of the peace settlement for Italy, France shall be regarded as a signatory to the terms of surrender for Italy. Other Members will be invited to participate when matters directly concerning them are under discussion.

(iii) Other matters may from time to time be referred to the Council by agreement between the Member Governments.

(4) (i) Whenever the Council is considering a question of direct interest to a State not represented thereon, such State should be invited to send representatives to participate in the discussion and study of that question.

(ii) The Council may adapt its procedure to the particular problem under consideration. In some cases it may hold its own preliminary discussions prior to the participation of other interested States. In other cases, the Council may convoke a formal conference of the State chiefly interested in seeking a solution of the particular problem.'

B. It was agreed that the three Governments should each address an identical invitation to the Governments of China and France to adopt this text and to join in establishing the Council.

. . .

II.—*The Principles to Govern the Treatment of Germany in the Initial Control Period*

A. *Political Principles*

1. In accordance with the Agreement on Control Machinery in Germany, supreme authority in Germany is exercised, on instructions from their respective Governments by the Commanders-in-Chief of the armed forces of the United States of America, the United Kingdom, the Union of Soviet Socialist Republics and the French Republic, each in his own zone of occupation, and also jointly, in matters affecting Germany as a whole, in their capacity as members of the Control Council.

. . .

9. The administration in Germany should be directed towards the decentralisation of the political structure and the development of local responsibility. To this end:–

(i) Local self-government shall be restored throughout Germany on democratic principles and in particular through elective councils as rapidly as is consistent with military security and the purposes of military occupation;

(ii) all democratic political parties with rights of assembly and of public discussion shall be allowed and encouraged throughout Germany;

(iii) representative and elective principles shall be introduced into regional, provincial and state (*Land*) administration as rapidly as may be justified by the successful application of these principles in local self-government;

(iv) for the time being, no central German Government shall be established. Notwithstanding this, however, certain essential central German administrative departments, headed by State Secretaries, shall be established, particularly in the fields of finance, transport, communications, foreign trade and industry. Such departments will act under the direction of the Control Council.

10. Subject to the necessity for maintaining military security, freedom of speech, press and religion shall be permitted, and religious institutions shall be respected. Subject likewise to the maintenance of military security, the formation of free trade unions shall be permitted.

B. *Economic Principles*

11. In order to eliminate Germany's war potential, the production of arms, ammunition and implements of war as well as all types of aircraft and sea-going ships shall be prohibited and prevented. Production of metals, chemicals [,] machinery and other items that are directly necessary to a war economy, shall be rigidly controlled and restricted to Germany's approved post-war peacetime needs to meet the objectives stated in paragraph 15. Productive capacity not needed for permitted production shall be removed in accordance with the reparations plan recommended by the Allied Commission on reparations and approved by the Governments concerned or, if not removed, shall be destroyed.

12. At the earliest practicable date, the German economy shall be decentralised for the purpose of eliminating the present excessive concentration of economic power as exemplified in particular by cartels, syndicates, trusts and other monopolistic arrangements.

13. In organising the German economy, primary emphasis shall be given to the development of agriculture and peaceful domestic industries.

14. During the period of occupation Germany shall be treated as a single economic unit. To this end common policies shall be established in regard to:–

(*a*)   mining and industrial production and its allocation;
(*b*)   agriculture, forestry and fishing;
(*c*)   wages, prices and rationing;
(*d*)   import and export programmes for Germany as a whole;
(*e*)   currency and banking, central taxation and customs;
(*f*)   reparation and removal of industrial war potential;
(*g*)   transportation and communications.

In applying these policies account shall be taken, where appropriate, of varying local conditions.

15. Allied controls shall be imposed upon the German economy but only to the extent necessary:–

(*a*) to carry out programmes of industrial disarmament and demilitarisation, of reparations, and of approved exports and imports;

(*b*) to assure the production and maintenance of goods and services required to meet the needs of the occupying forces and displaced persons in Germany and essential to maintain in Germany average living standards not exceeding the average of the standards of living of European countries. (European countries means all European countries excluding the United Kingdom and the Union of Soviet Socialist Republics);

(*c*) to ensure in the manner determined by the Control Council the equitable distribution of essential commodities between the several zones so as to produce a balanced economy throughout Germany and reduce the need for imports;

(*d*) to control German industry and all . . . economic international transactions, including exports and imports, with the aim of preventing Germany from developing a war potential and of achieving the other objectives named herein;

(*e*) to control all German public or private scientific bodies, research and experimental institutions, laboratories, &c., connected with economic activities.

16. In the imposition and maintenance of economic controls established by the Control Council, German administrative machinery shall be created and the German authorities shall be required to the fullest extent practicable to proclaim and assume administration of such controls. Thus it should be brought home to the German people that the responsibility for the administration of such controls and any breakdown in these controls will rest

with themselves. Any German controls which may run counter to the objectives of occupation will be prohibited.

17. Measures shall be promptly taken:–

(a) to effect essential repair of transport;

(b) to enlarge coal production;

(c) to maximise agricultural output;

(d) to effect emergency repair of housing and essential utilities.

18. Appropriate steps shall be taken by the Control Council to exercise control and the power of disposition over German-owned external assets not already under the control of United Nations which have taken part in the war against Germany.

19. Payment of reparations should leave enough resources to enable the German people to subsist without external assistance. In working out the economic balance of Germany the necessary means must be provided to pay for imports approved by the Control Council in Germany. The proceeds of exports from current production stocks shall be available in the first place for payment for such imports.

The above clause will not apply to the equipment and products referred to in paragraph 4 (a) and 4 (b) of the Reparations Agreement.

III.—*Reparations from Germany*

1. Reparation claims of the U.S.S.R. shall be met by removals from the zone of Germany occupied by the U.S.S.R., and from appropriate German external assets.

2. The U.S.S.R. undertakes to settle the reparation claims of Poland from its own share of reparations.

3. The reparations claims of the United States, the United Kingdom and other countries entitled to reparations shall be met from the Western Zones and from appropriate German external assets.

4. In addition to the reparations to be taken by the U.S.S.R. from its own zone of occupation, the U.S.S.R. shall receive additionally from the Western Zones:

(a) 15 per cent. of such usable and complete industrial capital equipment, in the first place from the metallurgical, chemical and machine manufacturing industries, as is unnecessary for the German peace economy and should be removed from the Western Zones of Germany, in exchange for an equivalent value of food, coal, potash, zinc, timber, clay products, petroleum products, and such commodities as may be agreed upon.

(*b*) 10 per cent. of such industrial capital equipment as is unnecessary for the German peace economy and should be removed from the Western Zones, to be transferred to the Soviet Government on reparations account without payment or exchange of any kind in return.

Removals of equipment as provided in (*a*) and (*b*) above shall be made simultaneously.

5. The amount of equipment to be removed from the Western Zones on account of reparations must be determined within six months from now at the latest.

6. Removals of industrial capital equipment shall begin as soon as possible and shall be completed within two years from the determination specified in paragraph 5. The delivery of products covered by 4(*a*) above shall begin as soon as possible and shall be made by the U.S.S.R. in agreed instalments within five years of the date hereof. The determination of the amount and character of the industrial capital equipment unnecessary for the German peace economy and therefore available for reparations shall be made by the Control Council under policies fixed by the Allied Commission on Reparations, with the participation of France, subject to the final approval of the Zone Commander in the Zone from which the equipment is to be removed.

7. Prior to the fixing of the total amount of equipment subject to removal, advance deliveries shall be made in respect of such equipment as will be determined to be eligible for delivery in accordance with the procedure set forth in the last sentence of paragraph 6.

8. The Soviet Government renounces all claims in respect of reparations to shares of German enterprises which are located in the Western Zones of occupation in Germany as well as to German foreign assets in all countries except those specified in paragraph 9 below.

9. The Governments of the United Kingdom and United States renounce all claims in respect of reparations to shares of German enterprises which are located in the Eastern Zone of occupation in Germany, as well as to German foreign assets in Bulgaria, Finland, Hungary, Roumania and Eastern Austria.

10. The Soviet Government makes no claims to gold captured by the Allied troops in Germany. . . .

[*Author's note*. There are a number of conflicting versions of 19, second paragraph, of point Section II.B. In the CAB 66/67 copy, this paragraph states that 'The above clause *will not only apply* to the equipment and products referred to in paragraph 4(a) and 4(b) of the Reparations Agreement'. The copy of the Protocol which was given to the Cabinet after the Paris Council [CP(46)292, 23 July 1946, Cab 129/11], quotes as the second paragraph of Section II.B.19: 'The above clause *will apply* to the equipment and products referred to in paragraph 4 (a) and 4 (b) of the Reparations Agreement', which unintentionaly would have made the British case against the priority of reparations payments over German economic self-sufficiency a very much stronger one. (Italics added)]

APPENDIX B
CAB 129/17
Extracts from C.P. (47) 68
20 February 1947*

CABINET

MAIN SHORT-TERM PROBLEMS CONFRONTING US IN MOSCOW: SUMMARISED CONCLUSIONS AND RECOMMENDATIONS

Memorandum by the Secretary of State for Foreign Affairs

1. I ask my colleagues to agree:–

   (i) That we should resist any claims which may be put forward for current reparation deliveries either from Eastern or Western Germany.

   (ii) That as a principal condition of economic unity we should obtain Russian agreement to bearing a reasonable share in the burden already borne and to be borne by the Occupying Powers in respect of relief imports and external costs of occupation of Germany as a whole.

   (iii) The demand for reparations from current production should not be refused outright. It should, however, be made clear that it cannot be considered until Germany has established a favourable foreign exchange balance and has met the expenses incurred by the Occupying Powers.

   (iv) That we should insist on an upward revision of the level of Industry Plan with a minimum steel production level of 10 million tons, the steel using industries being adjusted to a level appropriate to this steel output.

   (v) That we should insist on associating the discussion of economic problems with the consideration of the future political structure of Germany.

   (vi) That for the purpose of dealing with points raised in (i)–(iv) above we shall table, at the earliest opportunity in Moscow,

---

* Reproduced with the permission of the Controller of Her Majesty's Stationery Office.

a new set of political and economic principles dealing with the treatment of Germany during the second control period.

2. The most crucial part of the Moscow discussions is likely to concern the short-term problems of Germany, political and economic. The political problems, so far as they can be treated independently, are discussed in detail in separate papers circulated in the O.R.C. At the same time, the immediate political problems are very closely connected with the immediate economic problems and can only be considered in relation to them. The main economic topics likely to be discussed in Moscow are three, namely, economic unity, level of industry and reparations.

3. The background of long-term policy against which these immediate problems must be viewed is as follows: Our aim in Germany is the creation of a single State decentralised on federal lines, with her pre-war boundaries substantially unchanged except for the cession of some territory to Poland and Russia in the east, and the inclusion of the Saar in the French Economic area. She should be left with a sufficient industrial potential to ensure a reasonable standard of living, but this should be so designed as to interfere as little as possible with our own export policy. German basic industries should be socialised. The west bank of the Rhine and the Ruhr should be occupied, the former by the forces of the limitrophe Powers and the latter by the forces of the western Powers, the United States and the United Kingdom. An international control should be set up over the socialised industries of the Ruhr. The question of Russian participation in this control should be deferred for later consideration.

4. The first problem with which we are likely to be faced in Moscow is the demand by Russia that we should recognise her right to take current reparation deliveries from her own zone and should agree to her receiving current deliveries from the Western Zones in exchange for an upward revision of the Level of Industry Plan. These demands can only be met at the cost of considerable additional sacrifice by the British taxpayer. In our fusion agreement with the Americans we accepted with some misgiving certain financial commitments which in our present economic condition represent the absolute limit to which we can afford to go. The Russian demands must therefore be rejected.

5. In the unlikely event of the Russians being prepared to accept economic unity and waive their claim to reparation deliveries, both from Eastern and Western Germany, there is still no guarantee that economic unity would cost us less than it would if we were to

continue to run the British and American zones as a combined area separated from the rest of Germany. Although on present ration standards the Russian zone has a surplus of food-stuffs, it is substantially deficient in industrial raw materials. Moreover, industry in the Russian zone has been largely depleted and what is left is badly in need of repair. Under these circumstances, there is likely to be a net outflow of goods from the Western Zone and, if Russia were in practice to ignore the powers of German Central Administrative Agencies throughout the whole country, these goods from the Western Zones could easily be shipped across the Eastern borders of Germany into Poland and Russia. In other words, Russia would continue to take reparation deliveries from current production but in a disguised form.

6. To safeguard ourselves against this position we should only accept unity if Russia is prepared to bear a fair share of the net liability of the Occupying Powers as a whole, including a share of the liability that has already been incurred by the United States and this country. This share might be equivalent to her 50 per cent. claim of total reparation deliveries from Germany or at least equivalent to the proportion of the population of her zone to the population of the whole country.

7. We should further insist on a substantial upward revision of the Level of Industry Plan to ensure that Germany is left with sufficient industrial capacity to render her economically viable. While we should not try to settle the details of the plan in Moscow we should at least seek to reach agreement on the level of German steel capacity and of the related steel-using industries. We should not accept a lower figure for steel production than 10 million tons.

8. We shall almost certainly be faced with demands for current reparations at some future date. We should not refuse these demands altogether, but should take the line that the question cannot be considered until Germany has established a favourable foreign exchange balance and the expenses incurred by the Occupying Powers have been repaid. Should this position ever be reached the question could then be re-examined.

9. Further general points on which we must insist as preconditions for economic agreement are the removal of restrictions on the inter-zonal movement of German and Allied personnel and of goods, and the establishment of genuine freedom of assembly and expression, subject to the minimum agreed requirements of security.

10. Agreement on the terms outlined above will certainly meet
with strong Russian opposition. We may find ourselves faced with
a position in which we are urged to make small financial sacrifices
in exchange for certain politico/economic concessions. The attitude
of the other Occupying Powers and of the Germans and an account
of the particular problems with which we are faced are elaborated
in Part II of the attached paper. In brief they suggest that if the
discussions were to be confined to economic unity alone we might
in certain circumstances find ourselves in a minority of one and in
the eyes of the world opinion which is anxious to see unanimity
amongst the Four Powers, regarded as the country responsible for
failure.

11. It is most important that this position should be avoided and
that the responsibility for failure of Potsdam and of quadripartite
agreement should be placed fairly and squarely on the shoulders of
the Russians, who are entirely responsible for the present state of
affairs. To achieve this end, it will be necessary to widen the
discussion in order to cover the whole field of the Potsdam
Agreement. By ensuring that the field of discussion is extended to
the political and economic principles which we wish to establish,
we shall reduce the risk of finding ourselves in a minority of
one on economic questions. The Russians are known to favour
a centralised form of German Government. On the other hand,
the American views are very similar to our own, while the
French, who favour a confederate rather than a federal form,
would support us against the Russians if faced with an exclusive
choice.

12. A comprehensive account of our policy towards Germany,
which must emerge from such discussions would be desirable
not only for immediate tactical reasons. By taking the initiative
and putting forward comprehensive proposals, both political and
economic, with regard to Germany, we will supply a need long felt
by the British public and anticipate what will be an increasingly lively
demand for a further statement of policy.

13. We should, therefore, table at an early opportunity a statement
of the political and economic principles which, in our view, should
govern Germany during the second period of control. This will be
a logical sequel to the Potsdam Agreement which covered the initial
control period and should be designed to lead up to an eventual peace
treaty. A draft statement of the general sort which I have in mind
is attached at Appendix "A."

In the event of Russian acceptance of these new political and economic principles I should feel that we had made considerable progress. In the event of failure, the Russians are far too concerned with preventing Germany from being split into two and the resources of the Ruhr from being incorporated within a Western *bloc*, to counter a failure to reach agreement by abandoning the principle of quadripartite control. They would prefer to continue under the present uneasy arrangements and would probably try and avoid loss of face by asking that certain contentious points should be referred to the Deputies. In the meantime we and the Americans, perhaps with the French, would continue to operate Western Germany independently of the East, bartering the steel and industrial products of the Ruhr for food-stuffs and other essential relief imports from the East. This would reduce our dollar commitments and thereby hasten the recovery of our Zone. As this economic recovery developed we should find ourselves in a stronger bargaining position with the Russians, whose one zone of occupation is likely to change from an asset into a liability as time goes on. If events take this course, greater economic co-ordination will be necessary, and the consequent problem of closer political co-ordination will have to be faced.

Foreign Office, S.W.1,   E.B.
  20th February, 1947.

Principles for the Second Control Period

Preamble

In the text of Part III of the Potsdam Agreement published on 2nd August, 1946, were laid down the aims of the Allied occupation of Germany and the political and economic principles to govern the treatment of Germany in the initial control period.

The Controlling Powers reaffirm their acceptance of the aims and principles contained in this Agreement. It is their purpose to extirpate German militarism and Nazism. It is not their intention to destroy or enslave the German people. It is their intention that the German people should reconstruct their life on a democratic and peaceful basis. They consider, however, that the initial control period for which the Potsdam Principles were framed is now closed, and that the developments of events call for a further statement of the principles which should guide them during the second period of control which is now beginning. They are agreed that it will be their main task, and that of the Germans, during that period to achieve the following aims:–

(1) To establish political conditions which will secure the world against any German reversion to dictatorship and any revival of German aggressive policy.

(2) To establish economic conditions which will enable Germany to make good the damage done by Hitler's war; and will further enable Germans and the world outside Germany to benefit from German industry and resources without re-establishing the economic foundations of an aggressive policy.

(3) To establish constitutional machinery in Germany which will ensure these ends and which will be acceptable to the German people.

(4) To establish, with this end in view, the maximum responsibility for and interest in political, administrative and economic developments along democratic lines on the part of the Germans themselves.

With these aims in view, the Controlling Powers have agreed upon the following principles which shall guide them during the second period, and in the execution of which Germans shall play a major part.

A.—*Political Principles*

1. In furtherance of the policy of decentralising the political structure and developing local responsibility laid down in paragraph 9 of the Potsdam Principles, the objective of the Controlling Powers is to see eventually established in Germany a constitution based on the rule of law and providing for the division of powers between the constituent States or Länder and the Central Government. This division of powers will be made on the following principles:-

(a) All powers will be vested in the Länder except such as are expressly delegated to the Central Government, as set out in paragraph (b).

(b) The Central Government as finally constituted will have legislative and executive responsibility in the subjects essential to secure:-

(i) *The necessary political unity:* especially nationality, naturalisation, immigration, emigration and extradition; foreign affairs and the implementation of treaties.

(ii) *The necessary legal unity:* especially criminal, civil and commercial law and procedure; copyrights, patents and trademarks; negotiable instruments, bills of lading and other documents of title to goods.

(iii) *The necessary economic unity:* especially customs and foreign trade; import and export control; the maintenance of nationally important communications by road, rail, water; posts and telegraphs; weights and measures.

(iv) *The necessary financial unity:* especially currency and coinage; certain powers for co-ordination of banking: the national public debt and guarantees; certain powers of taxation to be agreed; foreign exchange control.

2. The following principles will govern the ultimate form of the central German Government:–

(a) There shall be a President and two Chambers, one representing the nation as a whole, and the other the separate Laender. Both Chambers shall be elected at regular intervals of not longer than five years.

(b) The rights and duties of the President shall be limited to those exercised by a constitutional head of State without independent executive authority. He shall hold office for not more than five years.

(c) The Chamber representing the nation as a whole shall be popularly elected and shall be responsible for initiating and passing central legislation.

(d) The Chamber representing the Laender shall be elected on the basis of equal representation for each Land. Its main concern will be to ensure that legislation takes fully into consideration the interests of the Laender.

(e) The members of the Central Government need not be members of the Chambers, but shall be individually responsible to the popularly elected Chamber for the exercise of their functions.

(f) A Supreme Court shall be established to safeguard the constitution and determine questions of dispute between any two Laender or between any Land and the Central Government.

3. The following will be the principal stages in the establishment in Germany of a constitutional democracy, as outlined in paragraphs 1 and 2:–

(a) Central Administrations, as envisaged in paragraph 9 of the Potsdam Principles, will be established to discharge the immediate tasks most necessary to ensure the economic unity of Germany.

(*b*) A German representative body will be nominated at an early stage to advise the Controlling Powers on the general aspects of the work of the central administrations and on the number and size of the Laender, and to work out within the framework of principles agreed by the Controlling Powers on the basis of paragraphs 1 and 2 the details of a provisional constitution.

(*c*) The recommendations of this advisory body will be submitted to the Controlling Powers and on the basis of them elections shall be held and a provisional Government formed to operate the provisional constitution.

(*d*) When due trial has been made of the provisional constitution under these conditions the constitution will be amended after taking into account the recommendations of the provisional Government and ratified by the German people and the Controlling Powers. At this stage a new Government will be duly elected.

4. As pre-conditions for the establishment of the rule of law and for any democratic development in Germany the following rights shall be freely and immediately exercised by all Germans throughout Germany subject to the minimum agreed requirements of security by the Occupying Powers: freedom of speech; freedom of the press and radio; freedom of assembly; freedom of movement and communication; freedom in religious affairs; freedom of the judiciary; freedom from arbitrary arrest and imprisonment; and constitutions of the Laender (and, as necessary, the constitution of the Central Government) will be so framed as to safeguard these rights.

5. The Controlling Powers will reserve to themselves full authority in respect of the following subjects:–

(*a*) Demilitarisation and disarmament.

(*b*) Denazification.

(*c*) Decartelisation.

(*d*) Security.

(*e*) Reparations.

(*f*) Restitution.

(*g*) Prisoners of War and displaced persons.

(*h*) War Criminals.

(*i*) Immunities and requirements of the occupying forces and of the control authority.

(*j*) Foreign relations.

Policy in the above subjects will be jointly laid down by the Controlling Powers, the execution of which shall be supervised by the Zone Commanders.

6. The Controlling Powers will retain forces of occupation in Germany adequate to ensure that Germany is, and remains, disarmed and demilitarised. A quadripartite Allied Inspectorate will be established to ensure that the work of disarmament and demilitarisation is completed and maintained. The officers and agents of this Inspectorate shall conduct in any and all parts of German territory all necessary inspections, enquiries and investigations.

7. The central administrative agencies refered [*sic*] to in paragraph 3 (a) above will be established by 1st April 1947, and will exercise executive functions in the fields of transport and communications, finance, foreign trade and industry and the distribution and production of essential materials and food-stuffs. Their executive functions shall extend over the whole of Germany; their agents and any Allied supervisory staff will be free to travel throughout Germany. In accordance with paragraph 16 of the Potsdam Principles it should be brought home to the German people that the Central Agencies will operate under the policy direction of the Controlling Powers. The Controlling Powers will, however, aim at devolving full executive responsibility on these central agencies as rapidly as circumstances permit. As soon as the provisional German Central Governments [*sic*] has been formed, it will assume the powers of the central administrative agencies in so far as these are consistent with the definition of powers to be delegated to the central authority contained in paragraph 1 above.

8. Control at this stage will be exercised as follows:–

(*a*) The provisional Central Government, when established, shall exercise legislative powers in the fields assigned to it by the constitution subject to the joint approval of the Controlling Powers and shall supervise the execution of any such legislation by the appropriate authority and of any instructions, in the fields for which it is competent, of the Controlling Powers.

(*b*) The Controlling Powers may, when they think fit to do so, authorise the provisional Central Government to enact legislation in any matters for which it is competent subject only to veto by the Controlling Powers.

(*c*) The method of control over the exercise by Land Governments of powers for which they are exclusively competent shall be determined by Zone Commanders.

9. The Controlling Powers will exert their efforts to accelerate the repatriation of prisoners of war and surrendered German personnel held outside Germany and to complete the process at the earliest practicable date. They further reaffirm the decision of the Allied Control Council that no German shall be removed to work outside Germany without a contract signed voluntarily and before his removal.

B.—*Economic Principles*

10. It will be the aim of the Controlling Powers during the second control period, subject to restrictions required in the interests of security, to enable Germany to make good the damage done by Hitler's war and to effect such further restoration of her economy as may be necessary:–

(*a*) to achieve as soon as possible a balanced economy which will permit her to pay for her essential imports from the proceeds of exports without external assistance;

(*b*) to repay as soon as possible to the occupying Powers the sums advanced, since their armies first occupied German territory, on account of the import requirements of the population of Germany and to pay for external occupation costs;

(*c*) to play her part in the restoration of a healthy economy in Europe as a whole.

11. Steps shall be taken to ensure as from 1st July, 1947, the full and immediate application of paragraph 14 of the principles laid down in the Potsdam Principles, which relates to the treatment of Germany as a single economic unit. Accordingly as from the same date all restrictions on the movement of goods between the different zones of Germany shall be abolished and, in pursuance of paragraph 15 (*c*) of the Potsdam Principles, the resources of each part of Germany and all goods imported into Germany shall be used for the benefit of Germany as a whole.

12. The appropriate Central German Administration will draw up a common Export-Import programme for Germany as a whole with effect from 1st July, 1947. This programme, which will allow for the equitable distribution of indigenous resources throughout Germany, will be designed to achieve a sufficient balance of exports over imports and thus fulfil the objective set out in paragraph 10 above. It will take into account the need to maximise coal production and agricultural output, improve housing conditions and restore the transport system. The export-import programme will be subject to the approval of the occupying Powers.

13. In order that appropriate German Central Administrative Agencies may be in a position to estimate the volume of export trade needed to achieve the objective in paragraph 10 above, the occupying Powers will render to these Agencies within a period of three months an agreed statement showing the amounts owing to them up to 30th June, 1947, in respect of all imports into their respective Zones for the population of Germany from the date on which their armies first occupied German territory. They will also furnish an agreed account showing the value of all exports from current production and stocks which have been exported from each zone since the same date. The difference between exports and imports will be the amount owing by Germany on this account to the four occupying Powers and the export-import plan will be based on the assumption that this amount, plus any further sums that may be advanced in respect of imports for the civilian population and displaced persons or otherwise, will be repaid.

14. The occupying Powers shall also render to the appropriate German Central Agencies an agreed account of their external occupation costs up to 30th June, 1947, and shall render further agreed accounts at three-monthly intervals thereafter. These sums shall be regarded as debts due from Germany to the occupying Powers, ranking for payment after the sums mentioned in paragraph 13, and the manner of their repayment shall be determined in the Peace Treaty.

15. The financial burden already incurred and which may in future be incurred by the occupying Powers will be divided between those Powers in equitable proportions as may be mutually agreed.

16. Until Germany shall have attained a balanced economy and until the sums referred to in paragraphs 13 and 14 above have been repaid to the occupying Powers, Germany will not be called upon to make any reparation deliveries from current production or stocks.

17. The appropriate German Central Administration shall present for the approval of the occupying Powers proposals for financial reform in Germany. The aim of these proposals shall be to place on a sound basis the German currency, the systems of taxation and banking, the national debt and the wage and price levels, to diminish the danger of inflation which arises from the present excess of purchasing power, and to provide for an

equitable sharing among the German people of the financial burdens of the war and its aftermath.

18. The appropriate German authorities shall put forward as soon as possible for Allied approval proposals in regard to the breaking up of concentrations of economic power as exemplified by cartels, syndicates, trusts and other monopolistic arrangements. Proposals to socialise certain industries will be taken into consideration by the occupying Powers and regarded by them as one method of carrying out this provision.

C.—Reparations

19. The Controlling Powers confirm the Potsdam Agreement on Reparations. Since, however, the determination of the amount of equipment to be removed from the Western Zones on account of reparation was agreed upon only subject to certain assumptions, not all of which have been fulfilled, a fresh determination will be made by the Control Council not later than 1st July, 1947, and not later than 15th August 1947, the Council will issue a final list of the plant and equipment to be removed from Germany. Germany will be left with sufficient capacity to produce annually 10 million ingot tons of steel and this will also be the permissible production of steel in Germany. Other limits on the capacity to be left in Germany of other restricted industries will be subject to similar upward adjustment. The Controlling Powers will co-operate in expediting the delivery to the recipient of the plant and equipment to be removed from Germany.

20. Any Allied Power which acquires, by way of reparation (or otherwise), title to the German ownership interest in an enterprise located in Germany shall possess all the rights pertaining under German law to the ownership interest so acquired and such enterprise and the ownership interest shall be subject in all respects to German law. Enterprises in which any ownership interest is so transferred shall remain a part of the economic resources of Germany.

6th February, 1947.

BIBLIOGRAPHY

Archives

Public Record Office, London
CAB 21; 65; 66; 78; 79; 80;
  81; 120; 128; 129; 130; 131;
  134
FO 181; 371; 800; 941; 942;
  943; 944; 945; 946; 1030;
  1039; 1049
PREM 5; 8
T 236; 242

Private Papers

Attlee Papers, Bodleian Library, Oxford
Inverchapel Papers, Bodleian Library, Oxford
Bevin Papers (BEVN), Churchill College, Cambridge
Brimelow Papers, Churchill College, Cambridge
Hynd Papers, Churchill College, Cambridge
Ingram Papers, Churchill College, Cambridge
Strang Papers, Churchill College, Cambridge
Harvey Diary, British Library, London
Dixon Papers and Diary, Private collection of Piers Dixon
Cairncross Letters, Private collection of Professor Sir Alec Cairncross

Newspapers and Periodicals

British Zone Review; *The Economist*; *Observer*; *The Times*;
Listener; *New Statesman*

Official Publications

Hansard, 1945–1948
Selected Documents on Germany and the Question of Berlin,
  1944–61 (Command 1552) (London: HMSO, 1961)

Butler, Rohan, and Pelly, M. E. (eds.), *Documents on British Policy Overseas*, ser. 1/vol. i (London: HMSO, 1984).

Bullen, Roger, and Pelly, M. E. (eds.), *Documents on British Policy Overseas*, ser. 1/vols. i and ii (London HMSO, 1986 and 1985).

Foreign Relations of the United States:

1945 Conference of Berlin, vols. i and ii: (Washington: United States Government Printing Office, 1960).

1945 vols. i, ii, iii (Washington: United States Government Printing Office, 1967).

1946 vols. ii, iii, v (Washington: United States Government Printing Office, 1970).

1947 vols. i, ii, iii, iv (Washington: United States Government Printing Office, 1972).

Theses

BAGGELEY, P. A., 'Reparations, Security and the Industrial Disarmament of Germany', (Ph.D. thesis, Yale University, 1980).

BLACKWELL, MICHAEL, 'Attitudes Concerning Britain's World Role Held by Policymakers in the Aftermath of the Second World War, (1945–47)' (Ph.D. thesis, University of East Anglia, 1981).

DEIGHTON, ANNE, 'Britain, the German Problem and the Origins of the Cold War in Europe: A Study of the Council of Foreign Ministers, 1945–1947', (Ph.D. thesis, University of Reading, 1987).

GORMLEY, JAMES LEROY, 'In Search of a Postwar Settlement: London and Moscow Foreign Ministers Conferences and the Origins of the Cold War' (Ph.D. thesis, University of Connecticut, 1977).

LYNCH, F. M. B., 'Political and Economic Reconstruction of France 1944–47 in the International Context' (Ph.D. thesis, University of Manchester, 1981).

NEWTON, C. C. S., 'Britain, the Dollar Shortage and European Integration 1945–50' (Ph.D. thesis, University of Birmingham, 1982).

RYAN, H. B., 'Vision of "Anglo-America" and the Origins of the Cold War: Some Aspects of British Foreign Policy, 1943–46', (Ph.D. thesis, University of Cambridge, 1978).

SHAW, E. D., 'British Socialist Approaches to International Affairs 1945–51' (dissertation, University of Leeds, 1974).

Books and articles

ACHESON, DEAN, *Sketches from Life* (London: Hamish Hamilton, 1960).

—— *Present at the Creation: My Years in the State Department* (New York: Norton, 1969).

ADAMTHWAITE, ANTHONY, 'Britain and the World, 1945–9: The View from the Foreign Office', *International Affairs*, 61/2 (1985).

ALPEROVITZ, GAR, *Atomic Diplomacy: Hiroshima and Potsdam* (New York: Vintage, 1967).

ALPHAND, HERVÉ, *L'étonnement d'être, Journal 1939–1973* (Paris: Fayard, 1977).

AMBROSE, STEPHEN E., *Rise to Globalism: American Foreign Policy since 1938* (Harmondsworth: Penguin, 1983).

ANDERSON, TERRY H., *The United States, Great Britain, and the Cold War: 1944–1947* (Columbia: University of Missouri Press, 1981).

ANSTEY, CAROLINE, 'The Projection of British Socialism: Foreign Office Publicity and American Opinion, 1945–50', *Journal of Contemporary History*, 19/3 (1984).

ATTLEE, C. R. A., *As It Happened* (London: Heinemann, 1954).

AURIOL, VINCENT, *Journal du Septennat, 1947–1954*, i. *1947* (Paris: Armand Colin, 1974).

AVON, RT. HON. THE EARL OF, (Anthony Eden), *Memoirs: The Reckoning* (London: Cassell, 1965).

BACKER, JOHN H., *Priming the German Economy: American Occupational Policies, 1945–1948* (Durham, NC: Duke University Press, 1971).

—— *The Decision to Divide Germany, American Foreign Policy in Transition* (Durham, NC: Duke University Press, 1978).

—— *Winds of History: The German Years of Lucius DuBignon Clay* (New York: Van Nostrand Rheinhold, 1983).

BALABKINS, NICHOLAS, *Germany under Direct Controls: Economic Aspects of Industrial Disarmament, 1945–1948* (New Brunswick, NJ: Rutgers University Press, 1964).

BALFOUR, MICHAEL, and MAIR, JOHN, *Four Power Control in Germany and Austria, 1945–1946* (London: Oxford University Press, 1956).

BARCLAY, Sir RODERICK, *Ernest Bevin and the Foreign Office, 1932–1969* (London: Sir Roderick Barclay, 1975).

BARKER, ELISABETH, *Britain in a Divided Europe, 1945–70* (London: Weidenfeld & Nicolson, 1971).

—— *Churchill and Eden at War* (London: Macmillan, 1978).

—— *The British Between the Superpowers, 1945–50* (London: Macmillan, 1983).

BAYLIS, JOHN, *Anglo-American Defence Relations, 1939–80* (London: Macmillan, 1981).

—— 'British Wartime Thinking about a Post-war European Security Group', *Review of International Studies*, 9/4 (1983).

—— 'Britain, the Brussels Pact and the Continental Commitment', *International Affairs*, 60/4 (1984).

BELOFF, MAX, *The United States and the Unity of Europe* (Westport: Greenwood Press, 1976).

BERNSTEIN, BARTON J. (ed.), *Politics and Policies of the Truman Administration* (New York: Franklin Watts Inc., 1974).

BIDAULT, GEORGES, *Resistance: Political Autobiography of Georges Bidault* (London: Weidenfeld & Nicolson, 1967).

BLACKBURN, R., 'Bevin and his Critics', *Foreign Affairs*, 25/2 (1974).

BOHLEN, CHARLES E., *Witness to History, 1929–1969* (London: Weidenfeld & Nicolson, 1973).

BOLSOVER, GEORGE H., 'Soviet Ideology and Propaganda', *International Affairs*, 24/2 (1948).

BOWER, TOM, *The Pledge Betrayed* (New York: Doubleday, 1982).

BOYLE, PETER, G., 'The British Office View of Soviet–American Relations, 1945–46', *Diplomatic History*, 3 (1979).

—— 'The British Foreign Office and American Foreign Policy, 1947–48', *Journal of American Studies*, 16 (1982).

BRYANT, ARTHUR, *Triumph in the West 1943–1946* (London: Collins, 1959).

BULLOCK, ALAN, *Life and Times of Ernest Bevin: Minister of Labour 1940–45* (London: Heinemann, 1976).

—— *Ernest Bevin: Foreign Secretary, 1945–1951* (London: Heinemann, 1983).

BURRIDGE, TREVOR, 'Great Britain and the Dismemberment of Germany at the end of the Second World War', *International History Review*, 3/4 (1981).

—— *British Labour and Hitler's War* (London: André Deutsch, 1976).

—— *Clement Attlee* (London: Jonathan Cape, 1986).

BYRNES, JAMES F., *Speaking Frankly* (London: Heinemann, 1947).

—— *All in One Lifetime* (New York: Harper, 1958).

CAIRNCROSS, ALEC, *Years of Recovery: British Economic Policy, 1945–1951* (London: Methuen, 1985).

—— *The Price of War: British Policy on German Reparations, 1941–1949* (Oxford: Basil Blackwell, 1986).

CAMPBELL, JOHN, *Nye Bevan and the Mirage of British Socialism* (London: Weidenfeld & Nicolson, 1987).

CAMPBELL, J. C., 'The European Territorial Settlement', *Foreign Affairs*, 26/1 (October 1947).

CARDEN, ROBERT, 'Before Bizonia: Britain's Economic Dilemma in Germany, 1945–46', *Journal of Contemporary History*, 4/3 (1979).

CHARLTON, MICHAEL, *The Price of Victory* (London: BBC, 1983).

CHARMLEY, JOHN, *Duff Cooper: The Authorized Biography* (London: Weidenfeld & Nicolson, 1986).

CLARK, RICHARD (ed. Alec Cairncross), *Anglo-American Economic Co-operation in War and Peace* (London: Oxford University Press, 1982).

CLAY, LUCIUS D., *Decision in Germany* (London: Heinemann, 1950).

CLEMENS, DIANE S., *Yalta* (Oxford: Oxford University Press, 1970).

COLE, G. D. H., *An Intelligent Man's Guide to the Post-War World* (London: Gollancz, 1947).

COOPER, DUFF, *Old Men Forget. The Autobiography of Duff Cooper (Viscount Norwich)* (London: Rupert Hart-Davis, 1953).

CROCKATT, RICHARD, and SMITH, STEVE (eds.), *The Cold War Past and Present* (London: Allen & Unwin, 1987).

CROMWELL, WILLIAM C., 'The Marshall Plan, Britain and the Cold War', *Review of International Studies*, 8/4 (1982).

CROSSMAN, R. H. S., *Planning for Freedom* (London: Hamish Hamilton, 1965).

DALTON, H. D., *High Tide and After: Memoirs 1945–1960* (London: Frederick Muller, 1962).

DAVIS, LYNN ETHERIDGE, *The Cold War Begins* (Princeton: Princeton University Press, 1974).

DE GAULLE, CHARLES, *War Memoirs*, iii. *Salvation* (London: Weidenfeld & Nicolson, 1960).

DEIGHTON, ANNE, 'The "frozen front": The Labour Government, the Division of Germany and the Origins of the Cold War, 1945–47', *International Affairs*, 63/3 (1987).

—— (ed.), *Britain and the First Cold War* (London: Macmillan, 1990).

DENNETT, RAYMOND and JOHNSON, JOSEPH E. (eds.), *Negotiating with the Russians* (World Peace Foundation, 1951).

DE PORTE, A. W., *De Gaulle's Foreign Policy* (Harvard: Harvard University Press, 1968).

—— *Europe between the Superpowers: The Enduring Balance* (New Haven, Conn.: Yale University Press, 1979).

DILKS, DAVID (ed.), *The Diaries of Sir Alexander Cadogan, 1938–1945* (London: Cassell, 1971).

DIXON, PIERS, *Double Diploma: The Life of Sir Pierson Dixon, Don and Diplomat* (London: Hutchinson, 1968).

DOCKRILL, MICHAEL, and YOUNG, JOHN W. (eds.), *British Foreign Policy, 1945–56* (London: Macmillan, 1989).

DREYER, RONALD, 'Perception of State-Interaction in Diplomatic History: A case for an Interdisciplinary Approach between History and Political Science', *Journal of International Studies*, 12 (1983).

DULLES, ALLEN W., 'Alternatives for Germany', *Foreign Affairs*, 25/3 (1947).

DULLES, JOHN FOSTER, *War or Peace* (New York: Macmillan, 1950).

EDMONDS, ROBIN, *Setting the Mould: The United States and Britain 1945–1950* (Oxford: Clarendon Press, 1986).

—— 'Yalta and Potsdam: Forty Years Afterwards', *International Affairs*, 62/2 (1986).

EISENHOWER, DWIGHT D., *Crusade in Europe* (New York: Permabooks, 1952).

ELGEY, G., *La République des Illusions, 1945–51* (Paris: Fayard, 1965).

ETZOLD, THOMAS H., and GADDIS, JOHN LEWIS, *Containment: Documents on American Policy and Strategy, 1945–1950* (New York: Columbia University Press, 1978).

EVANGELISTA, MATTHEW A., 'Stalin's Postwar Army Reappraised', *International Security*, 7/3 (1982).

FEIS, HERBERT, *From Trust to Terror* (New York: Norton, 1970).

FITZSIMONS, M. A., *The Foreign Policy of the British Labour Government 1945–1951* (Notre Dame, Indiana: University of Notre Dame Press, 1953).

FOSCHEPOTH, JOSEF, 'British Interest in the Division of Germany after the Second World War', *Journal of Contemporary History*, 21/3 (1986).

FRANKEL, JOSEPH, *British Foreign Policy 1945–1973* (London: Oxford University Press, 1975).

FRANKS, OLIVER S., *Britain and the Tide of World Affairs* (London: Oxford University Press, 1955).

FRAZIER, ROBERT, 'Did Britain Start the Cold War? Bevin and the Truman Doctrine', *The Historical Journal*, 27/3 (1984).

FREELAND, RICHARD M., *The Truman Doctrine and the Origins of McCarthyism* (New York: New York University Press, 1985).

GADDIS, JOHN LEWIS, *The United States and the Origins of the Cold War, 1944–1947* (New York: Columbia University Press, 1972).

—— 'Was the Truman Doctrine a Real Turning Point?', *Foreign Affairs*, 52/2 (1974).

—— *Strategies of Containment* (Oxford: Oxford University Press, 1982).

—— 'The Emerging Post-Revisionist Synthesis on the Origins of the Cold War', *Diplomatic History*, 7/3 (1983).

GARDNER, RICHARD N., *Sterling–Dollar Diplomacy in Current Perspective* (New York: Columbia University Press, 1980).

GEORGE, ALEXANDER, 'The Operational Code: A Neglected Approach to the Study of Political Decision-Making', *International Studies Quarterly*, 12 (1969).

GILBERT, MARTIN, *Road to Victory, Winston Churchill 1941–1945* (London: Heinemann, 1986).

GIMBEL, JOHN, *The American Occupation of Germany: Politics and the Military, 1945–1949* (Stanford: Stanford University Press, 1968).

—— *Origins of the Marshall Plan* (Stanford: Stanford University Press, 1976).

GLADWYN, Lord (GLADWYN JEBB), *The Memoirs of Lord Gladwyn* (London: Weidenfeld & Nicolson, 1972).

GORDON, MICHAEL R., *Conflict and Consensus in Labour's Foreign Policy 1914–1965* (Stanford: Stanford University Press, 1969).

GOWING, MARGARET, *Independence and Deterrence: Britain and Atomic Energy, 1945–1952* (London: Macmillan, 1974).

GREENWOOD, SEAN, 'Ernest Bevin, France and "Western Union": August 1945–February 1946', *European History Quarterly*, 14/3 (1984).

HALLE, LOUIS J., *The Cold War as History* (London: Chatto and Windus, 1967).

HARBUTT, FRASER J., *The Iron Curtain: Churchill, America, and the Origins of the Cold War* (New York: Oxford University Press, 1986).

HARRIS, KENNETH, *Attlee* (London: Weidenfeld & Nicolson, 1982).

HATHAWAY, ROBERT M., *Ambiguous Partnership: Britain and America, 1944–1947* (New York: Columbia University Press, 1981).

HAYTER, WILLIAM, *A Double Life* (London: Hamish Hamilton, 1974).

HEALEY, DENIS, *Cards on the Table* (London: Labour Party, 1947).

—— 'The Cominform and World Communism', *International Affairs*, 24/3 (1948).

—— 'Western Union: The Political Aspect', *Fabian Quarterly*, 58 (1948).

HENDERSON, NICHOLAS, *The Birth of NATO* (London: Weidenfeld & Nicolson, 1982).

—— *The Private Office: A Personal View of Five Foreign Secretaries and of Government from the Inside* (London: Weidenfeld & Nicolson, 1984).

HERRING, GEORGE C., *Aid to Russia 1941–46: Strategy, Diplomacy, the Origins of the Cold War* (New York: Columbia University Press, 1973).

HOFFMAN, STANLEY, and MAIER, CHARLES (eds.), *The Marshall Plan: A Retrospective* (London: Westview Press, 1984).

HOGAN, MICHAEL J., *The Marshall Plan: America, Britain and the Reconstruction of Western Europe, 1947–1952* (Cambridge: Cambridge University Press, 1987).

INGRAM, HAROLD, 'Building Democracy in Germany', *Quarterly Review*, 1947.

ISAACSON, WALTER, and THOMAS, EVAN, *The Wise Men: Six Friends and the World they made* (London: Faber and Faber, 1986).

JACKSON, SCOTT, 'Prologue to the Marshall Plan', *Journal of American History*, 65 (March 1979).

JONES, JOSEPH M., *The Fifteen Weeks* (New York: Harcourt, 1955).

JONES, ROY E., *The Changing Structure of British Foreign Policy* (London: Longman, 1974).

KAISER, K., and MORGAN, R. (eds.), *Britain and West Germany: Changing Societies and the Future of Foreign Policy* (London: Oxford University Press, 1971).

KENNAN, GEORGE F. ('X'), 'The Sources of Soviet Conduct', *Foreign Affairs*, 25/4 (1947).

—— *Memoirs 1925-1950* (London: Hutchinson, 1968).

KETTENACKER, LOTHAR, 'The Anglo-Soviet Alliance and the Problem of Germany, 1941-1945', *Journal of Contemporary History*, 17/3 (1982).

KIRKPATRICK, IVONE, *The Inner Circle* (London: Macmillan, 1959).

KOLKO, JOYCE and GABRIEL, *The Limits of Power: The World and United States Foreign Policy, 1945-1954* (New York: Harper and Row, 1972).

KRIEGER, LEONARD, 'The Interregnum in Germany: March to August 1945', *Political Science Quarterly*, 64 (1949).

KRIEGER, WOLFGANG, 'Was General Clay a Revisionist? Strategic Aspects of the United States Occupation of Germany', *Journal of Contemporary History*, 18/2 (1983).

KUKLICK, BRUCE, *American Policy and the Division of Germany: The Clash with Russia over Reparations* (Ithaca: Cornell University Press, 1972).

LAFEBER, WALTER, *America, Russia and the Cold War, 1945-1975* (New York: Wiley, 1976).

LARSON, DEBORAH WELCH, *Origins of Containment: A Psychological Explanation* (Princeton: Princeton University Press, 1985).

LAUREN, PAUL GORDON (ed.), *Diplomacy: New Approaches in History, Theory and Policy* (New York: Free Press, 1979).

LEFFLER, MELVYN P., 'American Conception of National Security and the Beginnings of the Cold War', *American Historical Review*, 89 (April 1984).

LIPGENS, WALTER, *A History of European Integration*, i. *1945-1947: The Formation of the European Unity Movement* (Oxford: Clarendon Press, 1982).

LIPPMANN, WALTER, *The Cold War: A Study in US Foreign Policy* (New York: Harper and Row, 1947).

LONGFORD, Lord (FRANK PAKENHAM), *The Search for Peace: A Personal View of Contributions to Peace since 1945* (London: Harrap, 1985).

LOUIS, WILLIAM ROGER, and BULL, HEDLEY (eds.), *The 'Special Relationship': Anglo-American Relations since 1945* (Oxford: Clarendon Press, 1986).

LUNDESTAD, GEIR, *The American Non-Policy Towards Eastern Europe 1943–1947* (Oslo: Universitetsforlaget, 1984).

—— 'Empire by Invitation? The United States and Western Europe, 1945–1952', *Newsletter 15/3* (Society for Historians of American Foreign Relations, September 1984).

MADDOX, ROBERT JAMES, *The New Left and the Origins of the Cold War* (Princeton: Princeton University Press, 1973).

MANDERSON-JONES, R. B., *The Special Relationship: Anglo-American Relations and Western European Unity, 1947–1956* (London: Weidenfeld & Nicolson, 1972).

MARK, EDUARD, 'American Policy towards Eastern Europe and the Origins of the Cold War, 1941–46: An Alternative Explanation', *Journal of American History*, 68 (1981).

MASON, EDWARD S., 'Reflections on the Moscow Conference', *International Organisation*, 1/1 (1947).

MASTNY, VOJTEK, *Russia's Road to the Cold War* (Columbia: Columbia University Press, 1979).

MAYHEW, CHRISTOPHER, 'British Foreign Policy since 1945', *International Affairs*, 26/4 (1950).

MCCAULEY, MARTIN, *The German Democratic Republic since 1945* (London: Macmillan, 1983).

MCNEILL, W. H., *America, Britain and Russia: Their Co-operation and Conflict 1941–46* (London: Oxford University Press, 1953).

MERRICK, RAY, 'The Russia Committee of the British Foreign Office and the Cold War, 1946–47', *Journal of Contemporary History*, 20/3 (1985).

MESSER, ROBERT L., *The End of an Alliance: James E. Byrnes, Roosevelt, Truman and the Cold War* (Chapel Hill: North Carolina University Press, 1985).

MILLS, WALTER (ed.), *The Forrestal Diaries: The Inner History of the Cold War* (London: Cassell, 1952).

MILWARD, ALAN S., *The Reconstruction of Western Europe 1945–51* (London: Methuen, 1984).

MOLOTOV, V. M., *Problems of Foreign Policy: Speeches and Statements, April 1945–November 1948* (Moscow: Foreign Publishing House, 1949).

MORGAN, KENNETH O., *Labour in Power 1945–1951* (Oxford: Clarendon Press, 1984).

MOSELY, PHILIP E., 'Dismemberment of Germany: The Allied Negotiations from Yalta to Potsdam', *Foreign Affairs*, 25/3 (1950).

—— 'The Occupation of Germany', *Foreign Affairs*, 28/4 (1950).

MURPHY, ROBERT, *Diplomat Among Warriors* (London: Collins, 1964).

NETTL, J. P., *The Eastern Zone and Soviet Policy in Germany, 1945-1950* (London: Oxford University Press, 1951).

NEWMAN, MICHAEL, 'British Socialists and the Question of European Unity 1939-45', *European Studies Review*, 10 (1980).

—— *Socialism and European Unity* (London: Junction Books, 1983).

NICOLSON, HAROLD, 'Peacemaking at Paris: Success, Failure or Farce?', *Foreign Affairs*, 25/2 (January 1947).

NICOLSON, NIGEL (ed.), *Harold Nicolson: Diaries and Letters: 1945-1962* (London: Fontana 1971).

NORTHEDGE, F. S., *Descent from Power: British Foreign Policy 1945-1973* (London: Allen & Unwin, 1974).

NUTTING, ANTHONY, *Europe will not Wait: A Warning and a Way Out* (London: Hollis and Carter, 1960).

NYE, JOSEPH S. (Jnr) (ed.), *The Making of America's Soviet Policy* (New Haven: Yale University Press, 1984).

OPIE, REDVERS, BALLANTINE, J. W., BIRDSALL, P., MUTHER, J. E., and THURBER, C. E., *Search for Peace Settlements* (Washington: Brookings, 1951).

OVENDALE, RITCHIE, 'Britain, the USA and the European Cold War, 1945-48' *History*, 67/220 (1982).

—— (ed.), *The Foreign Policy of the British Labour Governments, 1945-1951* (Leicester: Leicester University Press, 1984).

—— *The English-Speaking Alliance* (London: Allen & Unwin, 1985).

PATERSON, THOMAS G., *Soviet-American Confrontation: Post-War Reconstruction and the Origins of the Cold War* (Baltimore: Johns Hopkins University Press, 1973).

—— *On Every Front: The Making of the Cold War* (New York: Norton, 1979).

PELLING, HENRY, *The Labour Governments 1945-51* (London: Macmillan, 1984).

PICKLES, DOROTHY, *Government and Policies of France*, i: *Institutions and Parties* (London: Methuen, 1972).

PIMLOTT, BEN, *Hugh Dalton* (London: Jonathan Cape, 1985).

POLLARD, ROBERT A., *Economic Security and the Origins of the Cold War* (New York: Columbia University Press, 1985).

PRICE, H. B., *The Marshall Plan and its Meaning* (Ithaca: Cornell University Press, 1955).

REYNOLDS, DAVID, 'The Origins of the Cold War: The European Dimension, 1944–1951', *The Historical Journal*, 28/2 (1985).

—— 'A "Special Relationship?"': America, Britain and the International Order since the Second World War', *International Affairs*, 62/1 (1985/6).

RICE-MAXIMIN, EDWARD, 'The United States and the French Left, 1945–1949: The View from the State Department', *Journal of Contemporary History*, 19/4 (1984).

RIEBER, ALFRED JOSEPH, *Stalin and the French Communist Party 1941–1947* (New York: Columbia University Press, 1962).

ROSS, GRAHAM, 'Foreign Office Attitudes to the Soviet Union, 1941–45', *Journal of Contemporary History*, 16/3 (1981).

ROSTOW, W. W., *The Division of Europe after World War II: 1946* (Austin: University of Texas Press, 1982).

ROTHWELL, VICTOR, *Britain and the Cold War, 1941–1947* (London: Jonathan Cape, 1982).

RYAN, HENRY BUTTERFIELD, *The Vision of Anglo-America. The US–UK Alliance and the Emerging Cold War, 1943–1946* (Cambridge: Cambridge University Press, 1987).

SAINSBURY, KEITH, 'British Policy and German Unity at the end of the Second World War', *English Historical Review*, 94/373 (1979).

—— *The Turning Point* (Oxford: Oxford University Press, 1985).

SANDFORD, GREGORY W., *From Hitler to Ulbricht: The Communist Reconstruction of East Germany, 1945–46* (Guildford, Princeton, NJ: Princeton University Press, 1983).

SCHEER, JONATHAN, *Labour's Conscience: The Labour Left, 1945–51* (London: Unwin Hyman, 1988).

SCHLESINGER, ARTHUR, 'The Origins of the Cold War', *Foreign Affairs*, 46/4 (1967).

SCHMITT, HANS A. (ed.), *US Occupation in Europe after World War II* (Lawrence: Regents Press of Kansas, 1978).

SERFATY, SIMON, *France, de Gaulle and Europe: the Policy of the 4th and 5th Republics towards the Continent* (Baltimore: Johns Hopkins Press, 1968).

SHARP, TONY, *The Wartime Alliance and the Zonal Division of Germany* (Oxford: Clarendon Press, 1975).

SHLAIM, AVI, *Britain and the Origins of European Unity, 1940–1951* (Reading: Graduate School of Contemporary European Studies, 1978).

—— *The United States and the Berlin Blockade, 1948–1949. A Study in Crisis Decision-making* (Berkeley: University of California Press, 1983).

—— 'The Partition of Germany and the Origins of the Cold War', *Review of International Studies*, 11/2 (1985).

—— JONES, PETER, and SAINSBURY, KEITH, *British Foreign Secretaries since 1945* (Newton Abbot: David and Charles, 1977).

SMITH, LYN, 'Covert British Propaganda: The Information Research Department: 1947–77', *Millennium*, 9/1 (1980).

SMITH, JEAN EDWARD (ed.), *The Papers of General Lucius D. Clay: Germany 1945–1949*, 1 (Bloomington: Indiana University Press, 1974).

SMITH, RAYMOND, and ZAMETICA, JOHN, 'The Cold Warrior: Clement Attlee Reconsidered, 1945–7', *International Affairs*, 61/2 (1985).

SMITH, WALTER BEDELL, *Moscow Mission 1946–1949* (London: Heinemann, 1950).

SNELL, J. L. (ed.), *The Meaning of Yalta: Big Three Diplomacy and the New Balance of Power* (Louisiana: Louisiana State University Press, 1956).

SPANIER, J. W., *American Foreign Policy since the Second World War* (New York: Holt Rhinehart and Wilson, 1980).

STEININGER, ROLF and FOSCHEPOTH, JOSEF, *Die Britische Deutschland und Besatzungspolitik 1945–1949* (London: German Historical Institute, 1984), trans. Scott Langhorst.

STRANGE, SUSAN, *Sterling and British Policy* (London: Oxford University Press, 1982).

TANTER, R. and ULLMAN, R. H., *Theory and Policy in International Relations* (Princeton: Princeton University Press, 1972).

THOMAS, HUGH, *Armed Truce: The Beginnings of the Cold War, 1945–46* (London: Hamish Hamilton, 1986).

TRUMAN, HARRY S., *Memoirs*, i. *Year of Decisions, 1945* (London: Hodder and Stoughton, 1955).

—— *Memoirs*, ii: *Years of Trial and Hope, 1946–1953* (London: Hodder and Stoughton, 1956).

TURNER, IAN (ed.), *Reconstruction in Post-War Germany: British Occupation Policy in the Western Zones, 1945–55* (Oxford: Berg, 1989).

ULAM, ADAM B., *The Rivals: America and Russia Since World War II* (London: Allen Lane, 1971).

—— *Expansion and Coexistence: Soviet Foreign Policy, 1917–1973,* (New York: Praeger, 1974).

VANDENBERG, A. H. (ed.), *Private Papers of Senator Vandenberg* (Boston: Houghton Mifflin, 1952).

VITAL, DAVID, *The Making of British Foreign Policy* (London: Allen & Unwin, 1968).

WAGNER, R. HARRISON, 'The Decision to Divide Germany and the Origins of the Cold War', *International Studies Quarterly*, 24/2 (1980).

WAITES, NEVILLE (ed.), *Troubled Neighbours: Franco-British Relations in the Twentieth Century* (London: Weidenfeld & Nicolson, 1971).

WALLACE, WILLIAM, *The Foreign Policy Process in Britain* (London: Allen & Unwin, 1977).

WARD, PATRICIA DAWSON, *The Threat of Peace: James F. Byrnes and the Council of Foreign Ministers, 1945–1946* (Kent: Kent State University Press, 1979).

WARNER, GEOFFREY, 'The Truman Doctrine and the Marshall Plan', *International Affairs*, 50/1 (1974).

—— 'The Division of Germany: 1946–1948', *International Affairs*, 51/1 (1975).

WATSON, ADAM, *Diplomacy and the Dialogue between States* (London: Eyre and Methuen, 1982).

WATT, D. C., *Britain Looks to Germany: A Study of British Opinion and Policy towards Germany since 1945* (London: Oswald Wolff, 1965).

—— *Succeeding John Bull: America in Britain's Place 1900–1975* (Cambridge: Cambridge University Press, 1984).

—— 'Every War must End: War-time Planning for Post-War Security in Britain and America in the Wars of 1914–18 and 1939–45. The Roles of Historical Example and of Professional Historians', *Royal Historical Society Transactions*, 5th ser., (1978).

—— 'Rethinking the Cold War: a letter to a British Historian', *Political Quarterly*, 49/4 (1978).

WHEELER-BENNETT, JOHN and NICHOLLS, A. J., *The Semblance of Peace: The Political Settlement after the Second World War* (New York: Norton, 1972).

WILLIAMS, FRANCIS, *Ernest Bevin: Portrait of a Great Englishman* (London: Hutchinson, 1952).

WILLIAMS, FRANCIS, *A Prime Minister Remembers: The War and Post-War Memoirs of the Rt. Hon. Earl Attlee* (London: Heinemann, 1961).
—— *Nothing So Strange* (London: Cassell, 1970).
WILLIAMS, PHILLIP M., *Politics in Post-War France: Parties and the Constitution in the Fourth Republic* (London: Longman, 1954).
WILLIS, ROY E., *The French in Germany, 1945–1949* (Stanford: Stanford University Press, 1962).
WILMOT, CHESTER, *The Struggle for Europe* (London: Collins, 1952).
WINDSOR, PHILIP, 'Occupation of Germany', *History Today*, 13 (1963).
—— *German Reunification* (London: Elek Books, 1969).
WOODWARD, LLEWELLYN, *British Foreign Policy in the Second World War*, (London: HMSO, 1976).
WOOLF, LEONARD, *The International Post-War Settlement* (London: Fabian Publication, 1944).
—— *Foreign Policy: The Labour Party's Dilemma* (London: Fabian Publication, 1947).
WORSWICK, G. D. N. and ADY, P. H., *The British Economy 1945–50* (Oxford: Clarendon Press, 1952).
YERGIN, DANIEL, *Shattered Peace: The Origins of the Cold War and the National Security State* (Boston: Houghton Mifflin, 1977).
YOUNG, JOHN W., *Britain, France and the Unity of Europe, 1945–1951* (Leicester: Leicester University Press, 1984).
—— 'The Foreign Office, the French and the Post-War Division of Germany 1945–46', *Review of International Studies*, 12/3 (1986).
YOUNGER, KENNETH, *Changing Perspectives in British Foreign Policy* (London: Oxford University Press for the Royal Institute of International Affairs, 1964).
—— 'Public Opinion and British Foreign Policy', *International Affairs*, 40/1 (1964).
ZEEMAN, BERT, 'Britain and the Cold War: An Alternative Approach. The Treaty of Dunkirk Example', *European History Quarterly*, 16/3 (1986).
ZINK, HAROLD, *The United States in Germany 1944–1955* (Princeton: Van Norstad, 1957).

INDEX

Index 275

276 *Index*

Dulles, John Foster (*cont.*):
influential role of 142
on Molotov and Bevin 48
Dunkirk, Treaty of (1947) 38–9, 160

EAC (European Advisory Commission)
20
ECE (Economic Commission for
Europe) 172, 176, 178, 180,
186
Economic Council (bizonal) 199, 217
Economic Policy Committee 215
Economist, The 164, 174
economy 121, 133, 150, 167, 224
British 197; threat to 44
European 56, 106, 173, 176, 194
German 118, 141, 157, 197, 211;
action to improve 113; balanced
146–7, 152, 216
Soviet 126
Eden, Anthony 12, 16, 18, 21–4
passim, 216
EIPS (Economic and Industrial Planning
Staff) 63, 64, 65, 66
Eisenhower, Dwight David 25, 29 n.
Elbe, River 72, 75, 77, 92, 148
elections 11–12, 110, 144
Empire, British 3, 91, 129, 183, 196
Europe, United States of 64, 173
Executive Committee for Economics
(bizonal) 141
expansionism, Soviet 79, 127, 221,
231, 234
and communized Germany 5
dangers of 154
implications of 224
security and 83, 85
expenditure 56, 61, 109, 112, 154
concern over 105, 106, 125, 126,
174; and requests to reduce 74,
77, 109, 129, 138

federal system 114, 123–4, 132
Federal Republic, German, creation of
69
federation 20, 219
Finland 26, 37
First World War 17, 40, 122
débâcle following 17
lessons of 14, 24, 41
and reparations 24, 31, 39
FO (Foreign Office) 18–24 *passim*,
57–67 *passim*, 106–21 *passim*,

126–32 *passim*, 224–33 *passim*
and balance of power 47
and complicated negotiations 191
and economic problems 174
and Kennan Telegram 78–9
and Soviet Union 51, 140, 143,
161, 176; containment of 8, 50;
distrust of 28
food 89–91 *passim*, 106, 111, 112,
125
supplies of 29, 30, 35, 174–5, 176
Foot, Michael 13
Foreign Press Association 177
France 3–5 *passim*, 23, 27, 52, 53
aid to 210, 215
as ally 39, 41, 177
communism in 94, 131, 165, 194,
207; powerful role of 163; and
prospects for Western bloc 128,
187; threat of 191, 219
democratic government in 38
territorial claims of 164
Franco, Francisco 84
Franks, Oliver 47, 175, 178, 229
fusion, zonal 105, 116, 148, 152,
155, 162, 205
economic 100, 114
political 141, 198, 199
see also bizone
Fusion Agreement (1947) 156, 179,
195, 199

Gaddis, John Lewis 2 n., 6, 79,
229 n.
Gaulle, Charles de 39, 40 n., 145,
212
Geneva 176, 178, 218
German Advisory Council 145
Gimbel, John 2 n., 40 n., 84 n., 99,
136 n.
Gladwyn, Lord, *see* Jebb, Gladwyn
Great Power 17, 18, 135, 163, 215
Britain as 77, 78, 80, 229
and spheres of influence 37
see also Allied Powers; Western
Powers; world power
Greece 24, 129, 162, 163
Grotewohl, Otto 54

Halifax, Edward 41, 83, 85 n., 86 n.,
87 n.
Hall-Patch, Edmund 60, 66, 137–40
passim, 162, 205–8 *passim*

Index compiled by Frank Pert